# Don't Miss Your Life

## Find More Joy and Fulfillment Now

### JOE ROBINSON

**WILEY**

John Wiley & Sons, Inc.

Published by John Wiley & Sons, Inc., Hoboken, New Jersey
Published simultaneously in Canada

Design by Forty-five Degree Design LLC

**Library of Congress Cataloging-in-Publication Data:**
Robinson, Joe.
    Don't miss your life : find more joy and fulfillment now / Joe Robinson.
        p. cm.
    Includes index.
    ISBN 978-0-470-47012-1 (cloth); ISBN 978-0-470-90112-0 (ebk);
    ISBN 978-0-470-90113-7 (ebk); ISBN 978-0-470-90114-4 (ebk)
    1.  Happiness.  2.  Self-realization.  3.  Work—Psychological aspects.  4.  Quality of life.  5.  Conduct of life.  I.  Title.
    BF575.H27R625 2010
    650.1—dc22

                                                                        2010018491

Printed in the United States of America

10  9  8  7  6  5  4  3  2  1

*For my parents, John and Helen Robinson, who survived my passage through kickball, Little League, basketball, football, cross-country, stamp collecting, baseball cards, bodysurfing, bass guitar, and all that music*

Live!
And do not be ashamed
to be happy
Sing and sing and sing
The beauty of being
A lifelong learner.

—From the samba classic "O Que É O Que É?"
  ("What Is It? What Is it?"), Gonzaguinha

# Contents

# Acknowledgments

There's much to be grateful for at the end of the wrestling match of writing a book, such as being finished. I'd like to express my appreciation to everyone who lent his or her time, expertise, support, thoughts, and in the case of the life enthusiasts profiled here, passions, for this adventure to take flight.

I've been hashing out the intersection of work and life for years with Ran Klarin, covering topics all over the struggle-to-get-a-life map, from the siren of ambition to leisure motivation. His input and thoughts were very important to this project, bringing clarity and perspective when they were needed. Many thanks for the sounding board and support. Ran, who runs a workshop program called "Living the Dream Deferred," also steps up to the plate with his own story of cultivating a passion—painting—in chapter 8.

I'm very grateful for the help of Catherine O'Keefe, professor of leisure and therapeutic recreation at the University of Southern Alabama, whose feedback and insights for this project were invaluable. Her enthusiasm for the power of leisure to uplift lives on this planet is inspiring. I want to mention that there are hundreds of recreation and leisure instructors and researchers at colleges around the nation who provide an amazing and woefully undervalued resource to improve the national quality of life. This land would be a lot less racked and awash in medical bills if we paid attention to them.

Many thanks to all of the researchers and experts who were kind enough to share their time and work with me. Tim Kasser at Knox College and Kennon Sheldon at the University of Missouri provided great insights into the world of self-determination theory and goal motivation. A big "shake" to psychologist, prolific author, and brother in the ways of soulful and playful experience Bradford Keeney, for bringing together movement, play, and global traditions for me. Leaf Van Boven of the University of Colorado illuminated the fascinating realm of experience, while Lynn Barnett-Morris of the University of Illinois inducted me into the science of playfulness. I'm very grateful for the thoughts of Seppo Iso-Ahola of the University of Maryland, one of the seminal researchers in the slipstream where health, psychology, and leisure meet. The University of Utah's David Compton, a pioneer in the role of leisure and mental health, provided me with a storehouse of background and leads. Thanks to John de Graaf, author of *Affluenza* and national coordinator of the Take Back Your Time Campaign for bringing me into contact with many of these people and for his efforts to raise the value of time off-task and help Americans get their lives.

I want to give a big thank you to Suzanne Gluck at William Morris Endeavor for seeing the possibilities in this project and making it fly. Now it's time for those salsa lessons. Caroline Donofrio at WME provided great support and advice throughout. I'd also like to tip the hat to Elizabeth Tingue and Mina Shaghaghi for their contributions. I'm particularly grateful to Tom Miller at John Wiley & Sons, who made this book happen and who appreciated that a realm the world doesn't take seriously is seriously wonderful. I want to thank Lisa Burstiner at Wiley for all her efforts in making these pages clearer, and better, with a pro copy editing effort.

Thanks to all the life enthusiasts who were kind enough to open up their passions to me and let me join in with them:

orienteers Brad Wettmore and Werner Haas; kite flier Amy Doran; dragon boat paddlers Kathy King, Cindy Roberts, Tobi Goldberg Maguire, Linda Bloom, Karen Lynch, Nancy Glasgow, Vilma Mazziol, Robin Parker, Sheila McElwee-Witmer, Andrea Reiss, and the Hope Afloat team; rock climber Sara Lingafelter; mentor Mary Forgione; birder Eddie Bartley; badminton maniac Nao Kumagai; poet Adwin David Brown; cyclists Mike Valenti and Linda Imle; choir singers Sheila Gross, Felicia Kelly, and Laeticia de Lagasneri; inspiring hand-cyclists Oz Sanchez and David Lee; hockey player Sonja Rodriguez; equestrian Nellie Own; potter Tony Scott; dancers Briel Naugle and Richard Weinberg; kayaker Chris Joosse; painter Bill Selmon; aikido practitioners Gabriel Guzman, Erica Gipson, and Laurent McComber; surfer Ally Sycip; fly-fishing fanatic Darrell Kunitomi; kickballer Ariana Mayman; salsa dancer Kathy Smolik; softball coach Kim Travis; big band musicians Stuart Lease, Bob Edwards, Maggie McNeil, and Colleen Foster; potters Wade Lindsay and Mira Marshall; waterfall hunter Chris Shaffer; and tai chi chuan artist Ian Glazer. I had a great time and got plenty inspired by your lust for living.

I wouldn't have been able to find the life intelligence practitioners in these pages without a hand from a variety of instructors and advocates. Special thanks go out to Maggie Wheeler of the Golden Bridge Community Choir; Tommye Giacchino at Chicago Dance; Allison Hargis of the North Coast Band; Karl Grignon at Shoshin Aikido Montreal; Morty Bacar at Lakeside Pottery in Stamford, Connecticut; Scott Rodell at Great River Taoist Center in Washington, D.C.; and John Barresi at kitelife.com.

Designer Susan Dworski at theBlueOne.com provided graphic help on this project, in addition to her usual great advice and steady stream of "grist," as she calls it. One of the most inveterate life enthusiasts I know, she also tells the story of one of her host of passions in chapter 8. Imagineer and designer Sue

Baechler at Originaliti.com brings the spirit of play and fun to every day. She provided wonderful encouragement and insights throughout this process.

Finally, I want to acknowledge my good friends who have supported me along the way. Brazil-based Chris McGowan, coauthor of *The Brazilian Sound*, was instrumental in fomenting my passion for samba over the years and was a great supporter of this project, from editorial feedback to social media marketing tips. Many thanks, and to Monica Ferreira as well. Frida Silva brought a big burst of inspiration from Rio de Janeiro, guiding me through the samba highlights of my life in Rio, translating, and providing energy and love on a long and winding road. *Beijos* and *muito obrigado*. My special thanks to Tom and Kathy Freston for their encouragement for this project and my work. Jeff Sievert kept me supplied with a steady stream of references and food for thought, including the Alan Watts audio archives. Much appreciated, mate. Marty Herman, Michael Justice, David Langer, Anchora Siprosert and John Vasey all lent valuable feedback or assistance. Marty got me into salsa and provides us all with a lesson in determination in chapter 3, so he needs a special *gracias* here. As usual, my parents, John and Helen Robinson, were there 100 percent. There's no way I can thank them enough for everything. They've lived the philosophy of this book, from camping and road trips to long-distance biking into their seventies. Both did one-hundred-mile races known as centuries. My dad's not able to take his bike out anymore as a result of illness, but there's nothing he'd rather be doing than biking. This one's for you, Dad, and "the pass"—to hills joined and conquered.

I'll be most grateful, though, if this book sparks you to follow your heart and get out and live as you never have before.

# Introduction

If your keys vanish, you look under the sofa cushions. If your car disappears, there's LoJack. But what do you do when your life is missing—file a missing persons report? "Yes, officer, I used to be here, and then, uh, I was gone. Don't know where I went."

Have you lost that livin' feeling? When was the last time you were so excited by a passion that strangers wondered, What's up with the grin, friend? Where were you when you were so riveted by a new experience that you forgot you had a single problem? When did you last feel the tingle of a woo-hoo or a wow moment? This book is about that feeling—where it went, how you can get it back, and why the experience of it is more valuable than a truck full of Rolexes.

Many people would have you believe that being fully alive isn't that important, that it's a sideshow to the real measure of a worthwhile existence: external success and its engine in 24/7, nonstop productivity. A host of research says otherwise. The economic collapse of 2008–2009 revealed the transient nature of outward standards of success and how they keep you distracted from the source of true worth and the main event: life prosperity—full immersion in the experience of living. Times of crisis peel away the hype and restore our perspective, bringing us inevitably back to the real point of living. As psychologist Erik Erikson, famed for his study of life stages, put it: In the end, when you look back you'll want to know, "Did I get what I came for? Was it a good time? Did I do what I wanted?" Read on, and you will be able to answer a resounding yes to all of those questions.

## You Can't Play Hopscotch with a Flow Chart

The secret of life, a growing number of researchers are telling us, isn't in the symbols of success, but in participation in experiences that stir you. That's where you have the best chance to increase your happiness. And by the way, it's a much more cost-efficient way to get it. It costs me only ten bucks for a night of bouncing bliss at my local samba class.

More and more of us, though, have been cut off from sources of vitality and meaning that come from the nonprofessional side of life. Your interests and passions are what make life worth living and give brains what they need to keep from going stir crazy: engagement, discovery, and camaraderie.

The problem is a saboteur most of us are completely oblivious to—I sure was, for a long time—one that turns your very identity upside down. I don't want to alarm you, but within the fiber of your being a demon seed lurks. It's as diabolical as the chip inside the Manchurian Candidate, as relentless as the creature in *Alien*. I'm talking about your very real-appearing but mistaken identity, the performance identity, which makes you think you are what you *do*. It measures your worth by work output and the status of job or profession, rather than by your worth as a person. Its purpose is to keep you caught up in busyness and external worth, and it sabotages any natural urges that result in random acts of fun or nonproductivity. The result is a growing epidemic of life deficit disorder.

As long as you depend on performance for validation, you can't truly live, because the chip in your head is programmed only for output. The work mind can't play, because enjoying yourself is a realm of input—it's about experiencing, not about outcome. Using the work mind to produce fun is like having somebody keep minutes at your picnic.

Try to score quality living time when the performance killjoy is in charge, and you wind up antsy, fidgety, and guilty whenever you have a free moment. Time becomes something to fill with production, rather than something to make fulfilling. You find it hard to put play on the calendar or you think you have to go through a long period of intense, punishing work before you're entitled to take some time to enjoy yourself. You don't need a license from the government or a dispensation from the productivity police. You can grab the full force of life immersion now.

If that trip to the South Pacific you've dreamed about, that dance class or soccer team you keep meaning to join never seems to happen, it's because the rules you're playing by are made for a different game entirely—life denial. It's hard to play hopscotch with a flow chart. A growing body of science, however, shows that you can get your real identity back when you put your life in play, which is far from the path to slackerdom that we're led to believe. Instead, it's the path to life as good as it gets.

## The Missing Piece of Happiness

What nobody ever tells you is that making your world come alive takes a skill-set that is entirely different from what's on your résumé and requires entertainment that you, not Hollywood, create. For too long, many of us have left the living up to others—the experts, the athletes, the stars with the production values. We've turned into onlookers and lost touch with our capacity to develop abilities and express ourselves in ways that can vitalize our lives every day.

We assume that a scintillating life will emerge from work and external success. We don't think there's anything in particular we need to do to make it happen. So we wait—and wait. It's part of a mentality that always pushes living into the future. What if what you're waiting for is already here? What if the good life isn't off in a distant bump in status or fortune but in heightened life experiences you can have right now?

The science says that you don't have to wait any longer. You can exercise your birthright to be fully alive now. Swim with wild pink dolphins in an Amazon tributary. Pump rubber on an early Sunday morning cycling run with six of your new best buddies. Sing in a choir, even though your only vocal work is in the shower. Do whatever you imagine.

I've been following a tide of research from the social psychology, recreation and leisure, positive psychology, sports, and management realms that blows away the notion that R&R is substandard to productive hours. The evidence shows that participant leisure experiences are nothing less than the missing piece of life satisfaction. As a *New York Times* story reported in 2010, "New studies of consumption and happiness show . . . that people are happier when they spend money on experiences instead of material objects." One researcher in the piece, Thomas DeLeire of the University of Wisconsin, examined nine categories of consumption and found that only one was related to happiness: leisure, from vacations to sporting activities. Your passions and hobbies are the fastest track to the best kind of happiness: gratification that fulfills your core needs.

"The higher the frequency of participation in leisure activities, the higher the life satisfaction," says social psychologist

Seppo Iso-Ahola of the University of Maryland, a leading expert on the benefits of active leisure. Why not do more of this?

That's the idea here. In the pages ahead, you'll get the tools to activate this overlooked fount of life satisfaction where three major strands of social psychology converge—optimal experience, positive psychology, and the least known, self-determination theory—to tell us where life lives. We'll explore an area of happiness research that has gotten zero attention in the public eye but that shows us no less than where humans are at their happiest—when they're immersed in engaging play.

You're often told to follow your bliss, but it's never spelled out how in practical terms—until now. *Don't Miss Your Life* shows you how to put your life in play, with life skills and activation tools that put you in the middle of experiences so electric and sublime you'll need to be checked for illegal substances.

## Get What You Came Here For

Studies show that when you do things you like to do for no other reason than the pure joy or challenge of doing them, you get what a Guinness record's worth of work can't accomplish: experiences that lead to increased well-being and quality of life. Play is remarkably effective at this because it satisfies what we don't know are the engines of happiness and fulfillment: core psychological needs that make us feel independent, competent, and connected to others. Take care of these needs using the right motivation—internal, not external—and you can transform your life. You are off the missing persons list, rousingly present to get what you came here for.

The core-needs framework, developed by the University of Rochester's Edward Deci and Richard Ryan, is a remarkable tool, a psychological Rosetta Stone that decodes our innermost longings and links the worlds of science, spirit, and play. You'll learn how this veritable GPS of life satisfaction can guide you to a more dependable source of worth than the external hit parade and help you rediscover your real identity through its purest expression in the realm off the clock.

It's ironic that in a time of growing preferences for products that are natural and organic, what's going on inside our heads isn't organic at all. This book will show you how satisfying your core self-determination needs through play can restore your authentic internal compass, lost to external motivations. Follow your affinities for the experience of them, and you'll be as aligned as you can get with the true you.

I hope you're sitting down, because this may come as a bit of a shock. True success is in the living. This book will show you how you can get it, touch it, dance it, taste it, feel it to the tips of your hair.

All of the studies confirm what I feel in my bones when I'm in motion on the dance floor or trekking on a ridge top overlooking a secret canyon. Activation produces transformation. But stepping back from nonstop productivity to engage life has been so stigmatized by rabid performance identities—the term *leisure* has been twisted into a synonym for loafing—that most of us are in the dark about the crucial role leisure plays in health, happiness, and the excellence of our work. I'm not talking about vegging here but the opposite—active, self-selected engagement, your freedom to do or be whatever you want in your personal time. Without engaging leisure experiences, your life goes unexpressed.

This is more than good times calling you to show up for your life. In his history of the quest for respite from the grind, *Waiting for the Weekend*, Witold Rybcinski framed time away from task as the sacred versus the ordinary. You contact a deeper well when you pursue what matters to you—enthusiasms, wonderment, challenges—but meaningful personal time can easily be swamped even on weekends by the production default to errands, obligations, and to-do lists.

I meet people in my work-life balance and stress management workshops (worktolive.info) who have lost connection to the soulful space of engaged personal time. They are overwhelmed by stress and burnout and at the mercy of the performance identity—people such as Annie, an executive who called me at wit's end. She hadn't taken a vacation in seven years and was working ten- to twelve-hour days six days a week. "The thing is, I'm not really like this. I used to do yoga and get exercise," she told me.

At one time, I was just as oblivious to the grip of the performance identity. This book comes out of my own journey to escape that brain-lock. I knew there was a dazzling world beyond. The proof was right there in my passions—samba, salsa, hiking, and adventure travel. The thunder of a backcountry waterfall, a dazzling Fijian lagoon, or the thrill of dancing samba made it clear that there was another order of experience—and value—than that measured by the professional yardstick. Yet the performance mind-set is hard to shake.

A column I wrote on the psychology of travel opened my eyes to the myopia of external rewards and the power of experience and the research documenting it. I investigated many themes that will intersect here—the "stowaway" of the work identity that hampers our attempts to live, the refueling power of time off, the control-freak habit that keeps out the adventures that our brains demand, and why we are born to move. It became clear to me that what we seek through performance—acceptance, realization, even success—can't be wrung from that realm. Yet you *can* find all of it in the spirited experience of the last place in the world where they're supposed to come from: play. I became even more aware of how disconnected we are from the renewal and exhilaration of our living time when I started the Work to Live campaign to create a minimum paid-leave vacation law in the United States (which was introduced into Congress in 2009, thanks to the efforts of John de Graaf and Take Back Your Time). Americans give back $20 to $25 billion in untaken vacation days every year, say the folks at the travel Web site Expedia. That's like handing back your paycheck, or life.

It's hard to break out of the performance box to indulge in optimal living because of the lack of something most of us don't know even exists: leisure skills. If you don't have them, you default to boredom and entertainment chosen by others. Optimal off-hours don't happen without certain aptitudes and attitudes, tools I call life intelligence. You'll learn in the pages ahead how to develop these activation skills you can't live without.

Join me for a journey to the heart of the participant spirit, as I jump into full-tilt living with a crew of dragon boat paddlers, kickball players, rock climbers, choir singers, ballroom dancers, potters, adventure travelers, and folks who have discovered that liveliness, not livelihood, runs the well-being show.

"It's like total freedom and joy," says Amy Doran, a teacher in Bend, Oregon, who transformed herself from a fearful single mom to a confident festival entertainer by flying stunt kites. Rich and Amanda Ligato went from mild-mannered San Diego professionals to adventurers on a three-year, three-continent road trip.

Listen to what Richard Weinberg says about finding a passion and what it did for him. In his late forties, the Chicago real estate investor and entertainment producer thought he had pretty much done everything he needed to do on this planet. Then he discovered salsa, cha-cha, rumba, and foxtrot. "It's changed me totally," he declares. "It's really given me a— ," he pauses for the right word, "purpose. I went to the office, had a great family to care for, but dancing shifted my spirits and energy and direction in such an amazing way. I feel twenty years younger than I am." Find a hobby, and you discover a new universe.

David Lee's passion for cycling inspires me every time I think about it. A motorcycle accident at age twenty left him paralyzed and with a brain injury. At one point, he was declared clinically dead. He fought back to become a champion marathon wheelchair racer. Unbelievably, nine years later he was in another accident while training for an Ironman race. He lost a kidney and suffered more back injuries. But Lee's will to live every minute is unstoppable. Today he's a top hand-cyclist, racing in ultramarathons of three hundred miles and more. "I feel very blessed," he says. "I have life." See his amazing story in chapter 9.

## What's on Your Living Résumé?

It's been said that the greatest adventure is finding your life's work. No doubt, that's a saga, but the ultimate endeavor is finding your life's *worth*, which the research says happens in your living time. This takes as much focus as any job search, but we don't get that training. We're taught how to make a living but not how to do the living we're making. You've probably spent years planning your career and your professional future, but what does your life résumé look like? What do you do for fun? As with any job hunt, you can't land the life you want unless you acquire the skills, target what you want, and devise a strategy to get it.

This book equips you for the ultimate quest: the life hunt. It's a guide to the best gig you ever had—living it up. That doesn't come from happenstance but from a new concept for most of us: the conscious crafting of quality free time. I call it life optimizing, developing the skills and plans to turn formless off-hours into extraordinary times. In the pages ahead, you'll learn how you can direct the content of your life.

What do you live for? What are the passions in you right now that are just waiting for activation? Where are the interests that will lead to the highlights of your life? They're out there, if you are.

Landing the life you want requires an ability to play by rules the productivity identity has blinded us to: the laws of optimal life, your guide to life activation. These truths at the heart of optimal experience map out a realm as unknown to most of us as the bottom of the Sargasso Sea, a world unfettered by the clock and obligations that engages body, spirit, and mind. These laws connect you to another order of experience—visceral instead of cerebral; spontaneous instead of controlled; unknown instead of familiar; a realm of participation, not observation, where engagement triumph over comfort and eagerness, over cynicism.

Where do you find this elixir? How do you overcome the barriers to getting out there—no time, energy, bad mood, little money, too much stress, lack of play partner—and grab the good stuff? As you are about to learn, you can get there by (1) shedding the performance identity that keeps life out, (2) satisfying your core needs for self-determination with internally motivated experiences, and (3) acquiring the skills of life intelligence detailed in the laws of optimal life. You'll get the practical tools and a seven-day plan to optimize your life, plus an adventure in activation from folks who have figured out that the directions to success and adulthood are about as accurate as a divining rod.

The laws of optimal life show how you can override the task chip to activate off-hours, weekends, vacations, and dreams that are stuck on permanent hold. These truisms take you inside the participant dynamic that is essential for an extraordinary life—and the experiential wisdom at the heart of it. The keys to activation run counter to all of the schooling you get, but research says that this is precisely where you can find the quality of life you're looking for.

Chapter 2 and chapters 4 through 9 detail these precepts of optimal living, equipping you with the ability to offload external approval cravings that would have you believe that your life is a task to get done, instead of an experience to savor. You can toss this nonsense and follow your enthusiasms to success you can feel.

## Do You Have Life Intelligence?

Life intelligence gives you the behavioral skills to take charge of your life. Like emotional and social intelligence, skill-sets identified by Daniel Goleman as crucial to optimal functioning in society, life intelligence is a collection of traits that improve your odds of success, in this case, of tapping the most fun and fulfillment your brain's dopamine receptors can handle. Life intelligence harnesses skills that are mortal sins for the performance mind-set, such as not caring where the experience goes; relying on your internal locus of control, instead of on the crowd; seeking out novelty and risk, instead of security; and playfulness.

You'll find out which behaviors optimize your enjoyment and which habits keep it bottled up. We all get locked into a personality straitjacket, a code of conduct that we have a hard time breaking out of in the "rut race." Life intelligence rips those bindings off, freeing us from the prison cell of our own making. You can step out of the role of nonparticipant, the one who's too busy, too shy, too important, or too cool to join in. Coolness kills aliveness, because it's based on what others think. Fools have more fun, and you'll find out why. Are you too tired after work? Try the art of rallying. Are you grounded by your mood? Learn how to stop life-squelching attitudes in their tracks.

In chapter 1, you'll find out why having an activated life is as important to your health as watching your cholesterol or getting exercise. You'll learn how to stop renting your time on this planet and start owning it with time ownership, a tool that resets the relationship you have with your off-hours. You'll discover how to build aliveness into every day and reframe your expectations to pave the way for optimal experience.

To break the stranglehold of the performance identity, you have to leave behind false beliefs about self-worth that are, well, worthless. Learn in chapter 2 how to keep the performance gauges—how much you get done each day, how far you are up the ladder, how you're doing compared to others; in other words, the guilt—from being the sole arbiters of your self-esteem. There are more sublime yardsticks you can use when you embrace the path to improved life and work, the worth ethic.

All of the research, not to mention the grin on your face, says that the measure is in the experience. The squish of fingers in clay on a potting wheel. Sitting atop an ancient Mayan temple in Tikal, Guatemala, high enough to see only the jungle canopy below. The untangling of every tendon in your body as you soak in the steaming hot springs of Yellowstone's Boiling River.

When it comes to other aspects of a healthy life, such as diet and exercise, you can find plenty of information about what you need and when you need it, but there are few clues to the daily requirements of a fundamental component of mental and physical health: engaged enjoyment. You can finally get those building blocks in chapter 7, in a section on the fun pyramid. Its ingredients are as essential as those in the famous triangle of food groups. Learn how to build a strong foundation of active leisure, maximizing the novelty and challenging your brain craves.

Instead of all of those things you *have* to do, learn how to map out and mobilize what you *want* to do on this planet. Don't know what you want because you've been too booked up or guilty to dream? You can pinpoint your goals with the life portfolio. Start a to-live list to target a richer experience of life.

Zero in on the time drains that prevent you from participating in the high-value experiences your brain is screaming for. The free-time budget shows you how to carve out 20 to 50 percent more living time. That's way better than the cryonics folks can do. Use that liberated time for what you've always wanted to do, thought you couldn't do, or felt you weren't entitled to indulge in.

Where do you rank on the playfulness scale? Learn how you can boost your play quotient. You're not stuck with what you've got. Researchers say that you can expand your range of optimism and playfulness dramatically.

Along with the research and the adventures of our life enthusiasts, you'll get practical advice to help you plan, motivate, and chart your progress on short- and long-term living goals—from weekend planning to vacations and your big dreams. Identify potential new hobbies with the passion finder, a tool that transforms your affinities into pastime opportunities. Go to the interactive passion finder at dontmissyourlife.net to discover activities and connect with others who share your interests in everything from improvisational poetry to mountain biking.

Because free time is such an amorphous realm, you'll find techniques to nail down off-hours opportunities and overcome inertia to help you get out the door. You'll learn how you can

- Turn free time into tangible events in five steps.
- Lock in commitment to make it happen.
- Track your progress with photos of your activities in a special online scrapbook: the living résumé.

In chapter 10, you'll find a plan that puts together all of the skills you've learned in the book. "Seven Days to Your Life" shows you how to get on track to the fullest expression of your living time in one week. The "Optimal Life" program gives you the tools and exercises to activate an extraordinary experience on this planet. Put new passions on the calendar and overcome the bad habits such as time urgency and killjoy moods that prevent you from doing what your core needs want.

## Tomorrow's Too Late

I hate to bring this up so early in the proceedings, but we are dealing with a finite commodity: time. There are not many Methuselahs among us. Mortals have a very limited engagement. What do you want to experience while you still can? How much time do you have to do it?

Heather Burcham thought she had plenty of time. Then the Texan came down with cervical cancer in her twenties. A beautiful woman with long brown hair and a bright future ahead of her, she could have been bitter about her fate. But after learning that her illness was terminal, she decided to spend her remaining days living to the fullest. She took up skydiving, jumping in tandem with an instructor, and put her waning strength to work as a cancer activist, lobbying the Texas legislature for a vaccine that could prevent young women from contracting the human papilloma virus that caused her illness. I was moved by her determination to live with joy and purpose in her remaining days, and I hoped to interview her for this book, but she died at the age of thirty-one.

"How lucky you are. You get to enjoy each moment," she told an interviewer for ABC News, reminding us of the option we all have. Heather left a powerful message for us, one that I hope rings true from every page that's ahead: Tomorrow's too late. Get out and live.

# 1

## The Life Force

I got my arms, got my hands
Got my fingers, got my legs
Got my feet, got my toes
Got my liver, got my blood
I've got life
I've got the freedom
I've got life
—Nina Simone, "I Got Life"

Some people trek to Himalayan monasteries to find happiness. Others go to Vegas. Kathy King, a breast cancer survivor, paddles a dragon boat on the Schuylkill River in Philadelphia. Ad exec Mike Valenti cycles the back roads outside Chicago. I do samba. Anywhere. Actually, it does me. I don't really have much say in the matter once I'm in its proximity.

Samba is to me what spinach is to Popeye. When I hear the locomotive percussion and speed-strummed strings of the mandolinlike cavaquinho heralding this vivacious Brazilian rhythm, I am overcome by a surge of positive "affect," as they call it in the psychological trade, just this side of slap-happy. All imagined woes and moods run for cover from the joy brigade. My feet are in charge now, challenging gravity with every springing step. The key to samba is a bouncing motion, a subversive maneuver that breaks the spell of adulthood, releasing me from the straitjacket of things that must be done.

I never have to wonder what I'm doing here when the air is crackling with samba. It's obvious: to indulge in the sublime delirium of what I love. The sure bet about happiness is that you never find people looking for it when they're intensely alive. They're already there. It would make sense, then, to get in the vicinity of that vitality more often.

There is an aliveness inside us all that is buried but is yours for the taking. The kind of aliveness that can get you carded at forty-five. That makes you want to chest-bump a complete stranger. That puts a spring in your step again, like samba.

In Brazil, I went to a rehearsal in Rio de Janeiro of the Salgueiro samba school, one of the neighborhood groups that parades in the annual Carnaval blowout, three thousand members strong. In a hall as big as an airplane hangar, a throng of dancers, musicians, singers, and Salgueiro supporters were in full gyration to an earthquake of fifty drummers. I could feel the bass drums in my kidneys. I was overwhelmed to be in the thundering heart of samba. The whole neighborhood was there and in motion—kids; young couples; Vegas-style lead dancers called *passistas* in their gold four-inch platforms and not much else; and dozens of grandmothers shaking their rumps like there was no tomorrow. Everyone was singing along at the top of their lungs, as is the custom there, where everyone is in the band.

Despite the festivities, I hesitated to take the dance floor with these experts. The adult mind was doing its usual sabotage. It had gotten in the way of my aliveness many times through the years. What if I look like a fool? Will I be able to do it right? I'm gonna stick out for a mile. (I was a head taller than everyone there.) One of the grannies, who could see I needed to move and recognized the foolishness of trying to stand still amid this call of the samba gods, smiled and gestured for me to join in. I laughed and snapped out of the headlock. This was play, a judgment-free zone. It was all about the experience, no one and nothing else. The music surged, and I dove into the aliveness that's out there in the swirl of full engagement.

A consensus of brain researchers and social scientists, along with philosophers and spiritual guides from Alan Watts to Eckhart Tolle, say it doesn't get better than this: complete absorption in the moment. Brain neurons crave riveting, novel data; the mind seeks a soulful integration and meaningfulness in the only tense in which that can happen: the present. It all comes together in a nexus of concentrated action where skills meet challenge in optimal experience.

Abraham Maslow, a pioneer in the study of peak experience, called optimal moments times when we are most attuned, "more integrated and less split, more perfectly actualizing." He argued that these instants of sublime activation had all the hallmarks of the religious or mystical but were triggered by intensely felt secular experiences. Call it transcendental activation, transport to a higher plane of living.

Within seconds after I hit that dance floor, all that mattered for me was to move and keep moving to the freight-train beat. Once I dropped into the samba bounce, I was no longer on the outside of the window looking in, trapped in my cerebral bubble. I wasn't worried about what would happen tomorrow or what didn't go the way I wanted yesterday. I was 100 percent inside the unfolding present, thanks to the power of passionate play. In the moment of participation, I merged with the rhythm and the jubilant single organism that the hall of dancers had become. It was exhilarating to be in such effortless sync with the universe, which isn't how it usually goes, as you may know. But it can go that way a lot more often if you understand how these peak times occur and deploy the activation skills that get you in the middle of them.

Samba, like all passions, shows us that there's a deeper experience out there, one that can't be e-mailed, IM'd, tweeted, or texted but must be felt to the core, that makes it clear that the life satisfaction you seek is a participant affair. In Rio, I met a samba legend named Monarco, seventy-six, a singer and a composer for the Portela samba school, who had his own take on the power of personal enthusiasms.

"I have samba for breakfast, samba for lunch, samba for dinner! Samba is in my blood! It's a life force!" Monarco declared backstage before he and his group of septuagenarians, the Old Guard of Portela, turned into forty-somethings onstage at a local samba concert.

The psyched sage couldn't have put it any better. Life force—that's the vitality you can experience, if you know how to grab it. Vitality is the activation side of happiness, and it's a major marker and generator of well-being. This agent of aliveness has been shown to increase, no surprise, on the weekends and when you're doing things you love. Tap that animating spirit, and you come alive to the joy that's buried underneath all of the duty and self-consciousness.

I've seen that spirit make thousands of people rise from their desk chairs like Brazilian Lazaruses. In my workshops, I teach an impromptu samba lesson that transforms software programmers and sales managers into live human beings in a matter of seconds. It works every time, because infectious rhythms, laughter, and celebrating are part of our DNA; they simply need to be activated. Remember the letters S.A.M.B.A, and you can get there on a regular basis. They remind you to Seize the Adventure of the Moment with the Bounce of Activation.

Dive into your passions, and you blow past the heartaches and excuses that keep you from feeling pore-tingling fun without guilt. When you have the life force humming, you're not going through the motions anymore. You are the motion. You don't have to restrain your enthusiasm. You can be as excited as you want to be, shout without fear of breaking decorum, feel at home in your own skin. You realize that celebrating is not something to save for milestones but sustenance you can indulge in every week.

Most of us live in the soulless flatlands of adulthood, resigned to the loss of eagerness and joyful abandon. But you can bring that spark back from the dead through the life force of participant experience. Your brain, it turns out, doesn't want comfort; it wants engagement.

What are your life forces? Find out as we journey to the highlights of your life scrapbook. The thing about passions and vitality in general is that they don't spring fully born. They develop out of a process of exploration and skill-building. You will never find them unless you're immersed in them for a while. When I first heard samba, I didn't really hear it. I was interested in bossa nova and passed samba right by. Seattle-area attorney Sara Lingafelter was terrified of heights but wound up loving rock climbing more than anything else in the world. When San Pedro, California, journalist Mary Forgione volunteered to be a mentor to junior high school girls, she didn't even like kids and was doing it as a favor to a friend. A year later, it was her passion.

How do you get there from here? The activation system ahead takes you step by samba step to the life intelligence skills that unlock the experiences that make life most worth living. We get right to it in this chapter. First, we expose the false beliefs of the performance fixation that shove aside your living time, and then we revalue the free time you happen to own. Discover where you can find the missing link of happiness, and indulge it to satisfy your deepest aspirations. Change the default of life postponement in an instant, with a flip of the motivation switch, and suddenly you've got something to celebrate.

·················· ACTIVATE ··················

## Put a Bounce in Your Step

The first step to a richer experience of life is tapping the power of your body to lift yourself out of the usual mental cloister. Let's try it with an easy samba step you can learn right now (see a video lesson at www.dontmiss yourlife.net). Stand with your feet hip-width apart. Step your left foot forward about a foot length. Swing the right foot in front and around the stationary left foot, so your right leg is standing to the left of it. Now step the left foot to the side about a foot or more to the left of the right foot and a few inches behind it. Move the right foot to the opening standing position, hip-width apart from the left. Then swing your right to the front around the left and do it all over again, making sure to bounce on the balls of your feet and swing your arms forward with each step. It's like a speed walk in place, except with a bounce. Don't be alarmed if you suddenly find people asking whether you've gotten a haircut or lost weight. "No," you can tell them. "I got a bounce."

·····································································

### Test Your Vitality

What kind of shape is your vitality in? Let's take your aliveness temperature right now. The Vitality Scale was developed by Richard Ryan, of the University of Rochester, and Christina Frederick, of the University of Southern Utah. Answer each of the following questions that measure the state of your vitality, using a scale of 1 to 7, with 1 not being true at all about the way you feel, 4 being somewhat true, and 7 indicating very true.

- I feel alive and vital.
- Sometimes I feel so alive, I just want to burst.
- I have energy and spirit.
- I look forward to each new day.
- I nearly always feel alert and awake.
- I feel energized.

Add the numbers and divide by 7. This is your score.

## Obsessive-Compulsive Productivity

What would an optimal life consist of for you? Do you have a top-five list of things you'd like to experience during your time on terra firma? See the Northern Lights, maybe? Learn Spanish? Sail the Greek Isles? Don't worry, most people don't. That's "someday" stuff, daydream fare you're not supposed to take seriously, because it doesn't accomplish anything. It falls under the trivial personal life column, along with other "nonessentials" such as health, friends, and family that take us away from what we're here for—to get things done and display our prizes.

The world off the clock has been typecast as a squirmy place of shiftlessness, devoid of the purpose or importance of the job. Free time, we are led to believe, is inferior to the unfree time of performance. How's that for chutzpah? We are supposed to feel guilty in our off-hours and get them over with as fast as possible. The messages we do get about how to spend our free time send us on wild goose chases after momentary pleasures, instead of the lasting gratifications that fuel growth and life satisfaction.

The disinformation campaign comes via an impostor posing as your inner compass, who barks out orders to do the opposite of what can vitalize your life or bring happiness.

"Work twelve hours a day, so you won't get laid off."

"Get the seventy-inch flat screen TV, and your status will
be increased."

"Say no to overload, and you'll be a wimp."

"You've got two left feet, so don't think about taking that
dance class."

"You've got too much to do to take a vacation this year."

This barrage of garbage spewing all day, every day, is seldom
refuted by the facts. People who work sixty-hour weeks get
laid off just like everyone else. The thrill of owning a giant TV
will wear off, and you will have to buy something else to pad
the ego. Material things, researchers tell us, don't do anything
for our happiness. If you tell yourself you have two left feet,
you will.

The commands are coming from your inner Darth Vader,
the performance identity, a grim character who specializes in
hijacking the full expression of your life. It has decided that
you are what you do, and that if you aren't doing something
productive, you aren't worth much. The only value comes from
output and its yardsticks—money, status, popularity. The input
of renewal and amusement is considered some kind of character flaw. The result is an affliction that is widespread these
days—obsessive-compulsive productivity (OCP): the reflex to
be in continual task formation.

That has led to a spike in overscheduling and busyness, which
has turned leisure pursuits into endangered species. Mountain
biking has dropped 61 percent in the United States since
1999. Slow-pitch softball participation is down 30 percent, beach
volleyball 26 percent, and ice hockey 24 percent since 2000,
according to the Sporting Goods Manufacturers Association.
And for eye-opening numbers, try this one from U.S. census data:
78 percent of Americans over the age of thirty don't get any

regular exercise. Tent camping in national parks has dropped 23 percent since 1995. Only 14 percent of Americans take a vacation of two weeks or longer anymore, reports a Harris Interactive survey. The average holiday is now a long weekend.

Enabling all these trends is the OCP fallacy that says stepping back from 24/7 output is suspect. Researchers and people with life intelligence don't buy it. All of the evidence shows that active recreation increases health, happiness, self-determination, competence, and energy, and the experience of something that you should never have to feel guilty about: freedom. Sociologist Josef Pieper put it like this: "The power to achieve leisure is one of the fundamental powers of the human soul. . . . The power to know leisure is the power to . . . reach out to superhuman, life-giving existential forces that refresh and renew us. . . . Only in genuine leisure does a 'gate to freedom' open." Try getting that from your next e-mail or DVD. Engaged leisure is the freedom to live without controls, artificial ceilings, judgment, history, and self-consciousness. It liberates your inner longings, opening you up to the bigger picture of what's important, intriguing, and enthralling for its own sake. Its chief characteristics—a feeling of freedom and internal motivation—are the heart of human aspiration and self-realization.

The image of play as some kind of pointless diversion from what you're supposed to be doing couldn't be more bogus. What you realize in the exhilaration of losing yourself on the dance floor or snorkeling along the kaleidoscope of a dazzling reef is that there is no divergence at all. When you are at ease, the free you emerges from under the mask of your role, the professional you. It's me-time in the deepest sense.

"This is what I live for! I can come in here and be myself," exclaimed Kathy Smolik, a doctor's assistant and an ebullient mother of twins I met at a salsa class in Leesburg, Virginia. "I don't have to pretend."

"Leisure is the freedom to become your true self," says Catherine O'Keefe, a professor of leisure studies and therapeutic recreation at the University of South Alabama and an enthusiastic proponent of the power of play. "When freedom and leisure intersect, the result is a heightened or deepened experience of the self that nourishes the soul."

You can't fake fun. It's the genuine article, as are you when you're having it.

························· ACTIVATE ·························

### What Do You Live for?

We make lists of the things we consider important, and almost all of them have to do with one sphere of life—output. Activating the leisure side of your life is just as important. Keep a to-live list around, in addition to your to-do list, so that you know what you have to do on the R&R side. What interests, curiosities, and activities need to go on the list? Get a notepad and start jotting down ideas, big and small, to incorporate to-live-for opportunities into your life. See if you can come up with five ideas right now that could go on your life agenda—from concerts to social activities to trips.

·····················································

## Own, Don't Rent Your Life

The first step in your hunt for a more vital life is getting past the time barrier of OCP and understanding that you *do* have time. It's just not valued, organized, or deployed in a way that puts it on the calendar. The panic of time urgency, that chronic state of hurry-worry brought on by the performance compulsion, warps rational thought and triggers your amygdala, the home of the stress response, to send out the false alarm that every minute of the day is an emergency and has to be filled with productive endeavor, or else you're a derelict.

You can begin to reset the autopilot by acting as if your free time is really yours. I'd like to introduce a concept that can help you do that: time ownership. The idea is to stop renting your life and start owning it. This means taking possession of your stint on this planet by not burning up discretionary hours on any old busywork or rote "spectating" but by proactively finding and seizing the opportunities to activate life that are all around you. Time ownership removes you from the mechanical living-to-work yoke and restores consciousness. When you own your time, you realize that you're working for a reason: to live, and that free time is when you do that.

Own your time, and you can furnish it with the passions that give you pride of authorship. When you take title to your life, you set the stage for all of the skills that promote optimal life, because they are all rooted in the self-determined path. No one can direct your private hours for you. You're the entertainment director. Only you know what brings you joy, exhilaration, and gratification.

I'm happy to report that it's your lucky day. The deed on your free time is available for acquisition right now at a very reasonable offer: no charge. I'm sure you'll want to take advantage of this once-in-a-lifetime opportunity to officially control what's already yours. Please print out and sign the following time ownership agreement:

*Time Ownership Agreement:*
- I agree to use my time as if my happiness depends on it, which it does.

- I agree to seek out engaging activities for no other reason than the often delirious experience of doing them.
- I agree never to turn down an opportunity to live it up.

Congratulations, you've made a very wise choice. Now let's go to the next step in the revaluation. You can increase the worth of your time holdings by deciding how you spend that currency and what you spend it on. Don't pay everybody else off with your free time—the cable TV company, Sara Lee, the Internet—and forget about paying yourself. I'd like you to take advantage of your new role as free-time owner with a commitment to get your new life under way.

Start by paying yourself every week with at least one hour of active recreational activity. It can be anything from painting to dancing to hiking, as long as you're participating, not vegging. Begin to see these payouts as investments in life prosperity, not to mention a future of no regrets. Every time you jump into opportunities to feel joy, curiosity, and fun, you are building wealth in your life portfolio. You have to continually make investments of positive experiences, say researchers, to get the return of a happy life. The University of North Carolina's Barbara Frederickson, author of *Positivity*, says it takes a ratio of three positive events to one negative event to ensure a positive frame of mind—"the tipping point predicting whether people languish or flourish."

There's no better way to keep yourself life-positive than by having an active recreational life, one you take charge of as you would a financial portfolio. You can start doing that now by making weekly deposits to a balanced life portfolio. Begin by using the following chart to assess which areas of your life are low on reserves.

What kind of shape is your life portfolio in? Review the categories below and mark the areas of your life that are in the deficit column, which ones you're satisfied with, and which have a surplus. What category most needs your next deposit? When will it happen?

*The Life Portfolio*

| Category | Deficit | Satisfied | Surplus |
|---|---|---|---|
| Work | | | |
| Family time | | | |
| Social outlets | | | |
| Arts and music | | | |
| Relationships | | | |
| Travel | | | |
| Learning | | | |
| Exercise | | | |
| Service | | | |
| Spiritual | | | |
| Personal growth | | | |

Now it's time to see just how much value you have acquired in your time-ownership deal.

## The Free-Time Budget

We all have plenty of experience planning the professional side of our lives, but when it comes to our off-hours, it's a different story. Free time gets burned up without much advance thought. We wind up with halfhearted, last-minute attempts that seldom get off the ground. You can change that by taking your free time as seriously as you do your work, budgeting and planning it with a free-time budget.

Keep a log for a week (or use the one at www.dontmissyourlife .net) of where your nonwork hours are going. Include everything—

parenting, errands, chores, TV, Internet, and your free hours. What periods do you have open for free time? Wednesday nights, maybe? Saturday afternoons? Target those as activation zones. Great experiences can occur at any time, so don't get boxed into a certain time as being for leisure (only weekends, for instance) and ignore the rest of the week. Open up every part of your schedule.

Now dig deeper. How much more time can you free up? What time-draining activities could you cut down on (such as Web surfing, social media, TV)? What obligations or overscheduling could you retool to pump in more of what you want and need in your life? Try to increase the size of your free-time blocks.

Identify what percentage of your nonwork hours you currently use for engaged leisure activities. Now increase it by 20 percent. Can you do more? Could you increase your living time 30 to 50 percent a week? Excellent.

What experiences will you plug into those times? This depends on your interests and needs, which you can identify through the passion finder in chapter 3.

## Nothing Succeeds Like Recess

Brain surgeons have nothing on choir instructors, racquetball teachers, rowing trainers, and you, when you're immersed in active R&R. The surgeon has to carve into a cranium to restore brain functionality. Leisure can fix your head without touching it. Although you've probably heard little about these studies, a wealth of research shows that recreational activities can renew your brain in many ways. Engaged leisure can

- Reduce stress by buffering setbacks and building your coping mechanisms.
- Increase life satisfaction more than work does.

- Build self-esteem and confidence.
- Enhance social support and connection to community.
- Improve mood through increased self-control and cama-
  raderie.
- Help develop risk-taking skills.

Recreation and leisure professionals at colleges, clinics, and parks around the country have been trying to get it through our thick skulls for years: R&R is medicine. You experienced a "re-creation"—mentally, physically, and emotionally—when you play. There's clear evidence of the link between a sedentary life-style and chronic illness. Active living "maintains capacity over the long term, your capacity to seek novelty, to carry on a conversation, to physically perform, to create," says David Compton, a professor at the University of Utah's College of Health.

Physical exercise and the act of learning a new ability cause massive changes in the brain that result in improved health, memory, and problem-solving. High-quality leisure activities are one of the best stress buffers around; they interrupt anxieties and build emotional resources, such as a sense of mastery and social support, to keep burnout at bay.

This barely scratches the surface of what fully owned and operated free time can do for you. Knox College psychologist Tim Kasser has documented in multiple studies that people with "time affluence," sufficient time to take care of nonwork needs, report being happier than do those who work too much and have "time poverty." Kasser's research shows that as work hours increase and leisure time decreases, negative emotions and health problems increase and life satisfaction decreases. People with time affluence say they're more able to stay in the present and engage in activities they like that keep them healthy and socially connected.

Leaf Van Boven, a professor of psychology at the University of Colorado, has demonstrated that experiences such as vacations make people happier than material purchases do. Van Boven says that experiences have a much longer shelf life than possessions, which wear off quickly or are trumped by somebody else's shinier possession. That's why the giant-screen TV rush doesn't last very long. A great experience is around as long as your memory of it. "Experiences involve engaging activity, doing things that people find challenging and often perceive as fulfilling and meaningful life goals," says Van Boven.

The evidence shows that the missing link to happiness is right under our noses: the quality of our experiences. Half of your potential happiness is hereditary, say researchers. Not much you can do there. Another 10 percent is the result of your circumstances—geography, family, health. That leaves 40 percent of your happiness up to your own experiences, called "intentional activities." This is where you can improve your prospects with the power of active leisure.

It turns out that nothing succeeds like recess, that once-crucial part of your day. A landmark study led by Princeton's Alan Krueger and Nobel Prize–winning psychologist Daniel Kahneman analyzed how four thousand Americans spent their time and which activities led to unpleasant or happy results. As they and many others have demonstrated previously, money doesn't produce happiness. Income matters little to moment-by-moment experience. Once you have a sustainable level of income, money doesn't impact your life satisfaction. You adapt to whatever income level you're at, and it's not a big deal anymore. On top of that, wealth doesn't increase happiness because the fleeting satisfaction you get from it is based on what others think. That doesn't last, because it's not what you think. Active leisure, on the other hand, is 100 percent written and directed by you, so it sticks around.

Through the use of copious time diaries, the study revealed that people are at their happiest when they are involved in engaging leisure activities. Millions have lost their shirts and souls over the centuries in search of the hidden Klondike, always looking in the wrong place, but it's as near as the recreational and social pursuit of your choosing. Happiness is having a hobby.

The research tells us something as stunning as it is logical: happiness depends more on how you play, on your leisure skills, than on your business card or the car you drive. Engaged leisure gives you what a boatload of outward success can't: the actual feeling of "successfulness." It's not based on the fickle approval of others, but on the stirrings of something true and deep inside—authentic success, the sensation of life experienced and savored.

This requires that we make a quick change in the success calculus that drives the burnout model of overwork, overscheduling, and busyness.

> Old math: Performance + busyness + stress = material success, no life

> New math: Performance + sustainable pace + active leisure = authentic success, life experience

There's no question about success that you can feel. "It's a coming together of mind, body, and spirit," enthuses Linda Imle, a cyclist, grandmother, and computer technician in Fairbanks, Alaska, who says that when she's out on the road in the zone with her bike, "it's one of the highest of all highs." She recently cycled the entirety of Route 66, from Chicago to Santa Monica, California, for her sixty-sixth birthday.

In San Francisco, Eddie Bartley can turn his day around in an instant with a trip to a secret hideaway. "I hesitate to call it a religious experience," says Bartley, a fanatic birder and former telecom entrepreneur.

"Go ahead," I encourage him. It's pretty much how everyone with a passionate pursuit attempts to describe it. I tell him I've heard it from quilters, kite fliers, and rock climbers.

"It's a spiritual feeling," says Bartley. He tells me about a spot he found on the coast outside San Francisco where cliff swallows nest. He likes to go there and hang out with them. "They're flying all around you, building nests. I don't really know how to explain it. It just makes me happy to be there."

It may not be easy to describe, but immersing ourselves in experiences that intrigue, thrill, and evoke wonder at the joy and mystery in our midst seems to help us transcend the usual drumbeat of dreads and places us in the riveting tense we seldom visit: the present. It feels so good doing the tango or fly-fishing, you think you're in Valhalla.

"Something happens to you, and you know it, when you engage in something enjoyable," says recreation and leisure expert Catherine O'Keefe. "It elevates the human spirit. It's inspiring, heroic. Some might say if it just lifts me up, that's good enough."

The success you want from life, that we all want, has a template much different from nonstop performance and overload. It may be as near as the passion you don't know you have.

•••••••••••••••••••••• ACTIVATE ••••••••••••••••••••••

## The Goose Bump Test

When life lifts you to a higher plane, sometimes your skin will give you the experience of a standing ovation in the form of goose bumps. Your physiology is telling you that something has touched your core and that it wants you to remember it, leaving behind this derma-souvenir of an extraordinary moment. When was the last time you got goose bumps from something beautiful, thrilling, or transcendent? What caused that ovation?

•••••••••••••••••••••••••••••••••••••••••••••••••••••••

### Let's Hear It for Elation

If not suppressed, the elation of celebration finds its way to auditory climax through spontaneous bursts of exultation. We all have our own styles. Do you "Woo!" or "Woo-hoo!" "Yeah!" or "Yes!"? I range from "Woo!" to "Yeah!" when the moment hits the goose bump threshold. These outbursts help us do what we don't do enough of, truly rejoice in the secular arena, not only in the pews. In traditional cultures, celebrating was something people indulged in regularly. There were dozens of festivals in medieval days, a constant stream of opportunities for people to let off steam. We've lost the celebrating spirit, which these days is confined to milestone events—marriage, graduation—and the Hallmark traditions. Life is worth celebrating any chance you get. When your jubilance explodes to a crescendo of exclamation, you've reached a moment of true celebration. Don't let it go by unvocalized.

# To Smack or Not to Smack the Tetherball

You would think that if there were a source of happiness as reliable as engaged leisure, the riot police would be posted outside martial arts studios or sculpture classes to hold back the hordes. But some entrenched obstacles and, no doubt, a plot by antacid makers prevent an outbreak of sanity and your full savoring of the possibilities. One, you're an adult, and we're talking about, well, play. And two, leisure is equivalent to vagrancy for the poser who is calling your shots. Let's lose these killjoys, beginning with the grownup problem.

Have you ever had the urge to slide down a railing, plunge into a fountain, or join a game of Frisbee? But in an instant it was gone. You'd look like a fool, you're too busy, you're an adult, you've got problems. The play impulse is there, just not acted on.

Kids don't rule anything out as a potential opportunity to explore and enjoy. Adults rule very little in, because our culture has so many built-in biases against playing. "We think it's a waste of time or that we could be more productive doing other things— all sorts of dumb stuff," says Lynn Barnett-Morris, a professor at the University of Illinois, Urbana-Champaign, and an expert on the role of playfulness in personality. "Talking about adult play is kind of taboo in our culture." Grownups have the play urge, too, she says, as all higher mammals do, but we suppress it.

The reason kids have more fun than grownups do is that they know what we forgot: recess rules. So let's go back to a time before the amnesia set in and do a reset. You're standing in front of a tetherball pole on a school playground. Kids are flexing their lungs in all corners. You have a choice to hit the tetherball or not. Unlike an adult, you're not going to think about whether you can do it well enough to try. You're not going to pass it by because it's not important or you're too busy. No, without a thought, you walk over and send that ball into orbit.

Kids know why they're here: to smack the tetherball. Why would you want to just stand there when you could make a ball fly? It's a no-brainer. Researchers say we had it right in the first place, that we get the most satisfaction from experiences we do for the sake of doing them, for the "intrinsic," or internal, reasons, such as enjoyment or challenge, instead of an external payoff. We lose this crucial value when we learn that play, or leisure, as it's called for adults, doesn't have the outer rewards—money, status, toys—that are supposed to be the sum total of personal validity. We forget how to do things simply because we enjoy doing them, and that's a huge barrier to activating maximum life.

You can reclaim your innate ability to enjoy the moment by removing the external gauges of the performance identity that cramp the experience of living. It turns out that the real measuring stick is a pogo stick.

## What Do You Do for Fun?

The by-product of an active play life is a little item called fun, which is currently legal for all adults to partake in. Play is the route to fun, but grownups don't give it much thought, so the fun may be in short supply and not as stellar as it could be. You may have gotten into a play style that has become a rut—no fun anymore. Or you may have gotten out of the habit altogether. So, what do you do for fun? Or what did you do? On a scale of 1 to 10, how would you rate it for fun? For gratification?

### Not Your Father's Pogo Stick

If you really want a bounce in your step, the pogo stick is there for you. Invented back in 1919 by George Hansburg, the pogo took off in the 1920s, bounding its way into the popular culture via Broadway shows and contests. There's absolutely nothing productive about a pogo stick, which is why I like it as a metaphor for the joyful leap of play. Bouncing is simply a fantastical and therefore inherently pleasing thing for gravity-bound types to do, which is a good reason to do more of it.

You can get a kangaroo-size liftoff these days with the modern rendition of the pogo. The old style, still available, could get you off the ground six to twelve inches. The Flybar 1200 Extreme Pogo Stick springs you more than five feet into the air. You can leap over cars in a single bound. You have to see this to believe it. Watch this video of human springboks in action at www .youtube.com/watch?v=CiDDBCEsD5I. It's the closest thing to flying this side of a jetpack.

# Do It to Do It

The trick to revitalizing your life is to see play as you once did: as a rewarding activity, in and of itself. For that, you'll need to rewire your default motivational system. The point of dodgeball is in the throwing, catching, and leaping, not in receiving a citation from the National Dodgeball Council. The reward is the experience, paid off by the dance of gratification in your brain.

See it all as a game, about the woo-hoos instead of the outcome, and you start to see tetherballs everywhere. The goal shift gives you a deeper engagement in everything you do, whether you're at play or at work. The pressure's off. You can give it a go without having to know where it's going. It's just a game.

Welcome to the fuel of life activation, internal motivation— something it took me too long to discover. I used to be so externally driven that I was a walking production report, ticking off projects whenever anyone asked how I was. The human wanted out from automaton mode, though, and I discovered a much less exhausting and effective way to live.

Do it to do it. This is going to be our motto from here on out. Engage with what's in front of your face on its own merits, ignore the peanut gallery, and expect no payoff, and, boy, do you get one. The intrinsic goals of play have the power to vastly improve your odds of enjoyment. How could the following motivations improve your immersion in life?

- You participate because you want to. You're eager to be in the game.
- You play for the sake of playing.
- You jump in and try, even if you've never done it before.
- You play to learn and don't have to know it all.
- You play to be in the activity itself, not to get done with it.

> ## Life List: The Northern Lights
>
> The aurora borealis can leave even the most jaded people racking their brains for exclamations. Its dance of shimmering streaks, from greenish to turquoise, orange, and lavender (the result of charged solar particles meeting atmospheric gases), is a riveting cosmic experience. "No pencil can draw it, no colors can paint it, and no words can describe it in all its magnificence," said awed explorer Julius von Payer. Begin to fill out your bucket list, and consider the Northern Lights a worthy contender for it. It's featured every winter in the night skies of the northern latitudes. Give yourself a week or more to make sure you get a clear night, and take your pick from viewing sites in Alaska, the Yukon, Canada's Northern Territories, and Norway.

## *Brad Wettmore: How to Make Memories*

See whether this sounds familiar. It's December 30, and you're reviewing the year to see what notable things happened during the last twelve months. You rack your brain, but nothing out of the ordinary comes up. No times that left you grinning so hard you couldn't get to sleep. No trip to Hawaii. No poetry class. The whole year is a blank. No, you're not losing your memory, just the chance to have an indelible life.

It turns out that your brain neurons crave novelty so much that if you keep giving them the same data over and over, they literally stop noticing. They ignore the same-old same-old, as they cast about for some semblance of information they haven't digested a thousand times already. It's kind of passive-aggressive, but your brain is trying to tell you something: to make life memorable, you have to experience a life worth remembering.

When you're not paying attention to your life, it's gone without a neuronic trace. The life that could be can't be when you're caught in the loop of busyness and nonstop output. Breaking through that pattern takes conscious effort and leisure skills. Brad Wettmore has them, so he never has to worry about coming up short on memories. The Sunnyvale, California, computer security engineer would need a few weeks to download his annual highlights. In one year he played trombone and percussion with his fifty-piece marching band, the Repercussions, at various festivals. Almost every other weekend he was out orienteering, a sport that mixes trail running/hiking and map skills. And he and his wife, who plays alto sax in the band, traveled the back roads of the central African nation of Cameroon. To round things out, Wettmore took up pyrotechnics, working as a crew member for a huge Fourth of July fireworks display.

I caught up with him as this six-foot-seven poster boy for life intelligence sprinted across a field of amber knee-high grass to the finish line at an orienteering event in the mountains outside San Jose, California. He was winded and dripping with sweat after charging through the brush looking for hidden "controls," electronic boxes stashed behind trees and bushes that competitors locate with clues on a topographic map. Weed stickers covered his pants. He looked a wreck, but he couldn't be happier.

"I missed a control and had to go back," he said, grinning between gulps of oxygen. "But it was great!"

He got hooked on this treasure hunt in the woods, which is a hit in Scandinavia, six years ago, and it's been a major playground for him ever since. It gets him into nature, provides a physical but also mental workout—every course offers a different set of navigational puzzles to figure out while he's on the move—and has introduced him to a host of new friends through the Bay Area Orienteering Club. "I always have something to look forward to," he told me after he caught his breath. "A week before a meet I'll be thinking, I can't wait for Friday. That gives me something to work for."

Wettmore, forty-three, is working to live. Using skills that lie dormant in most of us, he cultivates a steady flow of fresh data to keep his brain neurons happy, and, as a result, so is he. The discoveries trigger the release of the neurotransmitter dopamine, the brain's pleasure chemical, which pays off new experiences with the glow of gratification. When the dopamine links with dopamine receptors, you feel good and want more. It's the reward system for making the unknown known, a process that was selected by nature to keep our species questing beyond the next ridge and expanding the dinner menu.

"The release of dopamine in response to novel information is the essence of a satisfying experience," notes behavioral scientist Gregory Berns, the author of *Satisfaction*. And that brings something quite significant to the party, he says: "When you are satisfied, you have found meaning." For life enthusiasts like Wettmore, passions bring purpose. That's value you won't find on any showroom floor.

If you want more satisfying experiences, you have to become more skillful at giving dopamine neurons what they need to go into action: novelty and challenge. These are the two most important ingredients in long-term fulfillment, says Berns, and both are at the core of something most of us don't give the time of day to: our play.

That can change, though, when you get in the habit of practicing time ownership. Since his college days, Wettmore has lived by the mantra "the weekend is mine." I'd like you to adopt that as one-quarter of your ongoing time ownership manifesto.

*The Time Ownership Manifesto*
- My off-hours are mine.
- The nights are mine.
- The weekends are mine.
- My vacations are mine.

It's a lot easier to play on your own field.

# Follow the Bouncing Experience

Your potential to make great memories has never been higher, because there's so much evidence on how and where to activate an extraordinary life. Billions of people throughout history have had to grope for happiness without a clue. They often wound up doing things they regretted in the morning or that their mothers wouldn't approve of. But you're on track here, because the heart of what makes life most worth living consists of experiences that engage, elate, and leave you in a state the land of samba calls "eating your ears." That's Brazilian for smiling ear to ear. You can get there by following the laws of optimal life, beginning in the next chapter, and when you

- Immerse yourself in the life force of direct experience.
- Extract yourself from obsessive-compulsive productivity.
- Exercise time ownership over your free time.
- Opt for success you can feel in your bones—authentic success.
- Enter the no-payoff zone of play by doing it to do it.

# 2

## Worth Is an Inside Job

We can secure other people's approval,
if we do right and try hard; but our own
is worth a hundred of it.
—*Mark Twain*

It's all in the wrists. Pull the handles under," says my flight instructor, a witch in a black cone hat. My runway is a beach; my craft, a kite, though not the one-stringed affair you might have floated with the kids next door. This one is a two-handled, four-stringed stunt kite known as a Quad, and it's a little temperamental. It rises about ten feet, flips to the left, and makes a kamikaze dive for the spectators, crashing into the sand on the northern Oregon beach.

It's clear to the observers here on the fringes of the Lincoln City Kite Festival that I am not one of the featured performers and that they'd better check their insurance coverage. The idea behind all of the handles and the strings is that you get the capability to make the kite perform any move this side of the mambo—if you know what you're doing.

After a few more crashes, my Halloween-costumed trainer, Penny Lingenfelder, one of the top fliers at the festival, gives me the crucial tip—hands close to the body as I tilt the handles under. The kite, which looks like a large pair of sunglasses with triangles for lenses, lifts straight up. I feel the grab of a ferocious wind, which crackles against the kite's ripstop nylon. I laugh out loud as I play tug-of-war with the heavens almost like the old days. The kite may be flying, but I'm the one who feels released from gravity. How is it that playing with a simple toy in cahoots with nature can deliver a cathartic experience in an instant? Then I lose control, and bystanders have to take cover.

If there's a pursuit that sums up the intrinsic joy of play, kite flying is at the top of the list. The innate delight built into this sky dance needs no payoff. You fly a kite for the pure pleasure of it—even if you're a festival performer at Lincoln City. Other than a few folks who design kites, everyone here has a day job.

I've come here to see how one of the oldest traditions of kicking back, dating to fifth-century B.C. China, can lift not only cloud-hopping nylon, but also people's lives. This activity would seem to be one of the least productive things you could do, as in "go fly a kite," get lost, scram. From what the fliers and the scientists tell me, though, if more people did it, there would be a lot fewer lost souls.

It's a wind-chilled day along the rocky bluffs of Lincoln City, a one-street town wedged between surf and pine-covered slopes. Several thousand spectators are bundled up to watch the performers—who will get nothing more than applause—do multiple acrobatic kite sequences. A forty-foot Macy's parade–size teddy bear and octopus float over the festivities, as Trilby multikites, with six diamond-style models hooked together, swish synchronized tails through the sky. I stop at the "Dancin' Al" banner, the roost of Al Jefferson, known as "twinkle toes" for his frisky-footed routines. Fliers choreograph their stunts to recorded music, everything from rock to hip-hop to country. But Jefferson's dance moves are on the injured reserve list today because of a knee issue. A state liquor commissioner in Portland who is hooked on kites, Jefferson always has a good flight.

"I can take my kite out, put my headphones on, and fly for hours," says Jefferson, a stocky man in a Raiders cap and black sweats who has taken his hobby to festivals around the United States and to the World Cup of kite flying. "It's like a therapy thing. I get a peace within myself that works for me."

Next to Jefferson, Amy Doran gets set for her routine. A petite youth program director for primary school kids in Bend, Oregon, Doran was at a low point when she happened upon the Lincoln City Kite Festival a few years ago. She had just gotten a divorce, was a newbie to the area from the Midwest, and faced growing challenges with a son who has epilepsy. When she saw the festival, she pulled an old kite out of her car and flew it off to the side of the event. Seven hours later, arms numb, she landed it. Jefferson came by and told her he'd never "seen anyone fly a kite that long. I think you're a born flier."

Doran was taken under the wing of local fliers like Jefferson and Lingenfelder and inducted into a welcoming tribe of fellow enthusiasts. She was too nervous to compete at festivals when she started. Now the crowd roars as the announcer introduces her. Dressed in the top hat and tails of Charlie Chaplin, she shuffles to center sand in the famed stuttery gait of the silent film star. She trips in a classic pratfall, gets up, and brushes the sand off. Then she picks up the handles of her kite, fumbles with them in mock confusion, and yanks the Quad up. The kite streaks, flips, and tumbles, all to Chaplin theatrics.

"Before I got into kites, I wasn't very happy," Doran told me earlier. "I had lost a lot of self-confidence and was really unsure where life was going to take me. Learning how to fly all styles of kites and perform in front of audiences taught me to believe in myself. It's opened up a whole new world for me, and it gave me a family."

## Get Higher at a Kite Festival

Because kite festivals don't attract big sponsors, they fly under the radar, but there are plenty of them from March to October every year. Visiting one is a great way to lift your weekend and maybe find a new hobby. Some events offer competitive stunt-kite flying, while many are only for fun, featuring expert flyers performing acrobatic maneuvers, kite-making displays, and mini-kites for the kids. The tandem kite team iQuad, led by champion flier and editor of kitelife.com John Barresi, is a favorite on the festival circuit, showing off the spectacular modern art of formation flying with six synchronized stunt kites. Check out a video of their aerial acrobatics at www.youtube.com/watch?v=6JjdJImATKM. For a festival near you, go to the American Kitefliers' Association site, www.aka.kite.org/.

The single mother who was fearful and alone has been replaced by a self-assured woman with a host of friends and an outlet for creative expression. She's become a top performer in competitions and recently started designing kites. Her boyfriend is also a flier. The kite effect doesn't end there. Doran's son, Connor, sixteen, recently took up flying and is now performing at festivals, even winning his division in competitions. "It's a major stress reliever," he tells me, as he ticks off the meds he used to be on. Anxiety triggers his seizures, but he hasn't had one now for months. "Kite flying works better than any anxiety medication," says the gangly teen. The proof was there for millions to see as Connor performed his indoor kite exploits in 2010 on the TV competition *America's Got Talent*, winning hearts with his courage and artistry. "My whole life I've been told I can't do things," he said. "But kite flying changed that. I have something I'm good at. That makes me feel I can do things."

An activity that the productivity mandate would have you believe is worthless has transformed the lives of Doran, Connor, and Jefferson. It's a lesson in how play expands not only spirits but skills that bolster self-worth. None of it would surprise psychologist Edward Deci, whose pioneering research in human motivation at the University of Rochester with colleague Richard Ryan has found that there are big rewards when you do things without regard to a payoff—everything from increased happiness and competence to a richer experience of life.

"Intrinsic motivation is its own justification," explains Deci in *Why We Do What We Do*, an extremely wise and important book that shows how to get out of the way of your own fulfillment. "Smelling the roses, being enthralled by how the pieces of a puzzle fit together, seeing the sunlight as it dances in the clouds, feeling the thrill of reaching a mountain summit: these are experiences that need yield nothing more to be fully justified. And one might go so far as to argue that a life devoid of such experiences is hardly a life at all."

As much sense as that makes, it's the external rewards that pull the strings, because there's something other than logic in control of our brains most of the time. That would be the identity thief who makes off with your life as surely as someone who's bagged your credit card information. Until you switch off the counterfeit you of the performance identity and the need to prove worth by output alone, you will continue to be relegated to the life onlooker column. You can shut down the heist by activating the first law of optimal life: worth is an inside job. You need a worth, as well as a work, ethic.

In this chapter, you'll get the life intelligence skills that lay the groundwork for the activation to follow. You'll learn how to reclaim yourself from the performance identity of the work mind and resist contingent self-esteem, which dictates that all value comes from polishing off tasks, none of which happen to be your life. You'll learn how to get out from under the thumb of work guilt and that sense of never being able to relax because there's always something to do next on the list. Best of all, you'll discover the skill that delivers true worth and identity: satisfying your core needs. A gratifying life doesn't come from external yardsticks of worth but from experiences that allow your core needs to take flight, such as a kite dancing in a blustery sky.

## Catch the Thief

Nobody wants to be a spectator to life, but the performance identity has other ideas. It snatches you from your life so stealthily you're on the sidelines before you even know it's taken over. In the guise of your inner voice, it shoves aside your personal life for what's assumed to be more important: making every moment productive. The only way to know you've been robbed is by the absence of a few items—fun, spontaneity, and new experiences, and the overwhelming presence of self-deprivation habits that make you:

- Fill free moments with busyness.
- Rule out a class you'd like to take because what would you really get out of it?
- Nix fun after work because you're not in the mood.
- Unable to relax when there's stuff to do.
- "Too busy" to get together with friends, so you lose contact.
- Feel guilty about taking a vacation.
- Not plan your leisure life or weekends.

The performance identity has no idea how to generate fun and aliveness. It knows only how to keep you running from the productivity police. You want fun? How about a little inventory

metadata? Or maybe some exciting product-to-category relationships? Don't you need to check e-mail that you just checked
five minutes ago? Once this mind snatcher has taken over, you
*are* your job—even on vacation. I know a woman in Arizona
who spreadsheets her vacations, planning out each hour before
she takes off. The performance identity never takes a day off. It
gets worse: Faye, a public relations entrepreneur in New York,
told me that she had a heart attack at the incredible age of
twenty-nine from her workaholism. "I realize I am completely
uncomfortable relaxing, which is quite frightening," she said.

You wind up uncomfortable with—and this is pretty crazy—
yourself. The performance identity seizes control of your self-
concept, swapping you out for the belief "I do, therefore I am."
Your value becomes dependent on the yardsticks of output—
what you got done, your latest job title, and the toys and status that are the metrics of success. It's identity theft, pure and
simple, a lose-lose proposition for life and work that results in a
lot of collateral damage.

- Chronic work weeks of fifty-one hours or more can triple
  the risk of hypertension.
- Untaken vacations and unexperienced life activities are
  gone forever.
- Productivity dives 25 percent with a sixty-hour week.

Contrary to the instructions of the performance identity,
your job is only a small part of who you are. It's what psychologists call a persona, a mask that describes your social role, but
it's not the real you. When you think it is, you lose track of the
authentic person behind the mask and that character's needs,
interests, and values. You wind up reaching what has to be
a zenith of futility—knocking yourself out to validate a fake
identity.

No doubt, work and performance are good things. They help you accomplish things, meet challenges, provide important services, and put dinner on the table. But the performance identity isn't satisfied with that. Its goal is to get you so caught up in the importance of doing and busyness that vanquishing tasks becomes the only path to self-value. Thinking all your worth lies in what you achieve and produce is an irrational belief. "A more rational assessment of your real worth would depend on such things as your capacity to experience being fully alive, feeling everything it means to be human," say psychologists Martha Davis, Elizabeth Robbins Eshelman, and Matthew McKay, authors of *The Relaxation and Stress Handbook*.

The evidence shows that the external success model is a flop when it comes to the creation of real worth, which stems from a broad, self-determined view that you are competent and worthy to enjoy life. A study of forty-nine of the Forbes 400 richest Americans found the most well off to be only marginally happier than the average person and 37 percent were less happy. More than a few Hollywood icons with a net worth larger than some small countries' feel only as valid as their latest kudos. One bad review can crush a flimsy exterior. It's time to build a broader, more resilient, and more fun basis of value than the daily public approval meter.

The initial skill of life intelligence is the ability to reclaim your identity from the performance chip. This requires that you separate your self-concept from what you do for a job and your value from what others think. Since input is where your life lives, staying on output in your off-hours isn't Phi Beta Kappa. Work is a square peg; life is a round hole. You can't produce fun; you have to experience it.

Switching off the output reflex at the appropriate times will take a certain presence of mind that comes from a departure from autopilot. You have to catch the identity thief in the act—when it drives you into burnout and overload, when it books up every second of your off-hours, when you can't enjoy yourself because you have too much to do, when you can't or won't let go of the day's headaches when you get home from work. You own your free time, remember?

•••••••••••••••••••••• ACTIVATE ••••••••••••••••••••••

### Hold the Applause

External validation keeps you on the hunt for approval to feed the performance chip. To get the upper hand on this habit, you'll need to start weaning yourself off the approval trough. This week, resist all impulses to seek others' praise or applause. Be immersed in your work and your life for the sake of whatever you're experiencing, not for a pat on the back. When someone doesn't respond to your effort, so what? If you act intrinsically, you do it to do it, so the stroke isn't needed. Write down how you feel when you don't get the approval. How could you retool your expectations to not need as much external validation? What can you do to catch yourself when you go into approval-craving mode?

•••••••••••••••••••••••••••••••••••••••••••••••••••••••

## Flip the Switch

The performance mind-set is obsessed with measuring. It insists that you're only as good as your last task or shot of approval. That locks you into the insecurity sweepstakes, chasing precisely what *can't* produce self-esteem. Pursuit of external goals leads to something called contingent self-esteem, which is a pseudo-esteem. It bases all of your worth on a particular domain that's important to you—job performance, wealth, beauty—which is dependent on the approval of others. Contingent self-esteem is shaky because it's subject to change, comparison, and somebody else's opinion. If job performance is your sole source of identity, and it takes a hit, you're vulnerable to a worth wipeout.

That's what happened to Tony Scott. After being laid off from a high-flying financial job on Wall Street, the engineer found himself devoid of an identity without the external yardsticks he'd always measured himself by. Who or what was he without the business card? "It was such a big loss," says Scott, who lives in a suburb in New York. "It was like, I'm totally useless now. I was very depressed."

A friend who had a pottery studio invited him to take a class, and with time on his hands, Tony did what he never would have done otherwise: play. Molding a blob of clay on the spot was strange at first for an engineer used to figuring out everything in

---

### Brush Up on Your Imagination

Expressing your life can take many forms, but one of the most direct lines to the inner reaches is through the arts. There are plenty of options to tap your creative spirit—via painting, pottery, jewelry making. Chicago's Lillstreet Art Center is a model for how to make the practice of art approachable for everyone. Inside an old gear warehouse, the center offers courses in ceramics, painting and drawing, textile and silk-screening, printmaking, jewelry, and metalsmithing. Greenhorns don't have to worry about being in a class where they're drawing stick figures and others are knocking out Picassos. Students are placed according to their skill levels. The ten-week First-Time Painter class is $150. See the Lillstreet Art Center Web site at www.lillstreet.com, or check the Web for an art class or teacher near you.

advance down to the most minute detail, but he soon got beyond the schematic instinct and went with creating in the moment.

"It was very revealing," he says. "I was able to express things I was feeling at the time. I might not be employable, but at least I could make a pot. It was very anchoring."

The validity Scott sought from the external realm had been there all along, on the inside. The artistic expression of his real identity let him know there was a person behind the career, one who didn't need endorsing. Now an entrepreneur with his own consulting business, Scott knows that job performance is only one aspect of his identity and that passions like pottery bring a broader base of value that can't be undermined by momentary disappointments.

Contingent self-esteem erodes true self-esteem by shutting down your sense of self-determination, the real source of personal value and a trait you tend to find outside the job. Without it, you are controlled by the external demands of others. In a study on workaholism, researcher Ronald Burke found that hard-core work addicts had "significantly lower self-esteem" than people who were enthused about, but not captive to, their work—which is not what we're led to believe. The thrill of a job promotion vanishes in two weeks. Then you're back to however you felt before the status bump. You get only a temporary boost from the rewards you receive from others, because their approval can't satisfy your core.

Nothing underscores the vulnerability of contingent self-worth better than research done by Mark Cullen, a professor at Yale's School of Medicine. The retired male executives he's studied have achieved just about everything possible in their careers, including huge financial success, but then comes retirement day. They walk out the doors of their offices for the last time, and by the next day they feel worthless. Their value is no longer fed by contingent self-esteem. "They're not producing anymore. They have no leisure skills and don't know what to do with themselves," Cullen told me. After working their entire lives for the time to live, when they get to that point, they don't know *how*. What's worse is that, devoid of identity and purpose, many die not long after they retire.

Compare that to four friends in their seventies who work out a couple of nights a week climbing ropes at the Los Angeles Valley College gym in Van Nuys, California. They train, joke, support one another, and indulge their passion for hoisting themselves up to the ceiling by ropes, something most twenty-somethings couldn't do. Sanford Werner, seventy-eight, a geologist by training, has been rope climbing for sixty years. It's a key part of his identity and self-worth that vitalizes his world with purpose and friendships.

The difference between the retired execs in Cullen's research and the rope climbers is identity. The rope climbers have one, not a pseudo-self based on contingent self-esteem. They know worth is an inside job. You can have that attitude at any age. At twenty-four, Briel Naugle already has life intelligence. "I like my job, but I'm working to feed my passions," says Naugle, who works in human resources in Chicago. Her biggest passion is Latin dancing, which she does three times a week. "I know that everything on my job is leading to my passion. My career isn't the only thing I can succeed at, and knowing that takes the pressure off."

Naugle has a healthy sense of what's important that people twice her age are missing. The skill of resisting contingent self-esteem makes sure she doesn't put all her worth eggs in one basket. Take her very wise cue and spread your esteem around to lots of sources. You can resist single-source worth by switching off the performance ratification equipment and turning on the true you.

*Turn off:*

- Externally driven self-worth. You are not an opinion poll.
- Guilt. It keeps others calling your tune. And it's optional.

- Compulsive busyness. Self-definition by how busy or consumed you are leads to booking up every free minute.
- Behavior that reinforces the performance identity, such as all-hours overwork bravado or asking, "What do you do" to someone you just met. How about "What do you like to do?" Then you get to the real self.

*Turn on:*
- Internal validation. Remove the external payoff and you shut down one-dimensional worth. The field is wide open to partake in what you want for its own sake.
- A mindful pace. Thinking expands the horizon beyond time-urgent production.
- Your real value. Separate your value as a person from your professional identity. Think of your work as the means with which you make your living, not the living itself.
- A broader self-definition, based on the mission of working to live, not living to work.

•••••••••••••••••••••• ACTIVATE ••••••••••••••••••••••

## Play Your Life Card

If you don't have an identity outside the job, your default will always be to the identity that provides the value: performance. But what else could your identity be beyond your job or professional designation? It's time to find out. I'd like you to create a business card for your life. In the card below, identify yourself by a hobby or an interest, something you would like to do or have always wanted to do. But it must be completely unproductive, something you do only for the sake of it, for its inherent fun or challenge. For example: John

Smith—Dog Whisperer, Laurie Collins—Tai Chi Artist, Jay Ellsworth—Rock Hugger/Climber. Pull your Life Card out as a reminder of your real business: to partake in as much of this planet as you can while you can.

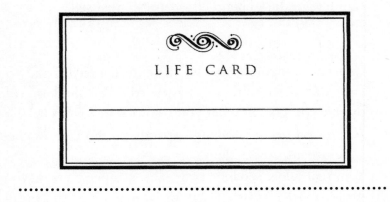

## Authentic Success

Sometimes I get a chance to watch the best surfers on the planet do their magic for free. I was walking along the beach recently and saw three dolphins peel at lightning speed across a wave. There was no professional reason for them to do it. It wasn't as if that was going to win them dinner. They were squealing across that glassy tube because they wanted to play. A break for a little surfing wouldn't prevent them from getting back to work when they were hungry. As we know, dolphins aren't dumb. They have it figured out. They play to live.

At the other end of the spectrum is a creature surrounded by beauty and the chance to have fun with it but that recoils from anything besides work: the bee. It spends its days commuting back and forth between luxuriant passionflowers or lavender blossoms, focused exclusively on the task without ever kicking back on a Posturepedic petal to take in anything except pollen and nectar.

## Know When to Say When

Your unconscious work style is a major factor in producing work guilt and a missing life. When you react to incoming demands and don't manage them, you wind up in mechanical overperformance mode, not knowing when to say when. A study at Harvard found that the main component for successful businesspeople who have true satisfaction in their lives is the "deliberate imposition of limits." These folks set boundaries, and you need to do this as well to have a successful balance of work and life. The key is developing your own guidelines to know when you've done "just enough."

"Even if you love your work, do too much of it, and you'll hate it," Yale overwork expert Mark Cullen told me. So, what are the guidelines that can tell you when you've done just enough? Does your productivity dive after eight hours? Knowing you don't have to finish everything on the to-do list today is another way of getting to the "just enough" point. Researchers say that, if you work excessively one day, the fatigue comes out of your hide the next day and the next. You can't throw your body at a 24/7 world. It's not physiologically possible. You have structural limits, as the engineers could tell you. Find those limits before they find you.

The dolphin and the bee both get their jobs done but in highly different ways. Which one does your work-life style resemble more? Are you a dolphin or a drone? The prevailing success mythology dictates that you follow the drone mode of the burnout model. But that's only one style of work. As the dolphins show us, there are other styles. For humans, I call it sustainable performance, meaning that we make adjustments to the way we work that allow us to manage and not simply react to the incoming tasks. There's another style of success as well, one that lets you exchange drone for dolphin mode—authentic success. The basis of authentic success is a shift of two letters in the famous phrase that feeds the performance identity: change the work ethic to the worth ethic.

Embrace the worth ethic, and value is no longer a function of whether you can get enough done or make enough bucks to be worthy but, instead, about what makes life and work worthwhile now—optimal engagement. At work, that means doing the job for the craft or the excellence of it. On the life side, it means diving into the experiences that let you express your core needs. What could be more successful than that?

The worth ethic reframes the premise of self-worth from something based on the approval of others to value you feel through the reality of your own experiences. Make the worth ethic your new governing principle, and you restore balance and the holistic reality that you are the sum of all your parts, not merely one sliver. Begin by treating your off-hours as seriously as your work. I'd like you to create a résumé for your life that will allow you to set goals, plan, chronicle, and savor memorable experiences.

•••••••••••••••••••••• ACTIVATE ••••••••••••••••••••••

## A Résumé for Your Life

To flesh out your real identity, create a résumé that documents the living you're making for yourself. You can do it on paper or go to www.dontmissyourlife.net to chart your life experiences and plans. As with any job résumé, step one is composing your mission statement. Instead of a job objective, detail what your life mission is. Instead of job experience, describe what you want to experience on this planet. List your interests and most memorable times, chart out your activities for next week, and keep a running tab of your latest classes, trips, and outings. Your off-hours won't be left to the afterthought column anymore. Use the living résumé as proof of the life you're making and a way to identify the activities and fun that let you know you've really lived. You were definitely here!

### The Living Résumé

- Name, real life identity
- Life mission
- What I want to experience on this planet
- Interests/favorite activities
- Most fun experiences
- What I've been up to lately (trips, outings, socializing, activities)
- Upcoming activities

........................................................

# Guilt Detox

The performance identity needs an enforcement mechanism to keep you on the straight and productive road, and I'm sure you are quite familiar with what that is. When you pull back from your job to try to enjoy a little downtime, you feel the twitchiness, the shame, the verdict from your commandeered brain: guilty! You should be getting something done! If guilt was gold, we'd all be millionaires.

Think for a second about what you've ever gotten for your hard-earned work guilt. Still thinking? The answer is: nothing. Work guilt stirs up turmoil and stress for zip.

It's not even guilt in the first place. Psychologists say that work guilt falls into the "unreal" guilt category. It's a false alarm.

You haven't punched anyone in the face or slashed his tires, or committed real harm. This guilt is an anticipatory anxiety—and a manipulation by others.

The voice in your head saying that you should work until eight p.m. or skip your vacation is not yours, just as the performance identity is not the real you. The "shoulds" come from others—parents, coaches, bosses, the culture—and get synthesized by the shadow identity into a bogus internal compass that feeds you nonsense. Guilt is optional. You can scrap it by refusing to let others make decisions for you. When you reflexively follow the "shoulds" of others as a result of guilt, you're letting someone else choose for you. The conflict between what you want and what the nag wants results in guilt, if you don't do what you're "supposed" to, or resentment if you do. In reality, there are no "shoulds," only choices. Make a conscious choice, and you resolve the conflict by making it your decision, so you don't feel guilty as charged.

One of the chief guilt inflictors is the false belief that free time has to be justified, because it's a lesser realm that takes you away from production. The angst you feel from this belief, since guilt is a stressor, comes from the same place that stress comes from, the primitive panic hub of your brain called the amygdala, a reason-challenged zone. Free time needs no justification—that's merely the performance identity's spin on it. You don't have to justify living your life. That's the goal of the work, isn't it?

• • • • • • • • • • • • • • • • • • • •  ACTIVATE  • • • • • • • • • • • • • • • • • • • • •

## Choose to Lose Guilt

Eliminate work guilt by making conscious decisions that take control out of the hands of manipulators. If you feel that you "should" work on a Saturday and follow the guilt inflictor's command in your head, you'll feel guilty if you

don't work and resentful if you do. If you instead make
a deliberate choice—even say it out loud—to opt for a
day of refueling or time with your family, because the
work can be done on Monday and staying healthy and
connected to family are priorities, you won't be racked
by guilt. You made the decision and had a reason for
it. Choose not to burn the midnight oil because you've
told yourself that your brain is fried and you know you
wouldn't get much of anything done in that state, and
you beat the guilt reflex that drives burnout.

## The Road to Living Well

Sages have been trying to get it through hard human heads
for centuries. All that glitters is not gold. The stampeded path is
the one to avoid. The externals we measure worth by are a mirage.
It's better to give than to receive. On the Greek island of Crete,
many still practice the concept of *philotemo*, a sense of gener-
osity that honors acting without regard to money, power, or
payoff. In the South Pacific, giving away possessions is a custom
in Polynesian and Melanesian societies, a relationship-building
tradition. Because baubles and glitter are the visible currency
of the modern realm, though, the shiny stuff has been able to
overwhelm folk wisdom. But now the philosophers have some
heavy hitters in their corner, scientists, who are demonstrating
in a variety of empirical ways that the road to "living well," as
Aristotle called it, is an unconditional one, a path well off the
track of the performance identity.

"When people are oriented toward goals for growing as a
person or goals for having good relationships or for benefiting
the community, they're happier," says Knox College psychologist

## Make Your Own Lottery

Like many people today, Rich and Amanda Ligato found themselves in a cycle of commuting and crashing on the couch. Amanda worked as a VP of human resources for a financial company in San Diego, and Rich was an office manager for KOA Campgrounds. One day on his way to work, Rich saw a billboard that would change their lives. It was an ad for the California Lottery pitching a $14 million jackpot.

No, they didn't rush out to buy a bunch of tickets. Rich came home and proposed a different scenario to his wife: "What would you do if you had $14 million and money was no object?" Her answer was easy: "Travel the world." That was his dream, too. Then came the next question. What if they didn't need a lottery jackpot to act on their dream? What if they could make their own lottery?

"We were on the success track, but the fun wasn't there," recalls the energetic Amanda. "We were thinking, Is this all there is?"

It wasn't. They decided to own their time. The Ligatos got their dream on paper and on a budget. They saved for six years, bought an old VW van, and made their break. They drove from San Diego to the tip of South America, then shipped the car over to Africa for more adventures on a three-year, 60,000-mile journey. The couple trekked the Inca Trail, hung out with mountain gorillas, and rafted the rowdy whitewater of the White Nile. That was just the beginning. On a follow-up adventure, they bicycled for a year and a half through Asia.

In the beginning, Rich was "terrified of everything. I was very much afraid at every border," he admits. "But all my fears were unfounded." The Ligatos listened to their guts instead of their fears.

The travelers discovered that the world outside the production bubble is the home of personal progress. When their van broke down in the Andes, they found themselves staring into the innards of an engine that neither one had any idea how to fix. So they pulled out a copy of *How to Keep Your Volkswagen Alive* and leafed through it. They were stunned when they were able to fix the engine themselves. "We started to realize that whatever the problem was, we could fix it," says Rich. "When you step out of your comfort zone and figure things out, you think, I can do this."

The Ligatos came back from their adventures brimming with confidence and resourcefulness, hallmarks of having ousted their impostor identities and reclaimed their authentic selves.

Taking a page from the Ligatos, if you won the lottery, what would you do? Make a list of the top possibilities. How could you start down that road today and make your own lottery?

---

Tim Kasser. "We want to act from a more intrinsic, enlightened place." That reflects our authentic nature, Kasser tells me, but we get tripped up by our fixation on external rewards.

Humans do better with internal motivation. Multiple studies in more than a dozen cultures have shown the power of intrinsic values to increase well-being, positive mood, vitality, and esteem. Act unconditionally, and you get the best return of all, life satisfaction, because you are aligned with your values and goals, says Kennon Sheldon, a psychology professor at the University of Missouri and a leading investigator of this realm. He calls that dividend "self-concordance," a harmonic state when goals reflect "the person's deeper or true condition."

This is where science and spirit meet, in the proactive experience of becoming who you already are, as Alan Watts might have put it. Watts, whose pioneering interpretation of Eastern thought laid the foundation for all of the current advocates of living *now*, would have loved the latest research. He argued that we could find our true natures only when we lose "the result-seeking mechanism"—the ego—which is what happens in the moment of full engagement. The result-seeking mechanism is useful for putting food on the table and a roof overhead, "but when the results the mechanism seeks are not external objects but states of itself, such as happiness, the mechanism is all clutched-up. It is trying to lift itself up by its own bootstraps. It is looking for results in terms of itself. It wants to get results from the process of looking for results."

External rewards sabotage your experience by placing all of the value on the finish line. This is like judging a meal by the last bite, or as Watts was fond of saying, a concert by the last note, when it's the melody we're here for. It makes behavior that has no external dividend attached to it seem as exciting as waiting in line at the DMV. Unfortunately, that includes all your fun and diversion.

Edward Deci conducted a study in which one group of subjects was paid to solve a puzzle, while another group got no money. The people who didn't get paid were interested in playing with the puzzle just for fun when the lab director left the room at a planned moment, while the financially motivated ones had no interest in playing unless they got paid. "Stop the pay, stop the play," Deci summed it up later. That's what happens to your play when the performance identity is at the wheel. It stops the play every day if there is no payoff. Sheldon and Kasser found that people who are focused on rewards have unsatisfying experiences marked by pressure and tension—not very conducive to enjoyment.

The way out of the external box is the life intelligence skill of satisfying your core internal needs. They know where the real value is.

••••••••••••••••••••• ACTIVATE •••••••••••••••••••••

### No Gain, No Pain.

The wisdom of acting without expecting an external reward might be obvious to sages and spiritual teachers, but for most of us, it flies in the face of logic and what we see happening around us on terra firma. When you do something, you want some reciprocity. If you don't expect anything, won't people turn you in to the authorities for suspicious behavior? Maybe. But it doesn't matter what anybody else thinks, only what *you* think. Identify three intrinsic actions you can take that would have no gain attached to them. Write down how you feel after performing each of them. What kind of external rewards do you normally expect? How long do they last compared to what you got from your intrinsic activity?

# The Ultimate Arbiters of Worth

No small amount of human duress is caused by a basic flaw in our perception. What we think will make us happy isn't necessarily what we need. What do we need? That's been a gray area that advertisers have happily filled in for us, creating needs where there weren't any, for designer water, military-sized SUVs, and athletic shoes with blinking lights in them. If we knew what really satisfied our deepest needs, we'd know where the real worth was hanging out. How valuable would that be?

The good news is that there is an empirically tested solution to this problem. The consensus among social psychologists is that humans have three basic psychological needs—for autonomy, competence, and relatedness. This is the triumvirate of what's known as self-determination theory, a model devised by Deci and Ryan. No matter how much external success you have, you will remain unfulfilled if even one of these core needs is not addressed—and they can be satisfied only when the goal is internal.

Gratifying your core needs switches on your real identity. They are the ultimate arbiters of self-worth, a built-in homing device for you to discover the person you are meant to be. These fundamental urgings take the guesswork out of wanting, not to mention the guilt out of living. When you're doing what you're supposed to be doing, satisfying your innermost aspirations, what's there to feel guilty about? What a gift, actually knowing where you can go to feel good besides to the refrigerator or the mall. I'd like to see these needs pasted on every refrigerator, bathroom mirror, and forehead in the land. Or maybe on a line of mugs. Follow these internal compass readings, and you obliterate the blathering of the performance identity. You know where the good stuff is now.

"When people are oriented to goals of doing what they choose, growing as a person or goals for having good relationships, they experience higher levels of the basic psychological needs and they're happier," explains Kasser.

The professional world is an external affair, for the most part, so core needs, such as autonomy and competence, find best expression in your private life. Active leisure has an uncanny ability to satisfy those needs.

As it is in physical fitness, psychological wellness is all about the core, in this case, what kind of shape your chief need-satisfaction muscles are in. These are areas that don't get much of a workout when your energies are devoted to the more glamorous external side of life, so if your muscles are a little scrawny, don't worry. You can build them up quickly with regular use.

The heart of the program is motive. You have to engage unconditionally. Intrinsic motivation is the scientific take on what Buddhists call "right resolve" or "right intention," or the

Taoists, "the course of nature." The intrinsic approach produces full engagement via internal goals—for creativity, excellence, growth, fun, exhilaration—focusing you without expectations. There are no barriers to your attention and immersion. Do it to do it, and you are in the highly concordant place where the chief ingredients of optimal living meet: experience, intrinsic motivation, and the moment.

> Intrinsic motivation + experience + now = optimal moments

Internal motivation interacts with your core needs as leavening does in a loaf of bread. You can have all of the ingredients to make bread, but without this fermenting agent, the dough doesn't rise to the occasion. Unless you're motivated by the right purpose, your potential to satisfy autonomy, competence, and relatedness can't lift off, either.

## The Washboard Core

The belief that our lives can be improved from the outside is rooted deep, from the times of Aladdin and his magic lamp to the lottery and the breathless hawkers on the Home Shopping Network. Our core needs tell us that we're waiting in vain, and that we are the ones who must make our lives fulfilled through self-determined actions. Our core needs are satisfied not by thinking, but by directly participating in life's meaningful experiences—by working them out as you would your body. Here's how you can keep your core needs as fit as washboard abs.

### Pumping Autonomy

To satisfy your need for autonomy, you have to feel as if you're making a free choice uncontrolled by others, which is the definition of free time. Being able to do the things you want to do is a key part of the well-being and worth picture. Autonomy comes from a desire to feel as if you are the author of your own script. When you feel that your activities are self-chosen, the autonomy is paid off with a sense of self-determination, which brings life satisfaction. The operative sensation with autonomy is freedom—not the kind you know as a concept or a symbol but something you can feel to your marrow. The more freedom you feel in your leisure activities, the more equipped you are to cope with stresses and setbacks in life, say researchers.

You can't feel true autonomy if you act because others want you to or if you feel pressured or forced to do something. This undermines the intrinsic element of doing it to do it that creates the sense of autonomy. If you go on a diet or start a kung fu practice, it has to be because you want to do it for yourself, not because of outside pressure.

How do you know if you're acting autonomously? Sheldon says you should ask these questions:

- Are my choices based on my true interests and values?
- Am I free to do things my own way?
- Do my choices express my true self?

*Act autonomously:* What do you want to do, apart from anyone else's opinion, that can give you a sense of autonomy? Learn how to cook? Sail? Where can you be in control of your actions, without constraints or concern for external rewards?

## Lifting Competence

Before Amy Doran stumbled onto the kite world, her need for competence was left solely to her job. That wasn't enough, so she had little confidence in her own ability to be successful at something other than what she had always done at work—until new capabilities blew in on a kite.

There's a slight catch here. Competence has to be combined with autonomy. You can be competent on an assembly line, but you won't have a true sense of effectiveness, because you're doing it for a purpose that is controlled by others. You have to feel that you're acting freely, and that there is a degree of challenge, or you won't feel your competence is being demonstrated.

The need to feel effective is essential to self-worth. Learning a new skill is one of the best ways to activate competence. In one study, first-time whitewater canoeists reported a surge in perceived competence as they took on and handled new risks. Your competence might be stuck in a professional rut, but you can always keep growing in your nonprofessional life. You're not dependent on every phone call or positive review for your worth, when you have skills outside the office.

*Pursue competence*: What would you like to be better at? What are you dependent on others to do? Take on these challenges, and competence will follow.

## Crunch Your Relatedness Muscles

Feeling connected to and cared for by others satisfies your core need for relatedness and intimacy. It's a well-vetted predictor of personal validity and well-being. David Myers, a psychologist at Hope College and the author of *The Pursuit of Happiness*, says that people who are content with their social lives are happier and healthier. Studies have also shown that folks with strong interpersonal connections live longer (married people outlive singles, for instance) and are physically healthier.

Unconditional involvement in active leisure is one of the best ways to satisfy your core need for relatedness. Everyone in the activity automatically has something in common with you, so it's easy to connect with people and make friends. The basis for the relating is the fun and the activity, not what anybody does for a living. You don't get the judging that goes on in the rest of our lives. Play keeps the yardsticks away.

*Build social connections*: Try a local interest group in your area, from wine tasting to hiking or philosophy. Find listings on the Internet or go to www.meetup.com, a site with a host of social activity groups to choose from.

## For What It's Worth

The engine of worth is fueled not by nonstop output, the approval of others, or any of the other external badges that keep life in a vise grip, but by the expression of your interests and aspirations. Follow your core needs, and you shut off the performance identity and the bogus instructions that come with it. Free up your core, and you can engage the world in the unconditional mode that creates optimal living. To recap, then, the keys to getting there are

- Untangling your true self from the counterfeit identity of performance
- Resisting the siren song of contingent self-esteem
- Beating the manipulation of guilt through conscious choice
- Embracing unconditional goals
- Satisfying your core needs for autonomy, competence, and relatedness through self-determined experiences

Now you're ready for the next stage of activation: learning the skills without which there are no thrills.

# 3

## No Skills, No Thrills

Note to self: See ophthalmologist. I'm watching a couples dance sequence demonstrated by my salsa instructor for the third time, and I have no idea how he's doing it. How is that possible? I'm staring right at him. Maybe I have some spatial defect that can't translate spinning arms and legs. Exasperation sets in, as I move along to the next woman in the class rotation, ready to showcase my Keystone Kops version of salsa. "I hope you're insured," I tell her. The voice in the adult mind says, "Hopeless—you'll never get this."

Loving the combustive mix of jazz and Cuban *son* that is salsa is no ticket to being able to glide on the dance floor. You need the combined talents of jujitsu, Twister, and a very good sense of humor to outlast your own klutziness. I remember a class where Gary, a reserved giant a little taller than me, at about six-six, got tangled up on a sequence that required one too many hook turns, which are tough on long legs. He hit the deck, crashing into the

Christmas tree at the dance studio, not once, but twice. He shook off the pine needles, kept practicing, and went on to become a very good dancer. Height, tallness or shortness—it doesn't matter. Look at Tommy Tune, the six-foot-six Broadway hoofer par excellence. It's all in the mind and the discipline.

The paradoxical thing about play is that you have to work at it to acquire the tools of enjoyment. In salsa, you need listening skills, dogged persistence, regular practice, and no ego. Sometimes a little support from your friends helps. I was tempted to chuck it a couple of times, but I got some remedial help from Marty Herman, a certified public accountant reincarnated in his fifties as an insatiable *salsero*. Marty went over a few of the moves and assured me that he had been equally clueless at the beginning. Dancing of any kind for him, in fact, was once a matter of high anxiety.

Before he had the skills, whenever he went to clubs and asked someone to dance to rock songs, it was always an intensely unpleasant experience. "I'm a very risk-averse person outside my comfort zone," he said. "I had to force myself to do salsa."

He started out with ballroom dancing but noticed that it was salsa dancers who seemed to have the most fun. Yet there wasn't much of that in his early days of trying to learn the footwork. "It was very frustrating," he said. "I'd look around the room and feel like I was the only one not getting it."

Determined to carve out a social life, Marty kept chipping away at it, until one night I witnessed a scene at a salsa club that in the past would have made him pull a muscle laughing at the preposterousness of it. The dance floor had been cleared, except for Marty, who was celebrating his birthday. He stood in the spotlight of the birthday dance, a ritual in which members of the crowd spontaneously jump in to dance with the guest of honor. The deejay slipped on a salsified "Happy Birthday," and it was go time. A woman took his hands, and the footloose CPA quick-quick-slowed into action. He launched into a cross-body inside turn, spinning the woman once, then went to a hammerlock and a reverse hammerlock and on to the smooth entwinement known as a pretzel, as the crowd clapped to the rhythm. Another half dozen or so women broke in to dance with him during the course of the song. He kept ticking on the beat like a metronome—because he'd put in the work.

That included a regimen of regular practice and overcoming major barriers to improvement, such as going out to clubs and asking strangers to dance. Getting out of the cozy house at night, dancing in public when you're still a greenhorn, and the fear of rejection were big obstacles, but Marty was able to push through them to develop his competence to the point where salsa could become a passion. He now hits the salsa floor four times a week and has a large network of live, nonvirtual friends he didn't have before.

Marty conquered a steep learning curve with something more powerful—the ecstasy of the dance, the gateway to celebration. The body knows what you need to do to contact the deeper rhythms and the life force of joy, but the head, captive to the performance mind of control and coolness, suppresses it. For millennia, letting the backbone slip was the order of the day, as it still is in the oldest culture on the planet, that of the Bushmen. Dancing has been at the center of their universe in southern Africa for tens of thousands of years.

"We dampen our feelings, but the Bushmen feel butterflies and they want to go deeper into it," says Bradford Keeney, a renowned family psychologist, cross-cultural explorer, and author of *Shaking Medicine*, *The Aesthetics of Change*, and a trove of other works. Keeney has lived and danced ecstatically with the Bushmen of Namibia's Kalahari Desert. "They remind us of something we've forgotten—how joyful and amplified our feelings can become."

During many all-night sessions of wild "shaking," as he calls it, with his friends in the Kalahari, Keeney has come to see that the Western world has cut itself off from one of the most vitalizing forces in life: the transformative and healing power of movement. "Excitation and arousal wake you up," he tells me. "You feel more fully aware of your presence in the world and desire to participate in it."

The experience of motion calibrates, attunes, and infuses you with spirit, maintains Keeney, who has studied and participated in ecstatic traditions from Bali to Brazil, to St. Vincent Island and the churches of Louisiana. He calls the shake the oldest medicine on earth, a resource that renews the spirit and, as a result, the body. With data showing that aerobic activity and passionate play lower stress and increase immune function, there's no doubt we all could do with some shaking all over. As with play, the key is letting go completely of what Keeney calls "the culture of being in control." Much of human longing, he thinks, is a quest for the spirited life that is locked out by the overpurposeful stranglehold of modern life. "You know you have the spirit when you have the shake," says Keeney with a laugh.

Or when you're in an improvisational salsa whirl. I eventually did learn salsa, which allows me to ride a wave of synchrony that borders on the telepathic. I'm playing a jazz solo with my body, no longer in the guard box of restraint. The joy we're taught never to show to strangers is loose and beaming on my face, as it is on my partner's. Movement unlocks it all, loose limbs forcing the mind to follow and stay a while. As Alan Watts wrote, "Life is a dance. And when you are dancing, you are not intent on getting somewhere." You are there.

The route to passions like salsa is what your mom said—"Do your homework, and then you can play"—and dancing is one of the most effective ways to play. "Why is dancing so good?" asks the University of Maryland's Seppo Iso-Ahola, whose passions are ballroom dancing and golf. "Sense of competence, social interaction, camaraderie. And you're doing it because you want to do it, so you have a sense of self-determination and freedom. You have all the elements of leisure right in it. So it cannot be any better than that as a leisure activity."

"I wish I'd known about this thirty years ago," Marty tells me, before heading out on a Sunday salsa doubleheader, afternoon and evening. "But it's never too late. I know I'll be dancing for a long time."

It's not too late for you, either. You can go from zero to a vitalized life by acquiring what you need to really live: leisure skills that develop a potential passion, help you sustain interest until you're competent, and optimize your experience in the moment. In this chapter I'll introduce you to those tools, which we'll explore through the activation process in the following six chapters. I'll also provide you with a road map to the type of experiences that deliver the most satisfaction—gratifications— and I'll take you through the steps of the passion-building process. The arousal and excitation essential to a spirited life are at your fingertips, when you know that passions take foreplay.

## School of Living

The conventional wisdom says that all you need to enjoy your off-hours is a padded backside. Maybe a full refrigerator. There's nothing to leisure, because you're doing nothing, right? Don't tell that to Sonja Rodriguez, a technology executive for Homeland Security, who, before she could discover her passion for ice hockey first had to learn how to ice skate and study the rules of a game she had no clue about while growing up in Puerto Rico. Don't tell Chicago ad executive and road racer Mike Valenti, a man who paid his cycling dues to learn the dynamics of riding in the pack. "It takes three to four years to get to be a good pack rider," says Valenti, founder of veloist.com. "Being able to sit in someone's draft is something that takes practice."

Whitewater kayaker Chris Joosse, a software developer for Microsoft in Tacoma, Washington, says you can't immediately hop into a boat and sail off waterfalls, as he does. He estimates that you'll "need two hundred to three hundred days on the river" to reach your prime paddling level. You have to know how to get in and out of eddies, recover from capsizing, and read the water, among other talents.

The notion that leisure is some kind of inert state is fiction. The real meaning of the term as defined by the ancient Greeks and college recreation and leisure instructors today is an active state of learning that allows you to realize your potential. The Greek word for leisure is *skole* ("school"). Aristotle argued that it was a realm for self-fulfillment, the ultimate in higher education. Leisure is the road to discovering the world around you and within you, an open university with the best teacher on the planet: experience.

The curriculum requires that you pick up some knowledge of, and aptitude for, the subject at hand. If you don't have the life intelligence skills to do that, it's easy to default to passive diversions—Web surfing, watching DVDs, checking e-mail, checking e-mail again. Participant skills are hard to come by in a world where the defaults are to consuming entertainment as opposed to making it, and to the spell of digital screens. It's as if life were a seat you could buy at TicketMaster to sit through to the final act or something that could be crammed into the window of a cell phone. More and more heads these days are stuck in the down position, buried in portable devices, oblivious to the sun in the sky, the breeze in the trees, the life draining from sedentary limbs.

# You Can't Text Goose Bumps

Many people today are afflicted with a problem that is a major barrier to any semblance of life participation. It's called Attention Deficit Trait, a condition identified by Massachusetts psychologist Dr. Robert Hollowell to describe the growing epidemic of shredded attention spans. Unlike Attention Deficit Disorder, you're not born with it. It's the byproduct of constant interruptions that undermine your ability to pay attention.

The average knowledge worker today checks messages fifty times a day and gets more than one hundred e-mails. Constant interruptions erode a part of the executive attention function in your brain called effortful control. That regulates your impulse control. The more interrupted you are from e-mails, texts, and cell phone calls, the more your ability to control your attention is damaged. In other words, the more you check e-mail, the more you have to check it. With friends like yourself, who needs enemies?

Under the influence of ADT, you can't control other bad habits either, because your self-regulation equipment is on the blink. This addiction to self-interruption makes it hard to pull away from distractions and disconnect from the almighty e-leash for the self-determined actions that are required for optimal living. It also makes it hard to bring any kind of focused attention to whatever you're trying to do to enjoy yourself. Limit your message-checking to four times a day (the most productive schedule, according to the research) and make sure you get daily disconnect time, and you can build enough attention again to experience the exotic world beyond e-devices.

## R&R Management

Becoming a participant in life requires that you have more awareness about how you make the decisions that bring about high-quality experiences. Let's look at how you're currently managing your R&R schedule. On a scale of 1 to 10, how active are you in making decisions about what to do in your free time? What percentage of your discretionary activities originates outside your own mind—for example, you turn on a screen or do what your friends suggest—versus ideas that you initiate? How does the quality of your experience change when the activity is something you initiate and participate in, compared to watching? What would make it easier for you to initiate and select ideas?

### Try This at Home

Human beings have been inventing objects to play with and challenge themselves from time immemorial. The earliest mention of a toy dates back to a Greek yo-yo in 500 B.C. In the early 1970s, a couple of friends in Oregon added a play device to the tradition that lets you kick up some skills around the house or the block—the Hacky Sack.

It began when John Stalberger and Mike Marshall kicked around a beanbag that Marshall had stitched together while Stalberger was recovering from a knee injury. They used their feet, soccer-style, to toss it back and forth and called it "hackin' the sack." Their makeshift game would turn a device that had never made it out of the carnival circuit into a personal fun tool and an international sport called "footbag."

You don't have a lot of excuses to stay on the couch with Hacky Sack. It's dirt cheap to pick up one of the crocheted and fabric bags filled with pellets, beans, or sand ($4 for a cool yin-yang or native Guatemalan patterned bag at globalmarketplacestore.com). You don't need anyone else to do it with, although you can make friends quickly if you start kicking the bag in a public space. The idea is to keep the bag aloft, kicking with the sides of the feet or the toes. There is no purpose here other than fun.

As your expertise increases, footbag becomes a combination of kung fu and ballet that's also a great workout. You can see what I mean by checking out Hacky Sack pioneer "Danceman" Steve Blough get down in these vintage videos at www.footbagging.com/free.htm.

## Oz Sanchez: No Excuses

The usual strategy for getting a life is one that we've all had at one time: the pseudo-vow. "I'll take that cruise when things aren't so crazy at work." "I'll get back to swimming again when I can find a partner to do it with." "I'll join that yoga class when I get some new sweats." It's amazing how long it can take to track down sweats when you're not really looking for them.

There's no shortage of alibis—too far, too expensive, you might not be good at it. Your spouse or friend doesn't want to go with you, so you can't do it, either. Why not? You could go by yourself to a class or an activity and meet all the people you'll need, folks who share a potential passion with you. Why let anyone else choose whether you live? If you don't cultivate life intelligence skills—a pursuit of competence, attention-directing, intrinsic motivation, and the discipline of commitment—the excuses win.

Oz Sanchez had plenty of excuses. He was riding a motorcycle when a car ran a stop sign and sent him flying off a twelve-foot embankment in San Diego. He landed on a pile of rocks, breaking his back. The former marine was paralyzed from his knees down at the age of twenty-five, just a few days before his wedding. He would be in a wheelchair for the rest of his life. "It really took a toll on me," says Sanchez. "I went into a very dark area, depression."

He "dwelled in self-pity" for a while and plunged into a period of deep despair. But Sanchez decided that he could not be a victim and started to climb out of the pit. He enrolled in college. Then one day he saw his first hand-cycle, a three-wheel bike you move with a hand-cranked pedal, and he thought it could be a way back to life.

After eighteen months in a body cast, he was euphoric at the freedom he felt being on a bike. But it was a whole new cycling experience with his his arms doing the pedaling. He had to learn how to steer, pedal, and brake with his hands and moderate his speed around corners or he would topple over. You can't lean as you would on a regular bike. Slowly, he began to build his upper-body strength and endurance. He kept training, and after a year of learning the ropes, he decided to enter a 10K race. The following year, he took on a marathon—and came in second. Sanchez was back among the living, thanks to play that became a passion.

"Hand-cycling helped redefine me, helped me get confidence and fulfillment again," he said. "It's such a rush feeling the speed and pushing yourself."

He trained so hard that he was chosen to be on the U.S. Paralympic team. A few years later, he won the gold medal at the Beijing Paralympic Games in 2008. He's now the best in the world at his sport.

Sanchez had every excuse to be a spectator, but he fought to be a participant in his life. Now he's helping others do the same, with motivational talks that inspire people to find the will within themselves to live to the fullest. "A passion is a very powerful thing if you can tap into it," he told me. "You've got to discover what yours is. You'll get from it a burning desire to achieve your goals. I sure did."

...................... ACTIVATE ........................

### Smoke Out Life Blockers

Many obstacles to life become so routine, we don't question them anymore. They're just part of our automatic behavior. Turning off that autopilot is your mission, as you clear a conscious path to a life of no excuses. The place to start is by taking an inventory of what stands in the way of a richer experience. What are the biggest obstacles to your living a more vital life? Money? Time? Exhaustion? Distance? Play venue? Social obstacles? Identify your chief life blockers. Come up with five excuses that keep you looking into the window of life. Now devise an answer to counter each excuse.

## Play to Seek

Plenty of pastimes (we should really call them present-times) don't require any skills this side of sentience, and this is where it's easy to get muddled about your off-hours choices. You don't need to be a prodigy to wield a remote control or feel your tensions melt under the hands of an artful masseuse. The body favors sensory and distracting enjoyments that require no skill

---

## Liquid Bumper Cars

There are a lot of paddling options these days, from kayaking to canoeing, rafting, and dragon boating, but all involve some level of skill to get the most optimal experience, whether it's navigating through sea waves or flashing through a whitewater chute.

One of the best places in the world to discover a paddling passion or improve your boating skills is the Nantahala Outdoor Center in the mountains of eastern North Carolina. With seven rivers to run in the vicinity, including its namesake, the center offers whitewater instructions for kayak, canoe, and raft at every level of ability on two-day and five-day courses from May to August. It's a liquid roller-coaster ride that sharpens your reflexes, wits, and confidence in the midst of uncertainty, while making you holler like a second-grader. See their Web site at www.noc.com.

---

and involve no challenge. The default is to choose what's easy, which feels good but doesn't fill you up.

Because passive entertainment is what gets drilled into us, this can easily wind up as the de facto downtime in your life. University of Pennsylvania psychologist Martin Seligman calls this realm of bodily delights and eye candy "pleasures." They require little in the way of participation or thinking, so their effect on well-being is ephemeral. "Once the external stimulus is gone, the positive emotion sinks beneath the wave of ongoing emotion without a trace," he says. If pleasures are your only life strategy, they leave you always wanting more.

Active hobbies and recreational outlets deliver experiences that stay with you. Dubbed "gratifications" by Seligman, they are part of a higher form of enjoyment that comes from engagement. Gratification is the long-term expression of satisfaction, a by-product of experiences that are challenging and involving. A major element of gratifications is that they tap into your own personal expressiveness, giving you a deep sense of identification apart from the work mind and other people's opinions as to who and what you're about. As you might expect, that feels pretty darn good. These more involving pursuits satisfy the brain-neuron mandate for novelty and challenge. They can include both mental and physical engagement, from astronomy or jewelry making to triathlons. The key distinction between the pleasures and the gratifications, of course, is the level of participation, as you can see in these examples:

*Pleasures/Passive Leisure*
Dining in a restaurant
Shopping
Watching a movie or TV
Hanging out at a bar
Watching a sporting event
Surfing the Web
Collecting

*Gratifications/Active Leisure*
Softball
Hiking
Chess
Volleyball
Quilting
Cycling
Line dancing
Diving

Unlike with off-the-shelf pleasures, you need to expend some effort with gratifications. Whether it's dragon boat paddling, mentoring kids, or sculpting, they are more challenging experiences that demand knowledge, dedication, and training. But if you make the investment, the dividends keep coming in the form of optimal experiences, self-expression, fun, and friends, rewards that top by a light-year or two what you get from zoning into the glow of your cell phone.

"You're constantly learning," says Werner Haas, a chemist in San Jose who gets his gratification from two activities that are a world apart—orienteering and ballroom dancing. He runs in an orienteering race every other week, scrambling through brush to find hidden controls with clues from a topographic map. "You get scratched up, muddy, dirty, fall on your butt, but it's a test every time you do it. It's that growth aspect that's fun. It's the same with dancing."

For Bill Selmon, a Chicago advertising tech, the challenge comes in a more creative form: painting. An oil painting class resuscitated his love for art and gave him an outlet that he spends twenty or more hours a week on. Even though he likes his job, Selmon says it's "not my idea. My painting is something I'm doing from beginning to completion on my own. My free time is my time to work on things I want to work on." Selmon, thirty-six, gets plenty of gratification from his passion for painting.

Gratifications are the kind of R&R you want more of. Iso-Ahola points out that they come from a seeking mind-set, as opposed to an escapist one typical for the pleasures. Recreation seekers, who are driven by personal and interpersonal goals, are less bored, more fulfilled, and healthier than people fueled by the escapist motive, he says. Spend too long in the latter mode, you become dependent on the entertainment served up until you don't know how to occupy yourself off the clock. Your self-determined core needs autonomous action.

## Avoid Diversionary Tactics

One habit that gets in the way of gratifying pursuits has to do with how you manage attention. The reflex to divert your attention to distractions in a free moment undercuts what your brain actually wants, which is engagement, directed concentration on novel and challenging experiences. Become aware whenever you have the impulse to shift your attention to a distraction. Instead, think about what you can focus your attention on before grabbing the cell phone or turning on the computer. That's where the engagement is. Ask yourself:

- What can I learn?
- What can I try?
- What can I experience?
- What's interesting in front of me right now?
- Where can I discover something?
- Why am I boring myself?

•••••••••••••••••••••••••••••••••••••••••••••••••••••••

# Life-Tasting

Show me someone with a lot of interests, and I'll show you someone who finds life interesting. Experts say it's the range of activities you're exposed to that gives you the best chance at a thriving life beyond work. When you get stuck in a rut—kids with ballet, soccer, or video games; adults with golf or poker—you limit the universe of what can really excite you because you limit your play and life skills.

Finding your passions is like wine tasting. The idea is to sample many kinds of activities, some of which grab your liveliness buds, while others may not quench your thirst. Where do you find the vintages that hit the spot? Start tasting, beginning with things that

- You used to love but dropped
- You've been wanting to try but haven't
- Make you happy
- Look intriguing
- Look fun but you think you can't do
- Are affinities and areas of interest
- Are out of left field, but you want to try

•••••••••••••••••••••••• ACTIVATE ••••••••••••••••••••••

## The Best of Times

Most of the play domain is ad hoc. We bump into this here, that there, and don't spend any time dwelling on what was fun, ecstatic, or satisfying about it. The more you zero in on what satisfies you in your off-hours, the more you can plant yourself in the vicinity of what really delivers the goods. Write down five of your most memorable leisure experiences. What did you like about them? What needs did they satisfy? Fun? Relaxation? Social connection? What's the common thread? What can you try that could provide more of that?

•••••••••••••••••••••••••••••••••••••••••••••••••••••

### How to Set a Volleyball

It gets lost in the big spikes and digs, but the central skill in volleyball is setting. The setter is like a point guard in basketball, making the right pass in the right place at the right time. Here's how to make a good set: Keep your hands close to your face, four to six inches above your forehead, with your fingers in the shape of the ball coming at you. Watch the ball in the window between your thumbs and index fingers. Face the direction you're setting to, and lift the ball with your fingertips—no palms—and arms and legs.

## The Passion Finder

Beyond the default of habit, there's a recreational option, likely several of them, with the power to make you feel so alive you'll need to look in a mirror to see if it's really you. You find them not through osmosis but by exploring and targeting activities that can bring the best internal return. The hunt for passions begins by identifying your participant style. What types of off-hours experiences do you like? Do you prefer social or more independent activities? Indoor or outdoor? Challenging or relaxing? Physical or mental pursuits? Competitive or noncompetitive?

Let's flesh out your participant profile further by zeroing in on the kinds of activities you're drawn to. Do you prefer hobbies and crafts? Sports? The creative arts? Maybe you've got multiple interests—all the better. You can pinpoint your affinities with the activity style test. Which of the following genres of R&R fit your interests? Which are you curious about? Which offer the most fun, challenge, or interest?

Outdoors
Hobbies and crafts
Creative arts
Travel
Games
Sports/physical games/fitness
Dance

Music
Science/mind play
Volunteering/service

The activity style test is part of a tool that helps you organize your life hunt: the passion finder. (See www.dontmissyourlife .net.) The idea is to discover potential hobbies and passions by choosing the genres you prefer and matching your participant style and goals with the pursuits. For instance, if your purpose is to socialize, you could find it in paintball, dancing, or stargazing parties with fellow astronomy buffs. Of course, not all of those activities might fit your genre affinities. The next step is to map out your chief R&R goals. They include:

Social connection
Mastering a skill/learning
Fun
Creative expression
Playing a sport
Fitness/exercise
Discovery/exploration
Service/helping others

Start with the genres that you have a preference for. Then look at the specific activities for the genres you like in the passion finder list and check off things you're interested in. From sports to social activities to volunteering, your options are vast, and you can mix and match, say, dancing and service. You'll be amazed at the number of volunteer programs that you can connect with. Check out http://www.volunteermatch.org/ to find an organization near you. Start brainstorming ideas here, concentrating on activities within genres that appeal to you, intrigue, or thrill.

*The Passion Finder*

**Outdoors**

- Archery
- Backpacking
- Bird-watching
- Bouldering
- Camping
- Canoeing
- Canyoneering
- Cycling
- Diving
- Fishing
- Fly-fishing
- Flying
- Geocaching
- Hang gliding
- Hiking
- Horseback riding
- Horseshoes
- Hunting
- Ice-skating
- Inline skating
- Kayaking
- Kite flying
- Kite surfing
- Mountain biking
- Mountain climbing
- Orienteering
- Paragliding
- River rafting
- Rock climbing
- Sailing
- Skydiving
- Snowshoeing
- Spelunking
- Surfing

**Hobbies and Crafts**

- Beadwork
- Calligraphy
- Candle Making
- Crochet
- Knitting
- Origami
- Quilting
- Scrapbooking
- Woodworking

**Creative Arts**

- Animation
- Calligraphy
- Cartooning
- Community theater acting
- Cooking
- Drawing
- Film/video making
- Illustration
- Jewelry making
- Gardening

Glass making
Landscaping
Metalsmithing
Painting
Photography
Poetry
Pottery
Sculpture

## Travel
Adventure travel
Barging
Cycling
Cruising
Freighter travel
Independent travel
Multisport
Rafting
Roadtripping
Trekking
Voluntourism

## Games
Backgammon
Billiards
Board games
Bridge
Chess
Dominoes
Go

Mah-jongg
Poker
Radio-controlled
    vehicles
Video games

## Music
Accordion
Bagpipe
Banjo
Bass
Cavaquinho
Cello
Clarinet
Composing music
Cuica
Deejaying
Drums
Dulcimer
Euphonium
Flugelhorn
Flute
French horn
Garage band
Guitar
Harmonica
Harp
Harpsichord
Lute
Mandolin

Marimba
Oboe
Organ
Percussion
Piano
Recorder
Saxophone
Singing
Sitar
Synthesizer
Trumpet
Trombone
Vibraphone
Violin

## Sports and Fitness
Aikido
Badminton
Baseball
Basketball
BMX
Bodybuilding
Bowling
Boxing
Capoeira
Cycling
Fencing
Football
Golf
Judo

Hacky Sack
Karate
Kung fu
Motocross
Paintball
Pilates
Running
Sailing
Skateboarding
Skiing
Soccer
Softball
Swimming
Table tennis
Tae kwon do
Tennis
Triathloning
Wakeboarding
Waterskiing
Weightlifting
Wrestling
Yoga

## Dance
Bachata
Ballet
Ballroom dancing
Belly dancing
Bolero
Cha-cha

Classical dance (Indian, Thai, Balinese)

Clogging

Cumbia

Folk dancing (Irish, Greek, and hundreds more from around the world)

Foxtrot

Hip hop

Hustle

Jazz dancing

Line dancing

Mambo

Merengue

Native American dances (hoop dance, rainbow dance)

Rumba

Salsa

Samba

Step dancing

Square dancing

Swing

Tango

Tap dancing

Waltz

## Science/Mind Play

Archeology

Astronomy

Botany

Entomology

Gemology

Fossil hunting

Geology/Rock hounding

Learning a language

Robotics

## Volunteering/Service

Animal shelters

Big Brother/Big Sister

Disaster relief

Greenpeace

Habitat for Humanity

Mentoring

Nature Guiding

Researching

Teaching

Maintaining trails

Marathon race volunteer

Tutoring

On the Web site, you'll also be able to see what level of effort is required for various activities, how long it takes to build up skills, and physical fitness levels that are required.

Finding what works is not just a question of your affinities and capabilities. The activity has to be one that is truly your choice. Why do you want to do the activity? To look good? Be cool? That won't work, because it undercuts the intrinsic motive. You have to be in touch with your true leanings. What are those?

- Which activities are the most fun?
- Which offer the most potential to learn?
- Which are the most meaningful?
- Which offer the most potential for camaraderie and friendship?

## Passions Need Foreplay

Some people lead lives in the shadow of the brilliance possible, while others bask in the bold strokes of primary hues, lit bright by the vitality of their passions. Having an enthusiasm that connects with you at a core level to look forward to energizes your life and provides purpose and meaning. The surfer checking the weather report every morning, the artist who can't wait to get home from work to return to a canvas, the table tennis player hooked on the Sunday pickup match at the gym—they have an extra gear or two of aliveness when a favorite activity becomes an extension of who and what they're about. They're excited to be here.

This is the bliss we're always told to follow. Not everyone can find it, though, because we're never given the facts of life, about how passions really work. Unlike romantic passions, they don't appear across the room, instantaneously setting your heart aglow. They're a vague glimmer that won't deliver thrills until you've gotten the skills.

The kind of passions that may someday be a source of rapture don't seem that way to begin with. For Sonja Rodriguez, it started with a hockey tournament that her boyfriend took her to. She had assumed that hockey was "all about fights," but she saw a few teams of women flying around the ice. "It looked kind of cool," she recalls, no pun intended. "I'm competitive. I could see myself getting into it." When she got home, she went online and started to research women's amateur hockey, although she had never ice-skated in her life. It took six months of learning how to skate and play the game before she joined a team. Nine years later, the Homeland Security executive plays on two teams, skating four times a week. "It's fast and exciting. Playing goalie is like life. It's all in the timing."

Passions take foreplay, which comes in the form of skill development. The passion that can transform your life from missing or just okay to extraordinary has to be built, says Robert Vallerand, a pioneer in the field of passion research and a psychologist at the University of Quebec. Vallerand and his colleagues have studied passionate cyclists, water polo players, music students, and synchronized swimmers in search of the keys to avid involvement. They discovered that healthy or, as they call it, harmonious passions spring from an autonomous personality that seeks out the goal of mastery in life activities. Mastery is an intrinsic aspiration that puts the focus on learning and drives "deliberate practice." A lot of it.

This jibes well with research findings on happiness that emphasize the role that effort plays in creating satisfying experiences out of the 40 percent of your happiness that you can affect through intentional activities. The two components of effort are initiating activities and then maintaining them (for more details on these, see chapters 4 and 9, respectively).

Repeated effort through practice operates as a self-propulsion agent, leading to improved ability and further interest, until the activity begins to define you. Vallerand boils down the passion process into three basic steps:

1. Select the right activity.
2. Increase the intensity of your interest with more competence/practice.
3. Internalize the activity by valuing it as a part of who you are.

For an activity to turn into a passion, it has to click with your core needs, especially autonomy and competence, providing meaning and a sense of growth that connect with you internally. "The more important [or valued] the activity, the more the activity will be internalized in the person's identity, and, consequently, the more passionate the person will be toward this activity," notes Vallerand.

Internal motivation is crucial to allow you to stick with the activity long enough for it to develop into a passion. So is autonomy. In a study of first-year music students who had never played an instrument before, only a little more than a third, 36 percent, developed a passionate interest in playing their instruments by the end of the term. The key difference for students who felt the sparks was that they didn't feel forced into playing. It's straight out of the self-determination playbook. The students who felt that it was their choice and interest they were pursuing were the ones who found the love.

Darrell Kunitomi is a practitioner of a pursuit known for its die-hard adherents—fly-fishing—which, in his inimitable style, he says is "chess to checkers, compost versus 3-in-1 Miracle Gro." He has thousands of flies, artificial bugs used as bait, scattered around his home, some he's collected and many he's made himself. The Los Angeles actor, director, and communications specialist has been at his passion, which is all catch-and-release, for twenty-five years and says he's still learning. His hobby is brimming with competence training. The food that trout eat is 90 percent underwater, but Kunitomi likes the challenge of trying to get them to bite on a fake bug on the surface of the water.

"You put yourself at a disadvantage with fly-fishing," he says. "The flow of the water will defeat you, the cast will defeat you, the wind will defeat you. It's more of a celebration when you finally fool this animal."

Passions pay off in a host of ways. They increase positive emotions and the optimal experience of flow during the activity and boost positive mood and decrease negative feelings afterward. Kunitomi likes the Zen aspect of fly-fishing: the repeated casting and hiking through the water is a moving meditation that stills the mind. People with passions add eight hours of joy a week to their lives on average, say researchers, which can have a big impact on well-being, because it's the cumulative effect of many positive experiences that creates happiness. It's no wonder that studies show that the strongest factor in perceived wellness is leisure satisfaction and that participation in crafts and hobbies strongly relate to high well being and low depression.

## The Toolbox of Optimal Experience

People with life intelligence get a lot more bliss and peak experiences, no matter what else is going on in their lives, because they have a few more tools of the ecstatic trade than the average person. They come equipped with behavioral traits and talents that propel an interest from square one to the passion stage. Over the next six chapters, I'll break down the key skills embodied in the essential truths of the experiential process: the laws of optimal life.

Each law distills a component part of the activation process. Like all truisms, these precepts spell out the way things really work or, in this case, play. They put you in the vicinity of participant R&R and supply the smarts you need at each of the three basic phases—the tools that get you activated, the skills that maximize your enjoyment once you're there, and those that sustain your commitment until the activity becomes a full-fledged passion.

## Phase 1: Priming Equipment

**Law of Optimal Life:** Safe is sorry

**Skills:** Risk-taking, venture aptitude, initiative, novelty seeking

Despite the assumption that happiness requires more and more security, the evidence shows that true gratification comes when you leave the comfort zone. Security is a red flag for the brain, where neurons are begging you to take a leap and bring back novel experiences. Yes, it can be awkward and hair-raising to venture beyond the cozy fortress, but that is the only path to the growth demanded by your core needs.

The key skill here is risk-taking. People with life intelligence know that the real risk is in *not* risking. That's what causes life deficits and regrets. You can develop your risk-taking ability by learning how to tame the caveman brain that keeps pushing the panic button. The way to do this is through preparation and venture aptitude: exploring.

In real estate, it's location, location, location. For optimal living, it's initiation, initiation, initiation. Initiating is a self-starter skill that launches you out the door to discover the passions of your life. This can lead you around the globe as you put your novelty-seeking tools to the test in one of the best training grounds for this talent—travel.

**Law of Optimal Life:** Expect no payoff (and you get one)

**Skills:** Intrinsic motivation, self-awareness, goal setting, curiosity seeking

The engine of activation is the motivation behind it. Your best-laid life plans will founder without the right intention. If you measure your goal by external performance criteria, you won't feel autonomy or competence, thus no satisfaction. Internal motivation is the path that leads to the passions and the purpose that bring you your best times. By not focusing on an external gain, you get an internal upgrade.

You can't deploy the right motive, though, without self-awareness of your values and the curiosity to uncover and pursue new directions. Research shows that higher curiosity leads to greater meaning in life—not a bad pickup to get from a little play.

## Phase 2: Optimizing Experience

**Law of Optimal Life:** It's the experience

**Skills:** Pursuit of competence, attention directing, problem solving, flow

The pinnacle of an engaged life is immersion in a supercharged here and now through experience. This is when you plug into a heightened enjoyment that you didn't know was possible for an adult. It requires that you do something that all of your programming resists—surrender to where you are and be completely absorbed in it.

Life intelligence practitioners are adept at letting go of the work mind, the adult mind, the future mind, and bellying up to the bar of the experiential process. The central tool is pursuit of competence, a skill that fuels their absorption in the intrinsic mission of mastery.

Next, you'll learn how to direct your attention to develop the focus essential to make peak experiences fly.

Problem-solving skills will get you through the stuck parts—the inexperience, the exasperation, or the inherent problems posed by the challenge itself. All of these skills come together in the state of optimal involvement known as flow, times when you are so absorbed in what you're doing that nothing else matters.

**Law of Optimal Life:** Play is where you live

**Skills:** Eagerness, playfulness, suspension of reality, positive affect, being socially proactive

We had these skills at one time, but adulthood took care of that. There's no better way to shift out of missing-person mode than to pick up play skills pronto. The process starts with an attitude shift, as you move out of the shut-down, jaded, grownup mode and back into the eagerness we all once knew. This primes the pump for positive experiences, putting you in the spontaneous frame of mind that leads to that great liveliness engine: playfulness. You can dramatically improve your playfulness and boost your play quotient.

Play requires that you escape from preoccupation and the worries du jour, so you need to cultivate a knack for suspending reality and forgetting about all the stuff you should do. You set aside the usual rules and enter a world that is its own reward. Developing a talent for play means that you also have to be socially proactive and use its chief tool and the true secret of the universe—positive affect.

## Phase 3: Sustaining Participation

**Law of Optimal Life:** You are the audience

**Skills:** Reframing performance anxiety, foolishness, internal locus of control, ignoring social comparisons

You're playing to the wrong audience when others determine your passions. The only one who counts is pictured on your driver's license. People with life intelligence share an important skill that allows them to stay focused on their goal of maximizing aliveness no matter who's looking. This is known as *locus of control* in the psychological trade. It's the belief that you can determine your own path and that it's the right one, and that as a result you don't need the approval of others to validate your actions. Learn how you can make this skill part of your life arsenal.

When you activate an interest, it's often something you do in front of others, and that's particularly true with the performing arts. The gaze of others can keep you from doing what you always wanted to, unless you shut this reflex down. Two skills help your do this—the ability to reframe performance anxiety and the ability to ignore social comparisons, including the albatross of being cool. The reality is, fools have more fun. People who are willing to go with life, instead of appearances, are free to live as if no one is watching.

**Law of Optimal Life:** Passions take persistence

**Skills:** Bias for action, vitality, tolerance for ambiguity, the discipline of commitment

You have to keep showing up in order for a passion to erupt, so creating a pattern of activation to sustain your interests is key. The skills at the heart of that process are a bias for action, tolerating ambiguity, and the discipline of commitment. A bias for action is the energy side of self-determination. It's a knack for trying a new course without cogitating it to death. You have to seize the adventure of the moment with the bounce of activation. The resource of vitality promotes readiness for action.

Sticking with the action pattern is the toughest part. You'll need to bring a couple of other skills into play here: tolerance of ambiguity and the discipline of commitment. Tolerating the learning curve and your uncertain progress takes persistent patience. You'll learn how to withhold judgment, control moods, and delay gratification to develop your tenacity.

## Skills Add the Spice

The difference between watching others dance and being able to jump in and join them is like comparing oatmeal to a feast of pad Thai noodles and Panang curry. Active leisure skills make it possible for you to taste the sumptuousness of life. Finding the right thing to taste is about shifting from spectator to participant, a journey you can begin when you embrace these keys to activation:

- The ticket to optimal experiences is skill building that you stick with.
- The more pursuits you try, the better your odds of finding a passion.
- Go for gratifications, which involve effort, over easy pleasures; choose seeking over escape.
- Identify potential interests with the passion finder process.
- Passions take foreplay, time, and effort to develop.

# 4

## Safe Is Sorry

We spend our time searching for
security and hate it when we get it.
—*John Steinbeck*

The antidote to a missing life may be buried inside an old *Seinfeld* episode. Maybe you remember it. George Costanza decides to do something radical to change his loser status. From now on, he will do exactly the reverse of his normal inclination. "If every instinct you have is wrong, then the opposite would have to be right," Jerry tells him, and George can't disagree. Going with the opposite, George winds up landing a girlfriend and working for the Yankees, which is unthinkable for normal George.

The Costanza Correction is not far off from what it takes to activate full-life engagement. So much of what we do is the complete reverse of what can deliver regular doses of vibrant living that a 180-degree shift from reflex is in order. Opting for intrinsic goals that produce growth and happiness is the polar opposite of the usual dash for external rewards. Seeing quality R&R as the engine of life satisfaction and productivity is the opposite of all the training you get. And few of us would ever suspect that what our brains and psyches want is engagement with the unknown, the reverse of the impulse to cling to safety at all costs.

It's one of the great, or maybe not so great, paradoxes of the human condition. In your brain every day the forces of safety and comfort are hard at work trying to squelch your craving for novelty and adventure, otherwise known as progress. No wonder you get headaches. The security default seems like the way to go, but it's completely at odds with the growth you need to be happy, as well as with the experiential process. Both of these demand that you stretch and take risks.

Yet security holds all of the aces, thanks to a deck stacked in its favor by a quirk of evolutionary history that places the primitive emotional center of the brain, the amygdala, in charge during moments of perceived threat. When fear is in the air, the amygdala hijacks your higher brain and rationality and sends out alarms to keep you from straying from the norm.

Some experts say we have an itchy security trigger because the species had to be hyperalert to threats to our survival when we were hunting for dinner on African savannas. As a result, we overestimate the cost of risk and underestimate the conse-quences of playing it safe. The payback for not acting comes in stagnation, boredom, and vital life forces that are walled off by the guise of comfort. You might be safe, but you're sorry.

That's the hallmark of regret, something about as welcome as a root canal. The fascinating thing about regrets is that the biggest ones tend to come not from what you did, but from what you didn't do—an opportunity unpursued, things left unsaid, life unexperienced. When you look back, you're disappointed more by the course not taken, known as the "inaction effect" in one study. The emotion of regret appears to have been selected by evolution to encourage you not to be a slug, to act on the opportunities of life.

Safety doesn't look so good from a distance, because what it's really holding at bay is you. It puts you at odds with your own nature and that of the planet around you—both of which thrive on perpetual change. Certainty seems like a bulwark against the chaotic forces of impermanence, but if you try to protect yourself from the flux of life, you isolate yourself from it, which triggers the very insecurity you're trying to prevent.

Optimal living comes from doing the opposite of your defensive reflex. Find out how to reverse that default behavior with the second law of optimal life and the trigger of the activation process: safe is sorry. You don't want to leave any living opportunities on the table. Act now or forever hold onto your "if only's."

The security reflex obscures the fallacy behind playing it safe: there is no such thing as security. Learn how you can outflank the illusion of the cozy bunker when you activate the life intelligence skills of risk-taking, venture aptitude, initiative, and novelty-seeking. But first, it's time for a reality check.

### Kathy King and Hope Afloat: Time Is the Real Money

Kathy King was driving across Philadelphia's Whitman Bridge, on the way to meet her sister at a train station, when she got the news by cell. Her doctor had the results from a biopsy of a pea-size lump under one of her breasts. He got right to it. "It's malignant," he said.

"The tears just started flowing," recalls King, a technical designer for a clothing company and the mother of two daughters. "I was only forty-two. The odds were so small that it would be cancerous. I got to the train station, and I had this out-of-body experience. I heard this voice saying you're different from anyone else here. You have cancer."

Radiation and chemotherapy treatments followed. King's hair fell out. Her marriage broke up. She fell into a deep depression. Then a friend told her about a group of breast cancer survivors who paddled dragon boats, a team called Hope Afloat. Dragon boat racing is a two-millennia-old Chinese tradition that has taken off internationally in recent years. Twenty-two paddlers sit two across in a fanciful canoe-like craft decorated with a dragon's head on the bow and a tail at the rear. A drummer sits at the front of the boat and bangs out the stroke rhythm for paddlers, and a steersperson in the rear helps navigate. King knew nothing about the sport when she went to a practice session with the team on the Schuylkill River. She had so little energy, it was hard for her to even keep the paddle in the water, but afterward she found herself as elated as she was exhausted. For two hours, all that she had thought about was the rhythm of her paddle stroke. She had forgotten all about her health and marriage problems. She had discovered the riveting power of direct experience.

"I felt like I really belonged here," she recalls. "I said, I'm going to really do this and do the best that I can."

Flash forward six years to Orlando, Florida, and I'm in a dragon boat on the lagoon in front of downtown Disney World with King and Hope Afloat, trying to keep my stick in the water. The women are training for tomorrow's dragon boat festival competition, which will pit them against other breast cancer survivor teams from around the nation. Lifting a paddle from the water and putting it back in seems pretty basic, but I find myself in a fencing match with the paddles behind and in front of me, tangled up in missed timing. I'm proving to be an excellent braking device. The coach at the back of the boat, Robin Parker, also a cancer survivor, has other ideas—such as fast forward movement. She's ready to show everyone what dragon boating is all about. "I'm going to count to ten, and I want hard strokes," she tells the team. "Okay? Bury it!"

I dig into the lagoon and get on rhythm, but she stops counting at three. By stroke twenty-five, I'm sucking wind. "Are we to ten yet?" I ask.

I had forgotten the key word in this exercise: dragon boat "race." This is a sprint and a serious workout for someone who's fit, let alone a recovering cancer patient. Many of the women on the team were advised by doctors that they couldn't do anything strenuous ever again, and paddling—forget it. Some in the group have had cancer recurrences. Three members of the team died during the course of the year. "Just doing this is a big deal," says Tobi Goldberg Maguire, a scientific researcher at the University of Pennsylvania, who had never participated in any sport and took this up after a three-year recovery from reconstructive surgery after a mastectomy. "I didn't think I could do anything anymore. I was incredulous that I could do this." She's now in her fifth season on the team. She shows me her paddle, which is decorated with a saying by her late father, an amateur boxer: "Keep punching."

## Are You Limiting Your Aliveness?

How annoyed are you that at this very second, you could be sitting on a potential passion or talent that will never see daylight because you think you're less capable than you are? Inside you, say experts, an adventurer is waiting to bust out. Studies have shown that once you participate in an adventure activity, such as whitewater rafting or climbing, you discover that the risk is lower and your competence higher than you thought. Sticking your toe in the water is the primary ingredient in boosting your risk-taking skills. The unknown becomes a momentary hurdle when you conquer something you couldn't have imagined yourself doing.

Over a couple of days at the Orlando Dragon Boat Festival I meet a bunch of courageous and spirited women who have learned by virtue of their brushes with mortality that they can live more intensely than they ever thought possible, without the security that they now know was never there in the first place. Every Hope Afloat member I talk to says that her life is richer and more satisfying now than before she got cancer. The women are energized by their passion for paddling and the team. The security reflex makes you think you have something to lose by stepping outside the bubble, but these women know that the real loss happens inside the bubble, with a life that's unexpressed.

"It was an awakening to take my time more seriously," says King, forty-eight. "Before, I'd be tired and I would stare down at my feet. Now I look up at the sky, the buildings. I don't want to miss anything. People tell me, 'You have this spirit and energy about you. You're so happy.' I've never been happier in my life."

Security no longer gets in the way of King's life or those of her colleagues. They know the future is as certain as a crap shoot in Vegas and that Emperor Safety has no clothes. They are messengers of the news we prefer not to hear: time is the real money.

"My priorities are way different," says Cindy Roberts, a broad-shouldered, athletic woman who only months ago was frail and sapped by a mastectomy, steroids, and depression. "What matters now is the time I have left on this planet and living my life," says Roberts, forty-seven. "I don't know if I'll make it to sixty-five. I'm not gonna wait twenty years I might not have. I want to see the world now." When these women talk about doing something, they do it. Roberts just returned from a trip to Argentina, her first international foray.

Dragon boat paddling has empowered all of the women on the team through the competence they've developed but also through the support and camaraderie, more than satisfying their relatedness need. "Life before paddling was just breast cancer and kind of being by yourself," says Karen Lynch, a blond, ebullient woman. "Now that paddling is in my life and all these women—it completes my life. It makes me a better person."

On race day, swarms of paddlers make last-minute preparations at tents that are set up outside the Cirque du Soleil building. They lather on sunblock and pop on shades. There are a few elite competitors, but most are amateurs out for the fun and the social outlet. Some teams are corporate crews, others were assembled by friends, and then there's the breast cancer division.

The squads head down the gangway to the dock, clutching paddles and shouting encouragement to each other. Hope Afloat faces off against the Tampa Bay Pink Dragon Ladies, Miami's Save Our Sisters, and Vermont's Dragon Heart Sisters in a five-hundred-meter contest. As I watch them step into their boats, Lisa Stanton, a leader of the Vermont team, points out Livona Allen, a particularly courageous teammate taking a seat behind the drum on the Vermont boat. "Her doctor made it possible for her to be here today," Stanton tells me. "She's very sick and may not make it another week, but she wanted to be with the team one last time. She doesn't have the strength to paddle, so she's going to drum."

I feel my throat catch as I watch Allen take the drumstick. A week left. I vow to remember this scene any time I imagine that I have a problem. We are far too oblivious to the privilege of our own breaths. As Allen drums the team to the starting line, I hear the beat of one tenacious heart.

There's a song that puts this moment and the opportunity before you into the proper perspective. It's a piece that jazz pianist Robert Glasper composed for his mother, who died at the very young age of forty-four in 2004, and it's affected me deeply since I first heard it. On "Tribute," Glasper blends a lyrical piano with a recording of the stirring funeral eulogy for his mother, Kim, a blues singer and a mentor to Robert, delivered by the Reverend Joe Ratliff. This song cuts through all of the dramas and delusions that hijack the realization of our lives. Ratliff winds up his remarks by citing the twin signposts of Kim's life, birth date in 1960, and passing in 2004, and then he says, "But neither of these dates are what brings us here today. It's the dash between the two. Ahhh, not that she was born, not that she died, but because of the dash. She lived! I mean, she lived! I mean, her dash is vibrant. It's not broken, it's full!" Take that sentiment and shove it down the throat of fear.

Back in Orlando, the air horn sounds, and the boats are off. At two hundred meters it's anyone's race, with Tampa Bay slightly ahead. The dragon heads on the bows lurch ahead, tongues flapping, then slide back as boats jockey for the lead. I can hear Robin in her childlike voice screaming, "Take me home," which is the cue to pour it on. At about a hundred meters to go, Hope Afloat turns on the gas and pulls farther ahead with every stroke, powering to the finish line for the victory. Fists and paddles punch the air. Hugs erupt.

Then comes a different celebration, not of victory but of life. The four boats glide near the dock and form a circle. In silence, the women toss pink carnations into the water in memory of teammates who have died. The moment is emotional for all of the paddlers, and particularly for King, who lost her seatmate, Sonya Adams, earlier in the year and wears a pin to commemorate her and another teammate who died, Fawn Vrazo. King's eyes well up as she walks up the gangway from the boat.

King has "learned to live in the moment, because you don't know what the next minute, hour, or day will bring." For the healthy, it seems that there's always time to get to it later. As the women of Hope Afloat know, there is no later. There is only the drumbeat of your heart now. Are you listening?

•••••••••••••••••••••••• ACTIVATE ••••••••••••••••••••••••

## Today Is the Day

The paddlers of Hope Afloat are messengers. They tell us that the problems we think we have are obscuring the point of what we should be doing here: living every moment as fully as we can. Imagine that you are told you have only six months to live. What can you do to live full-tilt, starting today? What plans will you make to ensure maximum living? Act "as if" and bring that urgency to your life now.

••••••••••••••••••••••••••••••••••••••••••••••••••••••••••

# What You Don't Know Can Thrill You

It happens to all of us. You wake up one day, and you realize that you have been here before, just like yesterday and the day before that. Most of us live inside a carefully controlled bubble of habit. It's safe, operating from the I-know mind, but it's also a numbing bore. Vitality and growth lie beyond the bubble, in the unpredictable world of the I-don't-know mind. Not knowing is the ticket outside the secure perimeter to the gratifications awaiting you.

The evidence shows that you are happier and healthier when you engage in new experiences. One study found that the need for novelty is so important to human development that the brain treats the unknown as it does a positive outcome. MRI scans showed that the right ventral striatum interpreted novelty as if it were a positive event that actually occurred, suggesting that novelty is its own reward, which ties in splendidly with the inherent payoff of intrinsic motivation.

That neurological reward happens for a reason: to impel you beyond the familiar. In a term that I love, researchers call the dopamine that is released in anticipation of novelty the "exploration bonus." We're all explorers if we simply follow the bouncing ball of our biochemistry. The novelty reward is a motivational cue that prompts us to learn and broaden our world.

Why do we pass up our bonus? "People so often stop growing and even actively resist change because they cling to the conceptions of the world and themselves that provided them maximum safety and security," explain psychologists Tom Pyszczynski, Jeff Greenberg, and Jamie Goldenburg in a state-of-the-science article, "Freedom versus Fear." That's "antithetical to the integrative processing of new information and experiences through which growth occurs."

It is the person or the passion you don't know that can get your core needs out of suspended animation. It's written in your gray matter. "Each network in your brain is striving against each other for feedback from the outside world," writes John Ratey in *A User's Guide to the Brain*. There's a cell-eat-cell competition for new data. "Couch-potato cells" that don't get enough signals will die off, while cells that stay active continue to grow and build in strength.

Dendrites, the conduits between brain neurons that keep information flowing, shrink or vanish altogether if they're not stimulated with new input. Active learning and physical exercise increase dendrite networks and also boost the brain's remarkable regenerating capacity, known as plasticity. "Neglect of intense learning leads plasticity systems to waste away," notes Norman Doidge in *The Brain That Changes Itself*. A pioneer of plasticity research, Michael Merzenich, says that "it's the willingness to leave the comfort zone that is the key to keeping the brain new."

The insatiable appetite of kids to explore their worlds or of scientists to spend decades trying to solve a mystery reminds us of the discovery impulse we all have when we don't pay attention to comfort zones or clocks.

## Do the Costanza

Comfort is a great seducer, a reflex that trumps the experiential magic that awaits you when you step off the known world. Break the comfort trap by challenging yourself to discover at least one new thing every day. When you feel yourself in replay mode, stop and go in the other direction. Do the Costanza Correction, instead of what the rut is telling you to do. Experiment with all of the things you can do differently in your day. Take a different off-ramp when driving home. Walk in a different direction on your lunch hour. Try a new coffeehouse. Practice catching yourself in mid-rut and aborting your habit. What will you discover this week?

# You Can't Live without Risk

In the classic noir thriller *The Night Has a Thousand Eyes*, Edward G. Robinson plays a man who can see the future. It's not a pretty sight. His gift becomes a curse, because he winds up knowing too much. Total predictability is not a recipe for a happy life. If you knew everything that was going to happen before it did, there would be no novelty, no autonomy, no punch lines. The uncertainty of life is the basis for the satisfaction that comes from uncovering the new or challenging yourself, which requires putting your nerves and ego to the test.

The surprising thing about risk is that we should be pretty good at it. We run a risk gauntlet every day. Every time you get in your car, there's a risk of an accident. At dinner, there's a chance you might choke on something. Take a shower, and you might slip and crack your head. Risk is an inevitable part of being the nonpsychic humans that we are—and of moving our self-determination needs forward. There is no freedom, as in autonomy, competence, or guilt-free aliveness, without risk.

Stepping out of the norm will naturally trigger some nerves. When you're trying something new, the thought of executing a salsa sequence in front of a crowd of onlookers or hurtling down a whitewater river on a raft is intimidating. It was for me. I was worried about being a klutz on the dance floor or winding up in the river. Both happened. Both were survivable lessons in the process of skill building. The problem is that we don't see process, only the performance identity's fixation on the end result: perfection.

The life intelligence skill of risk-taking lets you manage trial, as well as error. You're able to see risk, not as a dire threat but an incremental process of moving one step beyond the bubble and then another. It takes courage, yes, but it's only a temporary investment of nerves and ego in order to reap a lifetime of prizes: progress, passions, friendships. See the equation this way:

> Risk + temporary period of dripping armpits/
> exasperation/cluelessness = joy, progress, exhilaration,
> fun, competence, excitement, bliss

The aptitude here is managing uncertainty, which is a lot smarter than trying to avoid it at the cost of a life unlived. That's because risk, like the fear it produces, is very relative, subject to perceptions that change with your knowledge. What might be hair raising for you or me is not for others. And what's risky for them might be old hat for you. Wire-walker Philippe Petit has padded across cables strung high above windy valleys and skyscrapers (his walk between the Twin Towers in the 1970s, 1,350 feet above the streets of New York, is chronicled in the 2008 film *Man on Wire*). Yet he was afraid to swim until he was in his thirties. Petit says he doesn't think that his wire-walking is risky, because he researches it so thoroughly.

We can take more risks and feed our core needs with preparation and practice. Usually, we don't get that far, though. When a perceived risk appears in our consciousness, the primal impulse in the amygdala reflexively flashes the warning lights in less than a second. There's no time to get a rational thought in edgewise. Enter wild scenarios of what might happen should you step outside the bubble. You'll be a wimp if you don't stay on task. You'd be lousy at pottery or rock climbing. You might get mugged if you travel solo. There's no end to what the amygdala can concoct to keep you in a box.

Breaking away from the comfort zone touches off a discomfort zone, which sends us off on autopilot trepidation. We buy into these knee-jerk false alarms in the abstract without giving them real scrutiny. These are false choices kicked up by the amygdala.

The dread is all based on a very ballsy pretext—something that doesn't exist. Fear is a projected anxiety, a figment of your imagination that shuts down real opportunities for growth, aliveness, and meaning. Who's in charge here, you or a crystal ball?

The crystal ball is, actually, thanks to some bad brain architecture—until you activate the higher brain to rethink the situation. We react first and think later, thanks to the fact that the low brain that controls emotions was first on the scene and the portion of the higher brain that operates critical thinking evolved much later. You can overcome the fear reflex by contesting low-brain distortions and reassembling memories of them. Each time you recall a memory and add a detail by rethinking the event, you can change the memory's chemistry, say researchers, reducing the power of the initial fear.

The trick is to sort out the real risks—to your life savings, your health, your family—from events that merely upset your comfort zone. Let's draw the line right now on non-life-and-death fears that block the experience of optimal life. Projected fantasies will no longer be permitted to hold back a single adventure, a potential new friend, or a new discovery. No more opportunities to feel deliriously alive will be quashed by an irrational thought, by the false fright of a caveman brain that thinks the year is 200,000 B.C. Observe the fear—tell it, "Yeah, fine, I see you"—but act anyway.

The more you step out to be self-determined, the more you strengthen intrinsic self-esteem, which cuts down on the security reflex. People whose self-worth is based on intrinsic factors—internal validation, growth, choice—are much less defensive than those whose esteem is rooted in achievements and external approval. Once again, the performance identity is the culprit, making sure you stick to the training wheels and never ride the big bike of self-realization.

Play is a particularly good vehicle for overcoming fears, because it's a no-judgment realm that specializes in distracting you from limiting thoughts via concentrated activity. Vilma Mazziol, a member of the Hope Afloat team who was diagnosed with cancer at age thirty-seven, had an intense fear of drowning when she first tried out for the team. Now she's a veteran dragon boat paddler.

## ACTIVATE

## Defang Discomfort Zones

Identify a life risk you'd like to take but that you're blocked from acting on by a discomfort zone. What would you really like to do that would open up your life, but you're held back by the fact that you haven't tried it before, or you're concerned about how you might look? How mad does that make you? Zero in on the discomfort of that zone. Where is the aversion coming from? Every time you avoid confronting a fear, it imprints a pattern in your brain neurons that lock in the behavior. Step into the angst and look around. What's the root of the edginess? Keep digging until you find it. Now, identify why you have to break the avoidance pattern. Focus not on what could go wrong, but on what could go right. What would the internal benefits be for you if you took this risk? Feel what it would be like to drink in the fun, the camaraderie, or the challenge of this opportunity. What first step could you take today to move toward the goal?

......................................................................

## ⟿ Sara Lingafelter Hugs the Panic

Take on a risk, and you'll see that the fear is all bark, and you can bite back, even in some of the most high-risk activities. The barking was loud and ferocious for Sara Lingafelter, an attorney in Poulsbo, Washington. "I would describe myself as very risk-averse—make that, I have historically described myself as risk-averse," she says, laughing and correcting herself in mid-sentence. She has to reappraise her self-talk because Lingafelter is not the woman she used to be.

It all started when a friend talked her into trying a climbing wall one day at a local gym. Lingafelter, thirty-two, loved it, but climbing indoors was safe. Climbing in the wilds was another matter. She was terrified of heights and of falling— not a good combination for cliff-hugging.

Whenever Lingafelter tried dangling from ropes attached to towering rock slabs, she came face-to-face with her amygdala demons. "In the first years I'd find myself in a state of panic," she recalls. "I would hyperventilate and have to be lowered off the climb and have friends bring my gear back."

It was scary challenging the only fear that humans are born with: falling. But Lingafelter didn't run from it. She summoned up her courage and kept going straight at it, because she loved the outdoors, going on road trips to climbing hot spots around the Western United States, and hanging out with a growing tribe of friends who shared a passion for the rocks. She had to find a way to overcome the fear—of falling, of letting down a partner when she couldn't go any farther. She knew that most of her fears were irrational, but how could she turn them off? At the climbing mecca of Joshua Tree National Park in the Southern California high desert she fell, often as much as five feet down her rope, leaving her nerves swinging in the breeze. Rock climbing is a very mental affair. You have to convince yourself that your arm can span a gap you can barely reach to grab a crack or a piton hammered into the rock face while you stand with all of your weight on a nub in the rock face.

The solution didn't come overnight. Lingafelter kept reaching toward the fear. Little by little, she began to trust her own instincts, instead of giving in to irrational thoughts. Experience forged competence and then confidence, and that began to quiet the primitive brain. Today Lingafelter is boggled by what she can do that frantic brain burps once convinced her she couldn't. If the fear had won, she wouldn't have the anticipation of new adventures ahead at any time, a climbing blog that is one of the most admired in the field (theclimbergirl .com), a Twitter following in the thousands, "the most amazing friends," and the self-belief that tells her she can get through a climb, no matter what.

Lingafelter told me that one of her steady gigs, at an environmental resource nonprofit organization, may be numbered. "I'm not afraid," she says. "This is not six pitches up a rock face without a rope. It takes something much bigger

---

## The Challenge Course

If you want to build some risk chops, try a local challenge course. This experiential learning device gives you the chance to confront your fears and overcome inhibitions in a controlled environment. The activities can range from high-wire walking to trapeze swings, zip-line flights, and various other hurdles that can be anywhere from a foot or two off the ground to as high as fifty feet, all under the watchful eye of a trained professional. For the high courses, you'll be connected by a rope or climbing gear for your protection. Challenge courses build risk threshold, teamwork, and self-esteem. There are 8,000 to 10,000 challenge courses in the United States alone, so you should be able to find one nearby. The Association for Challenge Course Technology lists accredited companies at www .acctinfo.org/displaycommon.cfm?an=1&subarticlenbr=76.

---

than uncertainty to trigger a fear response now. That's a big change for me, because I've been a worrier my whole life. I feel like I've stepped off the moving sidewalk."

•••••••••••••••••••• ACTIVATE ••••••••••••••••••••

## The Other Cost of Risk: Not Risking

The primitive brain skews your perception of the cost of risk. It hogs the show, making you think only about the downside—in Sara Lingafelter's case, fear of falling and letting her friends down. But because she kept challenging her fear, she could see that there was a higher cost: what would happen if she didn't climb. She would lose the chance to enjoy adventures in nature with the people she loved to be around. Try to remember a life opportunity, an activity, or an experience in which safety prevailed and you didn't take it up or you bolted. What did you lose out on in that deal? What new adventure would you like to try, but you're held back by the safety instinct? Determine the cost of not diving in to the experience and facing down the fear. What's the price in potential fun, growth, or social possibilities?

· · · · · · · · · · · · · · · · · · · · · · · · · · · · · · · · · · · · · · · · · · · · · · · · · · · · · · · · · · · · · · · · · · ·

## The Exploration Principle

The essence of the self-determination at the root of your core needs is exploration, the need to move to a place that is more expansive, enriching, dynamic, where you can feel in your bones the progress of discovery. You can view risk in the same way. Stepping out of the comfort zone is merely exploration of a new skill or a destination—and of your own inner resources.

It's like the scientific process, merely a process of investigation. You find out what works by learning what doesn't. It took Thomas Edison sixteen hundred attempts to discover the filament that could conduct electricity in a lightbulb. I know you can light up your world quicker than that.

The life intelligence skill of venture aptitude is a powerful generator of participant experience. You turn risk into a quest to see what happens next, an experiment, an adventure. That way, the only failure is in not trying. The next time you're playing outside your comfort zone and start to feel jitters, tell yourself, I'm just exploring.

## Deploying Venture Aptitude

Risk-aversion wilts when you roll out your exploring mind. Here are five ways to step beyond the bubble and boost your engagement threshold by applying venture aptitude to whatever your risk is:

1. *Do it to do it.* This all-purpose intrinsic motivator ends the ego jeopardy that comes from the results-seeking mind-set. There's no harm to self-worth, because the objective is egoless—the pursuit of knowledge, challenge, or enjoyment.

2. *Make the unknown more knowable.* Knowledge trumps irrational fears. Talk to others. Do the research. Be aware going in that learning kung fu or tango will take a while, so you'll need patience. Start small.

3. *Don't look at the mountaintop.* Don't be intimidated by an overwhelming goal. Break it down to allow your competence to grow and don't dwell on unrealistic expectations. As you make progress, this will spur further risk-taking. Ed Viesturs, the first American to scale the world's fourteen tallest peaks, breaks down his climbs one base camp, one step, at a time. "You see this rock in front of you and say, I'm going to go to that rock and then I'm going to stop. And then I'm going to go to the next rock," he told me. His goal for the day is the base camp, not the summit. Make it yours, too.

4. *Advance into the fear.* You inflame fear by running from it, and you reduce it with every step that you take straight at it. As Mark Twain once said, "Do the thing you fear the most, and the death of fear is certain." Twain himself was deathly afraid of public speaking. He became one of the world's best live raconteurs.

5. *Dabble.* Put your foot in the water. Take a first step, and do it in an exploratory way. Try it and see what it feels like. Then dabble some more.

## Learn All about It

Active not-knowing is the route to knowledge and optimal living. You let the I-don't-know mind venture out
and find out the new story. It's very much the way that
journalists operate. Consider yourself on the beat of your
life story. Pick an activity, a place, or a person you know
nothing about. Maybe it's cooking, a part of town you've
never been to, or an acquaintance you don't know well.
Go on the scene and investigate. Ask questions without shame. It's easy when you don't know the subject.
That's why you learned so much when you were a kid.
Dig out the most interesting things you can find and
learn from the person or experience. Write a paragraph
on what you discovered and where you could venture
next with the knowledge.

# Something in the Way You Move

The battle between security and engagement comes to an absurd
head with the default to repeat oneself via the rut. You know
the pattern. You take the same route to work every day. You
keep going to the same Web pages. You sit in the same chair in
the class every week, though you are free to choose any. Pigeons
have nothing on humans in the homing department. If you
are fed up with a life of reruns, it's because your brain neurons are
fuming that they're getting the same data and are pleading with
you to get out and do something new. You can escape the repeat
beat with the skill of novelty seeking.

   You'll need to operate less on autopilot and become more
at ease trying things you haven't done before. Half the battle is

breaking the entrenched reflex built up by the rut. You can do that by scheduling diversions that get you off the usual orbit, and by making spontaneity one of your new intrinsic goals. First, you'll need to control time urgency, which can keep you in continual déjà vu mode, making you think you don't have a minute to deviate. But mix it up you must, or you wind up with a gnawing void inside your brain and soul. As we have learned, the mere hint that something new and unpredictable is about to happen touches off the brain's party chemical of dopamine, your exploration bonus. That seems like something that's worth having more of.

Travel is one of the best ways to beat the control system that keeps the unfamiliar at bay. You have official permission to not know where you are or even where the heck you're going, because you're not on home turf. You're relieved of command and the straitjacket of ritual behavior that comes with it. You're no longer driving yourself crazy trying to steer fate; instead, you're dancing with it. "Let life carry me," sings samba star Zeca Pagodinho, and that's my feeling precisely when I take to the open road. Travel, and the gate swings wide for the life forces of awe, wonder, and resourcefulness as you are surrounded by a world of novelty.

The delights of independent travel taught me early on that the less I try to control things, the more I'm able to get out of the way of my own life story. The highlights of my travels are always the places I didn't expect to be, the people I had no idea I was going to meet, and the marvels of human and Mother nature I never imagined.

On a road trip to Sedona, Arizona, I wound up discovering an amazing petroglyph site off the beaten track, down a dirt track with no tourists, that contained a record on its canyon walls of some two thousand years of human habitation, from early geometric designs to figurative Anasazi etchings, up

## The Stranger on the Train Effect

Are you looking for a good conversation? Hit the road. Within hours, you can get to know a perfect stranger better than someone you've worked with for years. It's a weird, exhilarating quirk of the travel experience, the friendship version of time-lapse photography.

Meet someone on a plane or in a distant holiday locale, and all of sudden, the usual barriers to connection and revelation are gone. Removed from the ties that bind to the workaday world and the caution that comes with them, you're free to be who you are to whomever. In no time, I've had strangers share doubts, dreams, and life bios, a Vulcan mind meld–like experience that liberates the real self behind the mask through unconditional interaction.

Psychologists call it the "stranger on the train effect," a phenomenon driven by the fact that what you say can't come back to haunt you. It happened on a train to Jane Ayer, a public relations entrepreneur in Santa Ynez, California. Traveling from London to Paris, she and the Parisian woman next to her got into it. "We just clicked immediately," she says. "It was like finding a soul mate."

We all get typecast at home, saying the same things to the same people. Travel breaks us out of the bunker so that we learn how to navigate the epic trip of strangers in search of connection.

to depictions of the Spanish on horseback. I found the site by having a conversation with a ranger at the tourist information office in town and asking about interesting, less-developed sites. As I stood before this cliffside history book, I closed my eyes and tried to imagine the generations of lives who had walked on this dirt, on freezing nights and blazing summer days, folks with hopes and fears, swinging from disaster to laughter, just as we do. It was a reminder that we are but a flash; we've got to make it a bright one.

At a lodge in the Brazilian Amazon, I got a tip about an unplanned activity up the Rio Negro, the vast blackwater river that intersects the Amazon halfway upriver. This is what I travel for: what's not on my schedule. A girl at a small village had taken in an injured river dolphin and nursed it back to life. The word got out in the dolphin community, and a pod decided to hang out with their buddy and his new human friends. There was the possibility of swimming with these rare creatures, remnants of ancient brethren who were cut off from the sea millions of years ago. The trip was several hours out of the way, but this was an adventure I wasn't going to pass up.

After a couple of hours of travel upriver through dense jungle, we tied up at a small dock in a village where kids played on a steep, sandy shore. Someone asked again about piranhas. We were told that there were no worries about them here. It made sense. Gobbling up tourists could be bad for business. I dismissed my fears and waded in to the denser water. Because of the sediment that washes into the Negro, the water was as black as Coke. That made it exciting, because I never knew when a dolphin would pop out of the water with a Mona Lisa smile or—whoosh!—brush my legs. They jumped up when they sensed that they could startle a human and darted around at will. It was thrilling to share the exotic aquatic world of these creatures that seem to know better than any other how to squeeze the maximum pleasure out of existence. I swam back to shore buzzing with adrenaline.

Travel often, and the unfamiliar becomes not only less threatening but welcome for the discoveries it brings and the tests you conquer. You become less fearful, more open to the I-don't-know mind, more confident that you don't have to know it all, more able to live in the moment, more okay with being vulnerable. Letting others know that you're lost or in need of a hand opens up the possibilities—and lifelong friendships. People like you better when you don't have all the answers.

The catch is that you get the benefits only if you're a participant in your journey. The magic is in the interaction. Participant travel skills are another thing that we're never taught. Because travel is one of the easiest ways to jump start a first-run life, it's time to change that right now.

# Participant Travel Tips

Venturing into the novel and unrehearsed comes very organically when you travel as a participant, instead of as a spectator. Here's a quick primer on keys to interactive travel.

- Research and plan your travels several months in advance. That gives you time to put together a trip with the most experiential potential.
- Find the interactive possibilities. What can you experience on your journey? What could break you out of the spectator role?
- Where's the novelty? Identify new things you'd like to try.
- Travel close to the ground and people—by foot, bike, or local transit.
- Find the opportunities. Once you're at your destination, dig through the available publications for interactive, immersive activities. Look for musical and cultural events to break through the tourist wall.
- Talk to strangers. Locals and fellow travelers will give you the tips that lead to your best adventures.
- Take the detours. Jump on opportunities to meet local people and get off the beaten path.

- Get out of character. Leave the personality straitjacket at home, and allow yourself to be more adventurous.
- Dump the production yardstick. No measuring allowed. It's not how much you do or see but how fully you engage in the experience.
- Play. You're at recess.

···················· ACTIVATE ·····················

## Vacations Don't Just Happen

Miss your vacation, and that time is never coming back again. You lose not only the chance to live as freely as you can all year but also amazing benefits for your health and work. An annual vacation can cut the risk of heart attack in men by 30 percent and in women who take more than two vacations by 50 percent. Vacations cure burnout, the last stage of chronic stress—but it takes two weeks for that process to occur. You need real time. Studies also show that your performance increases when you return to the job. But your holiday will slip away if you don't actively plan how to make the most of your time. Try to work out details of your trip at least four months ahead of time. You get the best deals by making reservations in advance. To ensure that you have the funds to travel, start a holiday kitty. Set aside $25 or $50 from each paycheck, and by the end of the year, you'll have a financial base to work with. Another key strategy to getting away is cross-training: training your colleagues to handle various parts of your job so that they can cover for you while you're gone, and vice versa. This is one of the secrets of long vacations in Australia and Europe. Make a list of folks who you could share your tasks with. Now, where are you going, and when, on your next vacation?

# You Have to Initiate to Participate

The skill that activates the participant experience is initiative. The good stuff doesn't simply show up; it has to be dug out. This means stepping out of the role of audience member and becoming an instigator. Part of the task is doing the legwork to identify activities or destinations you're interested in, and the other part is getting yourself out the door to show up.

Initiating is one key to the effort side of intentional activities that leads to happiness, say researchers. You need self-discipline and willpower to deploy it, and you increase your odds of being successful the more inherently pleasing the activity is and the better fit it is for your personality.

Do your research, and you can transform off-hours and travel from generic to custom-made, from sedentary to spine-tingling. The planning becomes part of the fun, setting off the anticipatory dopamine before you've even left home. Plotting an event is also a big part of the autonomy rush that you feel when you set a goal, map it out, and execute it. When I get back from a great trip, I'm fired up by a feeling of manifest autonomy and competence that powers up my sense of possibility. I thought up the itinerary, figured out how to get from here to there, and made it happen. I determined my life content. It doesn't get better than that.

It's true for all venues of activation: you have to initiate to participate, and that goes for rousing friends and family members, too. Initiators have a much better chance of realizing their self-determination needs than people who hang back and wait for an invite. There are risks in being the ringleader—potential rejection, judgment ("This outing sucks"), and the work of putting it together, but taking the lead is an essential skill of activation. If you want to ensure a life that is fully lived, you can't depend on others to create it for you.

## Incubate Fun

I'm a relentless hunter of activity info. I've found interesting things to do even buried in those generic in-room hotel magazines. I like to ferret out the obscure bar with a blues band, a park's dance class, or a local guide to lead me on a trek. I found a guide in the Cook Islands who led me on a jungle trek across the mountains of Rarotonga barefoot. I was impressed. Try to set aside time every week for event reconnaissance. It's easier to do than ever, thanks to the Internet. Your travels and activity options will be as engaging as the effort you put into fleshing out the opportunities to discover and participate.

Putting in the time on the front end will make your activities cheaper, particularly travel. There's a widespread myth that it's too expensive to travel, particularly to other countries. This is bogus. There are all sorts of inexpensive lodgings, cheap flights, and cost-cutting deals in a world of global competition for your dollar. You can camp in state and national parks for less than a cheap dinner out. Here are a few resources that can help you do more, save more, and build your novelty-seeking skills.

> *One-stop flight Web sites.* Kayak.com lets you canvass all of the other booking sites to get the universe of offerings on wherever you want to go. You won't miss much here. You can also try Dohop.com (for cheap flights), Vayama.com (for international travel), and SideStep.com for more comparison shopping on airfares.

> *Personal tour and lodging sites.* Rentalocalfriend.com connects you with local residents who will take you on half-day or full-day tours of their cities, from San Francisco, to New York, Paris, Lisbon, Shanghai, and London. If you really want to save money, try Couch-surfing.com, a site that matches travelers with a host

happy to let you stay for *free* on their couch or in the spare room. It's hard to top that deal, plus you make friends around the world. Another way to save money on lodgings is through social bed-and-breakfast Web sites, where you can find a studio apartment in London or Paris for $40 to $80 per night. Try Crashpadder .com, AirBnB.com, and iStopover.com.

*Local listings on the Web or in your paper.* Scour listings of events happening in your town every week, from local plays to concerts to sports leagues. They fly under the radar unless you search the fine print and call around.

LonelyPlanet.com. To get the lay of the land wherever you want to travel, check out the forum on Lonely Planet's Thorntree. It's loaded with tips on things to do and inexpensive places to stay or eat from people on the scene, from Colorado, Hawaii, or Florida to exotic ports around the world. Before I traveled to Burma, I found the information I needed for travel in this politically oppressed country from travelers who posted comments on the Thorntree about their trips there. I took off and had a remarkable adventure, experiencing what Asia must have looked like fifty years ago and meeting brave and resilient people whose quest for freedom is inspiring.

*Hotel deals.* For deals on U.S. hotels, I use Priceline.com. Try Agoda.com and HotelTravel.com for deals around the world and Venere.com for Europe. I got half-off rates in Rio de Janeiro from Agoda.com and four-star hotels for $30 a night in Asia from HotelTravel.com.

*Community college course/activity schedules.* Unless you're on campus, the doings at your local college wouldn't come to your attention. Visit the college's Web site or stop by in person, and find out what's going on. There's always a batch of interesting events, from lectures to astronomical star-gazing parties, to sports and games.

*National parks.* Check out the National Park Service site (nps.org) for ideas for your next trip. This is a fantastic resource to discover the host of natural spectacles that we don't realize are in our midst. Search state by state for the parks within each, and you'll never run out of trip ideas. The money excuse won't fly here. It costs $10 to $15 to camp at most U.S. national parks, with an entrance fee of $10 to $25.

*Discounted airfares.* Check out consolidators, wholesalers who have volume discounts. Airlineconsolidator .com claims to offer international fares up to 70 percent off the rack rates.

*Parks and recreation activities.* Recreation professionals are out there to help you stay fit and get a life at your local park. It's a great place to find inexpensive activities, from tai chi classes to softball. I found free archery lessons at a nearby park. Find out what's going on in a park or a recreation facility near you.

BudgetTravel.com. You can find plenty of ideas and deals at this site, from travel guru Arthur Frommer's *Budget Travel* magazine.

*Activity blogs.* If you want to find out about badminton or Borneo, check the Web for blogs on the topic.

As you increase your initiating skills, you'll get more comfortable doing things solo as well, including travel. I know from many independent travels that going solo increases the possibility of making new friends and uncovering adventures. You're more inclined to reach out, which gets you out of the bubble.

# Be Immune to Fear-Mongering

Here's something I don't think will happen in your golden years. I doubt that you're going to say, "Damn, I wish I had been more of a shut-in." Even though the fearmongers are doing their utmost to keep you from experiencing life, you have to ignore them. Your core needs can't stand to be cooped up. Take a cue from the women of Hope Afloat and grab a paddle and dig into life, with these principles as your fuel:

- Don't leave any living opportunities on the table. There is no later. The biggest regrets are the risks you don't take.
- Use homework and preparation to deploy the skill of risk-taking.
- Venture aptitude turns risk into exploring, no win or fail.
- Increase your novelty-seeking through travel.
- You have to initiate to participate in a fully lived life.

# 5

## Expect No Payoff (and You Get One)

The true way to gain much is never to
desire to gain much.
—*Francis Beaumont*

There was a time when everyone had a hand in their entertainment. If you wanted a concert, you sang. You didn't need judges, record contracts, or even karaoke machines to participate. I visited a village on the Fijian island of Viti Levu where that ethic still lives. One night I joined about two dozen villagers for an impromptu sing-along. We sat cross-legged, knee-to-knee, in a tiny community room, as a guitarist strummed and a group of adults and kids sang a collection of stirring traditional songs. The men wore skirtlike *sulus*, and some of the Afro-coiffed women held infants. They sang tales of local legends, softly and torrentially, and I slipped into a timeless South Pacific reverie. It was as real as the rips in the men's T-shirts. They didn't have much, but they had something powerful—the ability to lift up their spirits with friends and neighbors.

These days, the chance to affirm, console, or inspire through songs you belt out yourself is slim to none, outside of church pews. Singing has been appropriated by the entertainment business. It's for those who are "talented." Recently, though, I stumbled on some who don't think that harmonizing together is only for pros. At a yoga studio in West Hollywood, I sat in with a recreational choir, a group of folks who gather every Sunday afternoon for a sing-out. There were about forty members of the Golden Bridge Community Choir on hand, who ranged from their twenties to sixties. Many of them believe that singing together is the most important thing they do all week. Their eclectic songbook spans folk standards to African call-and-response chants, to sixteenth-century hymns.

"Okay, altos, try this," said Maggie Wheeler, our instructor and the cofounder of the choir. A vibrant woman with long brown hair, she sang into a wireless mike held in one hand and directed with the other. The altos tried her harmony line on a verse of "Turn the World Around," an infectious calypso classic from Harry Belafonte.

Before there were motivational speakers, anthems like this allowed you to pump yourself up for free. But we've gotten used to others doing the entertaining for us, to high-gloss production values, and to something else, the belief that there has to be some kind of payoff for everything we do. What am I going to get out of it? How is this going to get me somewhere?

I'll let Felicia Kelly, a business coordinator in a head scarf and a long skirt, answer that. The choir fanatic never misses a Sunday of song. "It's my favorite thing in the world," she told me earlier. "It's a religious experience without religion, singing a joyful noise, really rejoicing."

I could hear what she meant as everyone joined in—sopranos, basses, and tenors surging with the altos in a sublime, multilayered harmony. I had been lying low in the tenor section to avoid someone hammering the big gong near the stage and bouncing me. But as the choir rose, so did my voice. Carried aloft by the others, it seemed to fit right in. Whether it was the singing-with-headphones effect—you're Pavarotti when you can't hear yourself—or not, it was exhilarating. A burst of goose bumps signaled my liftoff from the usual mortal plane. The group dynamic was definitely part of the rush. I was no longer a solitary voice in the wilderness but part of something larger.

Researchers say that shared emotions can produce a state of attunement that is powerful. The bond is aided by a brain designed for social alignment. One of the instruments of connection is mirror neurons, which simulate the actions of others in our minds and emotions. "Mirror neurons make emotions contagious, letting the feelings we witness flow through us, helping us get in sync," explains Daniel Goleman in *Social Intelligence*. "We feel the other in the broadest sense of the word: sensing their sentiments, their movements, their sensations, their emotions as they act inside us."

The emotional force multiplier of a shared activity, particularly a celebrative one such as singing, can sure enough stir the soul. Sheila Gross, a psychotherapist who was cutting loose in the soprano section, said before the session that the first time she heard the choir, "I was just crying. Tears of joy, awe. So much beauty." At the time Gross was "only working, not filling my soul." She believes, "There has to be joy, spirit, a sense that you're part of something bigger" besides just the occupational side. She found the choral group a perfect tonic for the stresses of her job, counseling clients laid low by depression and anxiety. "There's something about expressing an emotion that's healing on some level. You feel good."

I'll say. Singing may seem like a simple diversion, low on the priority list compared to all the productive things we should be doing, but the research shows that it packs quite a punch for our well-being. Singing can make us healthier and happier. Cal State–Irvine education professor Robert Beck and Thomas Cesario of the college's school of medicine tested the saliva of members of the Santa Ana, California–based Pacific Chorale in action and discovered that a protein that's essential to fighting disease, immunoglobulin A, increased 150 percent during rehearsals—and 240 percent during performances! My favorite finding from the report is that the immune benefits rose in direct relation to how passionate the participant felt. I guess that means Celine Dion never needs a flu shot.

Other studies link singing with an increase in positive mood, social bonding, and improved health in the elderly. So, joining others in song, something the harassed work mind would write off as inconsequential, delivers in a way that polishing off the to-do list never can.

The crucial element isn't whether you have a good voice or perfect pitch; it's your participation. The Irvine study elegantly demonstrates the dynamic of the interactive moment: you get as much out of your involvement as you put into it, the benefits mounting with the level of your passion. To feel the magic, you have to step out of the role of spectator, of someone who is too busy, shy, or cool, and let the enthusiasm of your true self fly. And there's one more thing: your motive for doing it can't be that you want to get a record deal or blow away your next karaoke audience. You won't feel the ecstasy and true passion, as Felicia and Sheila do, unless your motivation is internal.

Singing for the sake of it is the quintessential intrinsic experience. You do it not for any external reward, but for the sheer joy of expressing yourself and sharing the glow of synchrony with others. As you will learn in this chapter, acting without regard to outcome frees you up for a deeper engagement with

## Raise Your Voice

The Golden Bridge Community Choir is part of a growing movement of recreational singing for people of all ages and abilities. Known as *ubuntu*, a Zulu word that means "I am because we are," the choirs build connection where there's not enough of it, through song, largely music from folk traditions around the world. There's no sheet music, no prior experience needed—you don't even have to be able to sing. There are no auditions. I walked in, Maggie Wheeler gave us lines to sing, and we were off.

"We come from a society rife with judgment of ourselves and everyone else," says Wheeler, who leads the program with Emile Hassan Dyer. "This is an arena where you can let that stuff go. We build and support a culture of kindness. You add music, and you're an instant community."

Harmony isn't an abstract ideal but something you can live and experience in a community choir. Find one in your area. The Ubuntu Choirs Network, based in Victoria, British Columbia, offers training programs if you'd like to start a choir in your town. Go to www.communitychoirleadership, www.maggiewheeler.net, and www.ubuntuchoirs.net.

life, at play or at work, because you have no expectations to snatch you away from the experience of the moment.

Internal motivation is the engine that drives an extraordinary life. It's the conductor of your aliveness and happiness and the basis for perhaps the most important law of optimal experience: expect no payoff (and you get one). Choosing internal goals over external rewards can make the difference between a life of chasing, and being disappointed by, yardsticks set by others, or whether you call your own tune and savor every note of it. That's the good news. The bad news is that intrinsic behavior is about as instinctive for most of us as particle physics, so it's going to take some practice to revamp the motivational gear. It's a radical departure from the default of external approval, but you can find your true bearings with the skills of self-awareness, openness and readiness, intrinsic goal-setting, and curiosity-seeking. Let's dig in.

## Why It's Wise to Get No Prize

There must have been something in the water 2,500 or so years ago. Between the sixth and fourth centuries B.C., three men with time to think and no BlackBerrys to distract them came to the same conclusion by three different processes of reasoning. Their deduction: the right life depends on the right purpose—an intrinsic one. Aristotle extolled the inherent value of personal goals, such as excellence and the pursuit of knowledge, which he considered much more important than wealth and more capable of leading one to the good life. The worthwhile life was to be found in self-improvement and learning. "All men by nature are actuated with a desire for knowledge," he said in *Metaphysics*.

In the East, Gautama Buddha and the Taoist sage Lao Tzu had already identified purposes at odds with our inner nature as the source of suffering and bad decisions. External desires set us up to be miserable, Buddha explained to his flock, "When one is overcome by this wretched, clinging desire in the world, one's sorrows increase like grass growing up after a lot of rain." Lao Tzu (who may have been a compilation of wise men) put the rulers of the day on notice in the *Tao Te Ching* that power, station, and money are a fool's gold, deceptions that get us off the authentic, natural "way." A few centuries later the gospel of Matthew would echo these sentiments: "For what does it profit a man who gains the entire world and loses his soul."

Modern researchers agree. The wise choice comes from the right motivation. Goals of self-enhancement, inherent interest, or community involvement lead people to be happier, learn more, and achieve at a higher level than folks motivated by external rewards. The unconditional approach works because it satisfies your core needs for autonomy, competence, and relatedness, which puts you right in line with the sages. The intrinsic path inspires a pursuit of knowledge, eliminates the illusion of desire, and keeps you on Lao Tzu's way, following the true course of your own nature. Internal motivation puts the wisdom of the ages and the thrill of the moment at your fingertips.

External goals don't deliver what you want because they satisfy only your perception of what others want. This leaves you dependent at any given moment on the next badge, notch, pat on the back, designer watch, or real estate holdings. "Extrinsic" goals, such as wealth, status, and performance yardsticks, are great—if you like stress and insecurity. Researchers have mountains of literature on how lousy those outer standards are at providing worth:

- The more importance placed on wealth aspirations, the poorer the well-being.
- When self-esteem is based on external measures—appearance, performance, approval—there is more stress, anger, and substance abuse.
- The stronger the financial goal, the lower the satisfaction with family life.
- Higher extrinsic values are linked with increased insecurity and lower self-esteem and with greater anxiety and depression.
- Focusing on extrinsic goals crowds out intrinsic experiences, such as living.
- Pursuit of extrinsic goals can lead to contingent self-worth (you're only as good as your next possession or success).

- External approval concerns lead to an increase in social comparisons with others—and more insecurity as a result (a huge killer of well-being, as we'll see in chapter 8).

The biggest toll of the external reward track may come from the way that fixating on outcomes affects your experiences. "People lose interest in many of the activities they perform," notes the University of Rochester's Edward Deci. "They begin to see the activities merely as instruments for . . . rewards, so they lose the excitement and vitality they once had for the activities."

That's how the bounce in your step goes missing. The culprit again is the performance mind, the need to validate by measurable output. Deci calls it "instrumental thinking," when everything you do is an instrument to bring about some result. This is deeply ingrained behavior. In an age when every conversation and Facebook "friend" is a potential rung up the ladder, choosing goals with no outer payoff can seem like naiveté run amok. Yet there's nothing more realistic than satisfying your core needs, if you can dig them out from the ones foisted on you.

•••••••••••••••••••••• ACTIVATE ••••••••••••••••••••••

## Recognizing a Killjoy When You See One

We don't think too much about why we want things. We simply know we want them, usually as fast as possible. That nonthinking impulse of desire works to the advantage of external motives, which are instinctive in a world of nonstop sales pitches. Training yourself to recognize why you want the things you do will help you turn off the autopilot of the external default. Track your motivation during the next few days at work and at play. Keep a list of the things you do for external payoff. What are they and what are the rewards? How long does the payoff buzz last before you need another hit? In your R&R pursuits, train yourself to catch payoff signals such as: Where will it get me? Who's going to be there? What would it accomplish? Every time one of these killjoys pops up, see it as a dictator keeping you in onlooker mode.

••••••••••••••••••••••••••••••••••••••••••••••••••••••••••••

## The Reunion of Self-Awareness

New car ads get nowhere with the University of Maryland's Seppo Iso-Ahola. He drives a vehicle that he has no desire to trade in. It's a choice that allows him to use funds that would be spent on car payments for something much closer to his heart. "I could buy a better car, but I'd much rather use that money for a vacation to Scotland to play golf with my buddies and have a great time," he says. "That to me is much more important. I value those experiences much more than the car."

Knowing what you value, as opposed to what marketers or peers think you should want, is where it all starts for your life hunt. The bearings of your inner compass can get severely tweaked from years of calibrating the demands of others. You have some dim memory, perhaps, of once walking barefoot in a park, maybe cruising under big skies on a road trip, or wanting to learn another language. The yearnings get submerged, though, in the autopilot of the job-and-survival game. Your intrinsic goals can resurface only when you exit the mechanical track.

The skill that reunites you with your own goals is self-awareness. It requires that you step away from output mode and reclaim your aspirations through the input of reflection and assessment. When do you feel most alive? What kinds of experiences satisfy your core? What are you passionate about? Intrigued about? What do you really have fun doing? What's missing from your life right now? Challenge? Fun? Meaningful connections with others? Intensity of experience? Keep the antenna up all the time for things that align with your gratification equipment, and for things that don't.

Awareness doesn't just help you formulate internal goals; it also helps you prioritize them. You'll see that free time isn't a deviation from what you're supposed to be doing on this planet but the means to satisfy your deepest needs. When you know that, you can take the actions necessary to make your life goals happen. These are known as negotiation strategies in the recreation and leisure field. You need tactics to get around the obstacles holding off an optimal life. What kind of tactics? Here are some strategies to prioritize free time and make sure you get out to enjoy it, as reported by active life participants in one study:

- I plan ahead to make leisure activities happen.
- I make my free-time activities a priority.
- I try to organize my time.
- I set aside a specific time for recreation and leisure.
- I find people to join me.
- I work hard to get more free time to play hard. (That's working to live.)

What negotiation strategies can you use to push through the obstacle course to optimal living?

·················· ACTIVATE ··················

## Wake-Up Wednesday

When hump day arrives, the weekend is within sight. It's a perfect time to set the stage for free time in line with your intrinsic needs. Set aside a few moments for

Wake-Up Wednesday, an exercise that allows you to practice self-awareness. From your scenic vista overlooking the weekend, identify which internal needs are most pressing and how you could satisfy them in your free days. Take ten minutes and a pad of paper and sketch out what your core is craving this week. Inspiration? Competence? Novelty? Exploration? What is it? Now figure out what kind of activity can help you sate it.

## Motivational Jujitsu

The premise of life assumed to be the gospel is that of quid pro quo. You do something to get something. Almost everyone wants a payoff. Not getting one is treated as a personal failure. Rewards are the official scorekeeper of progress in an externally driven world, but they don't make you feel like you've moved forward at all. They only make you want more rewards. "It is the nature of desire not to be satisfied, and most men live only for the gratification of it," wrote Aristotle, summing up this timeless futility.

Desire's henchmen are expectations. You expect something with an expectation, an outcome. If you don't get the outcome you want, you're not happy. Expectations fuel the external rewards default—and probably not surprisingly, unhappiness. Modest expectations have consistently shown up as a key marker of folks who are happy. What we expect a lot of the time is to be satisfied by other people's approval.

What if you could measure progress based on your own approval? This is the dynamic of the unconditional approach. You advance where it counts, in your gut and in your head, through experiences you enjoy, feel, and learn from, instead of tally. "Getting" is so ingrained that it's going to take a little motivational jujitsu to turn advancement into an internal objective. The trick is redirecting your motivation and expectations to a larger purpose, such as being with others, having fun, or personal growth. You do it to do it.

External gauges of progress put you at the mercy of the performance metric. This hijacks a lot of fun by demanding that we satisfy ridiculous standards to simply enjoy ourselves. A woman I met recently told me that her husband, a business consultant, had trained as a concert violinist. She had never heard him play, though, because he hadn't picked up the instrument in twenty years. Why? He didn't want to play unless he could perform to the rigorous symphony standards he'd set for himself. This is nuts—and tragic. What a waste of joy and free expression.

Another new friend of mine, Josh, a home rehab entrepreneur in San Francisco, loves to run, but he kept getting injured while training for marathons. He wound up feeling burned out on his passion because he measured his progress by the times he ran and how many miles he trained each week. After one too many Achilles and fascia problems, he decided to dump the external yardstick and run for the fun of it. That changed everything. He now enjoys running again and isn't getting injured.

The intrinsic motive ends the self-sabotage of masochism that performance controls foist on us. The need to play the violin at a virtuoso level or run more than your body wants to are false barometers that can't measure the experience of enjoyment or living to the hilt.

Most of the rewards you're conditioned to crave—money, toys, clothes, house—are visible ones. It seems natural to want to have some tangible proof that you're going places. But, as you have learned, these are ephemeral trophies. You don't buy them inside, because they are based on others' opinions. The intrinsic progress you want can't be seen unless you have a brain scan of the light show going off in the fist-bumping section of your cranium.

You'll need to get used to a more lasting kind of reward that makes you feel satisfied and thrilled to be alive. That comes from another kind of goal, oriented toward experiencing, learning, socializing, and giving. You'll have no trouble believing this kind of progress, because it's coming from your own noggin.

## The Mentor

"You're brilliant, Aisha. I see you in an internship at USC," says Mary Forgione, the president of Motivating Our Students through Experience, a nonprofit group that helps bright, at-risk, inner-city girls go to college and illustrates the potent intrinsic motivation of service.

It's a Saturday morning, and Aisha and fifty other girls, primarily Hispanic and African American, are clustered around a table at Occidental College in East Los Angeles, getting the lowdown on college futures. Most come from chaotic, poor households in which girls quickly become moms and minimum-wage lifers. Aisha, a senior with a 4.0 average, says she doesn't know where she wants to go to college. Forgione later tells me that the girl doesn't think she's college material.

Forgione's group pairs professional women with a hundred junior high and fifty high school girls who have promise and no hope. They hang out with the girls and prepare them for college and life. When Forgione took her mentee, Laura, to a restaurant, the girl had no idea what to order. She'd never been to a restaurant before. She lives in a one-bedroom apartment with a single mom and three siblings, one of whom has two kids. Laura studies in the bathroom. She would fall through the cracks if it wasn't for Forgione, a former editor at the *Los Angeles Times* and a woman with a huge dose of life intelligence. She's also climbed the tallest mountain in the lower forty-eight states, Mt. Whitney, thirteen times, she thinks.

Forgione is stunned by what's happened since a friend asked her to mentor five years ago. "If someone had told me ten years ago that I'd be working with kids, I would have said they were crazy. I don't like kids; I like nature. I had no idea I had the power to open up somebody's life."

She had no idea, either, that she would find her life's passion here. "What I've learned from Laura and the girls is profound," she says. "It's absolutely fabulous to help other people on their path."

Getting the intrinsic choice right comes down to the life intelligence skill of setting goals. "My goals tell me how to live my life, so I engage in behaviors relevant to that goal," says Knox College's Tim Kasser. "If I have the goal of close intimate relationships, then I'm more likely to do the kind of things that are going to satisfy those needs."

If your motivation springs from inner values, it leads to autonomous activity. If it doesn't, external goals control you from the outside. Here are some examples of how the distinction plays out:

*Leading Goal Motivators*
Intrinsic
    Personal growth
    Fun and enjoyment
    Pursuit of competence

> Social connection
> Excellence
> Freedom
> Challenge
> Community/contribution

Extrinsic
> Performance
> Financial success
> Appearance/coolness
> Fame/popularity
> Material possessions
> Status/social comparison

The choir singers we just met run the table on intrinsic goals—fun and enjoyment, personal growth, social connection, freedom to do what they want, pursuit of competence, challenge, excellence, and, with a free concert to the public and underprivileged kids, they also reap the reward of contributing. They were able to find an activity in sync with their core needs. That provides them with the satisfaction that creates meaning in their lives. Even though they didn't seek a payoff, they got themselves quite a return.

······················ ACTIVATE ······················

## Control Expectations

The intrinsic option gives you the power to defeat a major saboteur of aliveness: your expectations. When you do things simply for the experience of them, you don't have to expect anything, so you don't have to be disappointed in results that don't match your projections. Expecting is a form of outright guessing, which isn't an effective strategy on which to base your happiness. From now on, instead of being run by expectations, try running them. Check external payoff expectations at the door before you head out to live. Let's start practicing. Choose two activities that you would like to put on your life calendar. What are your expectations for them? If they're internal, great. If they're external—you want to impress others, network, be skilled overnight—you have to change them. Which goals from the Goal Motivator list would be the best expectation busters for those activities?

. . . . . . . . . . . . . . . . . . . . . . . . . . . . . . . . . . . . . . . . . . . . . . . . . . . . . . . . . . . .

# Own the Goal

The programming starts early. For me, the quest for gold stars was already under way in kindergarten. Getting one meant that I could stay on my nap mat or recite my numbers better than other kids could. I had to get that five-year-old ego rolling. I wanted to be stellar, so I got hooked very early on performance rewards. This seemed to be what it was all about, knocking myself out and waiting for my banana like a trained capuchin. The external reward became the tail that wagged this dog until I realized it wasn't a payoff at all, but an endless come-on that delivered only need for more payoffs.

When I discovered the intrinsic option and started going for the experience, one thing jumped out right away. I wasn't marooned in the future anymore, waiting for the next result or a better place to be able to enjoy myself. I was free to be absorbed in the spacious moment at hand. It was the way I always feel when I travel: that the instant of experience contains all that is needed. The person across the table is enough. The scenes rolling by the train window are enough. It's life at face value. In my business workshops, I call it "content over clock," and it's the essence of full engagement in anything. You are not gripped by hurry-worry and the end result but are immersed in what you're doing.

It can feel very weird not going for the gold, whether it's money, praise, or a little adhesive star. You might have to be locked in a padded room for a few days to get through the shakes of reward withdrawal, but you will make it. Once you learn how to live without the validation (that isn't one) of future payoffs. You'll feel a lot lighter on the intrinsic diet.

There are few choices more important than the one you make to act from intrinsic motivation—in whatever you do, at work or at play. The key is to find goals and activities that are "concordant," or aligned with *your* interests, traits, and values, as opposed to goals that come from social pressures or guilt,

---

## Making Work Work

Intrinsic motivation also helps in the realm that particularly defines payoff mode: the workplace. Researchers say that when you work for the excellence or the craft of whatever you're doing, instead of for the praise or the promotion, you do a better job and you like your work more. Focus on the content of what you're doing, instead of on the back pats or getting done with it, and you'll have an entirely different level of engagement. You improve concentration and attention and evade the scourge of time urgency when you're fully involved in what you're doing because of its own inherent interest. A study by Judith Harackiewicz and Andrew Elliott found that "intrinsically motivated employees are continuously interested in the work they're doing." Full engagement upgrades every experience.

says Kennon Sheldon of the University of Missouri. To help you determine the right intention and stick with it through the siren call of external temptations, Sheldon suggests that you "own the goal" and "make it fun."

- *Owning the goal.* You take more responsibility when you own an objective, and this helps satisfy your autonomy need. Identifying your motivation and "the core values that the goal expresses" helps keep you at it.
- *Making it fun.* Fun is an all-purpose antidote to the reflex for external payoff. It reframes the goal to the experience, removing the need for comparisons and judgments that are the grim reapers of performance fixation. This is particularly useful for when it comes to the social component of your core needs, because it frees you up for unconditional interaction.

When you opt for enjoyment and play, you are automatically in the intrinsic mode. You can get a feel for the kinds of goals you can own or make fun from motives reported by participants on a wilderness canoe trip. They listed a number of internal goals that would work splendidly for your adventures as well. The canoe trippers were doing it

- For the fun of it.
- To do something different.
- For excitement and stimulation.
- For the personal challenge.
- To experience nature.
- To make friends.
- For the exercise.
- To do something new.

## ⌒ *The Smashing Time of Nao Kumagai*

External motivation can steal the enthusiasm right out of you, leaving gaping holes where the joy used to be. It happened to Nao Kumagai, forty-two, a man who was so smitten by badminton while growing up in Japan that he didn't date during his teen years. He just smashed goose-feather and cork shuttlecocks. He played competitively in Japan, and when he arrived in the United States to work as a salesman for an import-export business, he tried to keep playing at the top of his bracket. Once he started a family, though, he figured that he wouldn't have time to practice enough to stay competitive, so he stopped playing entirely.

This was a big mistake. The all-or-nothing performance criterion left Kumagai's stress with nowhere to go, and his spirit was grounded. "I thought I was too busy, but I wasn't," he says. "Now I realize how much I need badminton."

These days Kumagai plays for the fun and the social outlet, and he is enjoying it more than ever—the intrinsic payoff. No pressure, only play. He travels a lot, selling products to the restaurant and hotel trade, but wherever he goes, he takes his racket with him and tracks down a badminton court. Give him a spare hour after business meetings, and he's blasting birds and making friends at a local gym.

Kumagai's love for the game is sonnet worthy. Badminton is sport, art, refuge, teacher, and friend. "When I'm depressed or don't have confidence or fail at something, I know I can get over it with badminton," he says. "Each time you lose a game, you practice until you improve. I tell myself, Look how I did in badminton. I can improve. In business, you have to have confidence or you can't sell. Badminton gives me that. The smash is my confidence."

## Eye-Opening Experience

The internal route of participant play is often an eye-opener, revealing things about yourself you never knew, because you were stuck in the bubble. At a free archery class at a local park, I learned how to aim by letting go, instead of trying to control my arrows. I also found out that I had a dominant eye. We all have a favored eye, similar to right- or left-handedness. The archer's dominant eye, not his or her handedness predisposition, determines which side of the bow the person shoots from.

Here's how to figure out which eye is the boss: Take your right hand and, palm down, place the fingers of the right hand over the fingers of your left hand, positioning the right thumb over the left thumb to form a triangle between your index fingers and overlapping thumbs. Hold your hands up, palms facing forward, and place the "triangle" about six inches in front of your eyes. With both eyes open, look through that triangle at an object—a doorknob, a car, a lamppost. Now close your right eye. If you can still see the object, you are left-eye dominant. If you close the left eye, and the object remains in the triangle, you have right-eye dominance. I discovered that I was left-eyed, although I bat right-handed. Sharpen your focus with an archery lesson at a local parks and recreation facility.

"It's like when a baseball player hits a home run," Kumagai explains, trying to convey the exquisite feeling of the smash, whacking a high, fat bird over the net. "I know what that feels like. You know when you hit it well, and it just feels really good."

I find him in his element, playing doubles at a court in a park in West Los Angeles. There are three games in progress on a busy a basketball court. Birds are whipping back and forth across the nets. There are three sets for each game; the first team to get 21 points in each set wins. There's no setter as in volleyball, so it's very fast-paced. The bird comes at you, and you whack it back. Adherents claim that badminton is the second-most-played sport in the world, behind soccer, thanks to devotees in Asia, where it's the national sport of nations such as Indonesia and Malaysia and has millions of participants in China and Japan. Kumagai is in badminton nirvana on a long rally. After a winning smash, he punches the air with his racket to celebrate.

I haven't played badminton since I was twelve, but Kumagai won't be dissuaded from spreading the gospel. He patiently gets me and my friend Ran Klarin, a tennis player, up to speed. "You hold the racket like a handshake," he explains. "You can use the wrist better that way." I practice hitting the bird back and forth with him. My timing's off. I see that I need to swing earlier than I think I do. The fluttery, knuckleball-like velocity is deceptive. We split up into teams, with Kumagai and me against Ran and a local pastor. I have some deer-in-the headlights moments when the bird comes straight at me and I miss it completely, but I do much better than I expect. I'm pumped by a distinct buzz of competence and the joy of fun. I feel Kumagai's enthusiasm rubbing off on me and something else: the thrill of a team game.

There's an intensity and a camaraderie in playing with others that I now know I missed. Team games don't need to end after thirty. As I connect on a volley over my head or slide for a lob, I feel some long-absent sensations return-ing—the rush of split-second reactions, the tingle of total alertness, elation. Kumagai has made the sale. I've found a new game. After the session, my friend and I bought rackets and formed a team, and now the bird is the word.

Kumagai's passion keeps his life full of fun, competence, and gives him plenty of relatedness with his fellow badminton enthusiasts. He says that it even helps with his marriage. "When you play doubles, you have to learn how to support the other person." The telltale evidence of passion, the visible vibrancy of positive affect, is on his face and in his spirit. If only everyone had a transforming passion like Kumagai.

## Are You Recreationally Available?

Just as a relationship can't go anywhere if the two parties aren't emotionally available, you have to be recreationally available, or you'll wind up divorced from your life. You can snap out of lockdown with the aptitudes of openness and readiness, which invite the leisure skills into your life that put you in the activation column. Otherwise, you're stuck defaulting to performance mode and passive leisure. Being available to your life is a matter of being wide-eyed again, of losing the adult albatrosses of cynicism and knowing it all, of embracing the role of lifelong learner. This will require a new rhythm to the way you live, one without the automatic dismissal of anything that doesn't have an external prize attached and without the control reflex that shoots down everything that's not within your comfort zone.

You wouldn't miss a career or a financial opportunity. Why miss a chance at life? You won't when you're ready for it, which you can be by eliminating these behaviors that keep out your life:

- *Rut reflex.* The autopilot forecloses anything that is out of the norm. Break out of the schedule whenever you can. Every morning, ask yourself whether you're closed or open for the business of living today.
- *Time panic.* As Kumagai discovered, the "I'm too busy" mind-set is a false belief. He could be a parent, a husband,

## The Ride Is the Race

Roll across the Midwest with a few thousand new friends on one of the great recreational cycling events, the RAGBRAI (which stands for the [*Des Moines*] *Register*'s Annual Bicycle Ride Across Iowa), held each July. It's a weeklong road trip, with all ages, all costumes, some ten thousand strong, 476 miles across the Iowa countryside. Because it's not a race, there's no performance standard to worry about and measure yourself against. You can relax and take in the journey at ground level through small-town America. The event stops in eight hamlets along the way, whose residents inspire riders with marching bands, barbecues, and root beer floats. There's plenty of time to compare helmets and potato salad with other riders and locals. Check out the bike-cam video that Mike Valenti, the owner of veloist .com, shot of this event in 2008 as he rolled through it, and you'll want to be in the middle of the next one: www.veloist.com/video/661421: Video:24082.

and a traveling salesman and still play badminton. Time urgency is a false emergency. The real emergency is not living your life as fully as you can while you can.

- *A closed mind.* As we have learned, a closed mind makes no sense, because your core needs want the self-determined experiences that lead to learning and satisfaction. Expect no payoff, and there's no threat to the ego from the new or the unknown.

- *Controlling behavior.* If you're always in control, this guarantees a steady diet of the same old stuff. Letting go opens the discovery pipeline. It's exhausting and extremely limiting when you have to run the world.

# The Itch That Makes You Scratch

Kathy King heard about her future avocation of dragon boat racing from a friend in a poetry class. Richard Weinberg bumped into the activity that would change his life when the restaurant where he was eating dinner turned into a salsa dance party. Chris Joosse became a kayak fanatic after a guide on a rafting trip challenged him to try solo paddling. Not one of these people would have discovered what would become their central life pursuit if their interest hadn't been piqued. They were curious.

Curiosity is a powerful driver of intrinsic engagement, and it can make the difference between life opportunities taken or missed. It's part of the insistent urge from your brain neurons to see what's around the bend or on the other side of that yoga studio window, and it comes from the brain's mandate to experience novelty. Curiosity is the spark plug of interest, which ignites exploratory behavior and fuels the knowledge base, says the University of North Carolina's Barbara Frederickson.

The capacity to be intrigued is an essential skill of life intelligence. As children, most of us have lots of it, but that inquisitiveness is beaten out of us by the time we're adults. Research shows that people with greater curiosity expand their knowledge and skills, take on more growth experiences, and—crucial for life activation—have a better tolerance for the difficulties that come from trying new things. This makes them more apt to reach for the novelty that leads to gratifying discoveries. People with voracious curiosity seldom run out of amusements or interests, the quintessential intrinsic companion. The beauty of interests is that they make you think about things other than yourself, a subject that usually sends you off to other tenses and away from engagement.

An interest in birds led Eddie Bartley to take up bird-watching and then photography to document his discoveries. "It's a sense of peering into a secret world," he told me. "You feel as if you're part of that world that all humans once lived in."

Curiosity didn't kill the cat. It allowed the cat to increase its life experiences ninefold. "Curiosity motivates people to act and think in new ways and investigate, be immersed, and learn," write psychologists Todd Kashdan, author of *Curious*, and Paul Silvia, who specialize in studying curious behavior. They report that people with higher curiosity are more inclined to participate in activities that are personally and socially enriching. More curiosity on a daily basis also leads to something that is quite remarkable: greater "perceived meaning and purpose in life."

Researchers place curiosity at the center of the self-determination process, the inspiration for aspirations that lead to autonomy, competence, and connection with others. We all start out with a large supply of this impulse, but it gets waylaid by fear, the spectator habit, preoccupation, cynicism, and any number of externally controlled attitudes. Without your own interests in charge, you're left to follow the choices of others.

If you want to feel more alive, get curious. Curiosity fires up activation and immediate attention. "When curious, we are fully aware and receptive to whatever exists and might happen in the present moment," say Kashdan and Silvia.

The life intelligence skill of curiosity-seeking equips you to grab the leads and glimmers before they flit by—and then act on them. They may show up as "That's interesting" or "How does that work?" or "I wonder whether I could do that." Pretty unremarkable stuff, yet where it leads can be extraordinary. You can expand your inquisitive skills by boosting behaviors that drive interest, such as these:

- *Ask more questions*. Anyone you speak to is a potential lead to something fun or riveting. Ponder why and how more often.

- *Follow the learning.* What do you want to know more about?
- *Try new things.* Put yourself in situations that are out of your normal orbit, and instead of dismissing them, say, "What if I tried that?" Ask yourself, What have I tried lately?
- *Get out there.* Physically exiting the control bubble exposes you to new stimuli and sources of curiosity. Several people in this book found their passions while doing a different activity.
- *Research idle curiosities.* Google it. Then try it.
- *Kill jadedness.* The seen-it-all pose is the kiss of death for curiosity.

•••••••••••••••••••••••••• ACTIVATE ••••••••••••••••••••••

### Listen to Your Interest Detectors

Curiosity is a signal from your brain neurons to discover something. If you automatically disregard their pleadings, those signals become less insistent. Don't let these interest detectors be drowned out by preoccupation and distractions. What are you curious about at this moment that could lead to a life opportunity, new friends, or a great vacation? Follow it up with a next step. Keep a running list of curious musings. At the end of every week, take the most interesting prospects and see where they go next.

•••••••••••••••••••••••••••••••••••••••••••••••••••••••••

# How Curious Are You?

What state is your curiosity in? Take the Curiosity and Exploration Inventory, developed by Todd Kashdan, Paul Rose, and Frank Fincham. Respond to each of the following statements as you would usually describe yourself. There are no right or wrong answers. Rate each statement on a scale of 1 to 7, with 1 being a statement you strongly disagree with and 7 being a statement you strongly agree with.

1. I would describe myself as someone who actively seeks as much information as I can in a new situation.
2. When I am participating in an activity, I tend to get so involved that I lose track of time.
3. I frequently find myself looking for new opportunities to grow as a person (e.g., information, people, resources).
4. I am not the type of person who probes deeply into new situations or things.
5. When I am actively interested in something, it takes a great deal to interrupt me.
6. My friends would describe me as someone who is "extremely intense" when in the middle of doing something.
7. Everywhere I go, I am looking for new things or experiences.

Add up your ratings and average them for your score. Before you do that, though, you'll need to reverse-score item 4. If your answer to that statement is that you strongly disagree, you would rank it as a 1 and score it as 6 or 7. If you answer 3, score it as 5. If you answer 7, score it as 1. Numbers 1, 3, 4 and 7 test your exploration tendencies, while 2, 5, and 6 rate your talent for absorption, a key to paying the attention you need to be curious.

## No Strings Attached

You may feel as if you're floating free of all moorings without the external homing device of rewards. That's the idea. You have to cut the strings of marionette mode to immerse yourself in unconditional experience. With the right intrinsic goals you can taste the freedom of living without agendas or yardsticks and revel in the sublime symmetry that occurs when your actions are completely aligned with your core. The key themes to remember:

- The skill of intrinsic motivation, acting for no payoff, is the engine that drives self-determination and leads to full engagement and a satisfied life.

- Intrinsic goals lead to autonomy and competence; external goals—money, success, appearance, status—lead to the need for more approval *from* others and result in more control *by* others.

- Self-awareness reveals the intrinsic path and prioritizes the choices that lead to optimal life.

- The right motivation comes from skillful goal setting, as you shift from outcome to experience.

- Curiosity increases your participation in personally and socially enriching activities and generates greater meaning and purpose in life.

# 6

*～～*

# It's the Experience

The whole point of existence does not
lie in some future destination . . . this
particular instant in which we are living
is the fulfillment of everything.
—*Alan Watts, philosopher and author*

I'm getting a good feeling as I climb the wide wooden
staircase of Estudantina, an old dance hall off the Lapa
district in Rio de Janeiro that has been serving up happy feet
for more than eighty years. The building itself dates back well
into the nineteenth century and looks like it has been beamed
in from old Lisbon, with its giant arched windows and balco-
nies. It's exactly the kind of place I travel for—funky, off the
tourist circuit, filled with locals, and jamming with music that
cuts through all of the barriers to another culture. The admission price is $5. It's the kind of place where I can predict with
certainty that happenings and adventures are imminent. The
banner on the back wall reads, "Enquanto houver dança haverá
esperança" ("As long as there is dance, there will be hope").

Within seconds after I get to my table, the nine-piece band
unleashes a set of euphoric samba classics that doesn't stop

for an hour and twenty minutes. There are no breaks between songs, just one long medley that sends me, my friend Frida Silva, and a delirious working-class crowd into a rapturous explosion of free-ranging limbs and hips. Before the night is over, I meet Reynaldo, a man whose love of samba is literally unstoppable. In his white shirt, white pants, and white shoes, he puts on a dazzling display of intricate solo samba footwork for the entire first set. Whatever he's drinking, I want some. As Frida translates, I ask him how he can keep at it for more than an hour straight. My thighs are burning after fifteen minutes. "That's nothing," he tells me. "I've done samba for three hours."

Reynaldo dos Santos is seventy years old. When he hears a cavaquinho, the feisty, mandolinlike instrument that hyperactivates samba melodies, his skin tingles. If he catches a samba song coming out of a store, he'll start dancing right in the middle of a downtown sidewalk. This, I hardly need to point out, is someone who is fully alive. What is it about samba that is so intoxicating? I ask, though I already know the answer. Alegria! Joy, he says. It's written on his face and that of everyone in the room. I tell Reynaldo he is my new role model and ask whether he has any dance tips. "Don't have shame," he says. We hug as new friends and brothers in samba. Then the cavaquinho breaks out, and the tingling begins.

I take Reynaldo's advice and slip inside a dimension beyond time and self-consciousness. My feet answer the call, sliding and bouncing, telling gravity and the forces of control to shove it, responding to every tempo change. I feel my arms traveling up to the heavens, testifying the full ecstasy I have no shame in broadcasting. One of the songs the crowd sings along to is the anthem "What Is It? What Is It?" whose words amplify Reynaldo's message and say it all. "Live! And do not be ashamed to be happy."

Soon I am unaware of anything but churning rhythms and bodies and a bliss I don't want to end. Frida tells me later that while I was in the samba zone, the lead singer of the band yelled out from the stage to me, "Dance, gringo!" She says it was a

---

## Dance on the Head of Fate

Brazil's national song-and-dance form of samba emerged in the early twentieth century as African drum circle rhythms joined up with marches and guitar-based *choro*. The first officially registered samba song was "Pelo Telefone" ("On the Telephone") in 1917, although some say it wasn't a samba at all. Samba took root and blossomed in the slums, or *favelas*, of Rio, where songwriters chronicled the disappointments of life with music that danced on the head of fate. Samba's infectiousness boils out of propulsive cross-rhythms and call-and-response vocals. It's "we" music, not "me" music, born for celebration.

Samba became the official music of the Rio Carnaval, spawning an earth shaking version called *samba enredo* and the speed-samba dance made famous by those platform-wearing float dancers. There are a host of samba styles, but the rhythm is unique in Latin music for its bouncing lilt. Brazil's beloved songwriter Dorival Caymmi described it this way: "Anyone who doesn't like samba is sick in the head or sick in the feet." For more info, check out *The Brazilian Sound*, the best source on Brazilian music (Temple University Press, 2009). To listen, check out these albums: Beth Carvalho's *Ao Vivo Convida*, Zeca Pagodinho's *A Vera*, Maria Rita's *Samba Meu*, Arlindo Cruz's *Ao Vivo*, Dudu Nobre's *Roda de Samba*, Teresa Cristina's *Melhor Assim*, and Clara Nunes's *Para Sempre Clara*.

compliment, like, Go to it! My obliviousness was proof that I had reached the high end of the central ingredient in optimal aliveness: direct experience. I was riding the moment in flow, so absorbed that nothing else mattered, even ego, as I reveled in a trifecta of experiences: travel, music, and the skills-challenge component of dancing samba.

Nirvana is now, and experience is its stage, in moment-to-moment participation that anchors you in the unfolding present. That's usually a place we're sprinting past on the way to somewhere else. We don't think about being where we are so completely that there is no room for anywhere else, because the premium is on where you're supposed to get to: the prizes, the expectations, the better place that's always "out there." In the participant experience, you learn that what you already have—feet, hands, joy, friends—is more than enough to get what you're here for.

Experience can vault you into optimal states because it is a deeply personal realm that contacts authentic places within you: your core needs. "Experiences really satisfy desires for self-actualization," the University of Colorado's Leaf Van Boven explains to me. "They help people become the type of people they would like to be."

I certainly could feel that in that old dance hall in Rio. I could be the cross-cultural explorer, the musical discoverer, the *sambista*, the joyful celebrant, all core aspirations ignited by the experiential dynamic. The ability of experiences to feed the soul makes them the best route to happiness and fulfilling times, but they're a treasure trove we're largely unaware of. Van Boven, who studies the role that experience plays in happiness and well-being, knows why. The gratified life depends on our making a choice that is counter to our training: whether to buy material things or experiences. Objects are what we're used to spending our discretionary capital on. But if the money goes to material items, you'll be less happy, says Van Boven. If you purchase experiences, you'll be happier.

Experiences trump material items because they stick with you through the memories and the singular interactions they create. They're not external badges that depend on others' approval. Experiences can't be undermined by comparisons to anyone else's. They're your personal event, the participation and impact determined only by you. You don't habituate to experiences as you do to a new car or phone. The new car smell won't last, but the memory of screaming down a zip line in a forest will.

Another big reason experiences are so satisfying is that you tend to do them with others. That strengthens relational bonds, reports San Francisco State psychology professor Ryan Howell, so you're getting your need for relatedness met, which is a specialty of engaged play. And something else, he notes, something critical if you want to feel like more than a mannequin with a voice box: the interactive moment increases your vitality. The luxury car can't do that.

So experience is where the liveliness is. I got an excellent description of where we can find that zone from Adwin David Brown, an improvisational poet and teacher I caught dancing with words one night at a packed Santa Monica coffeehouse. Brown's long braids jumped as he delivered what makes for a splendid ode to the life force of experience.

> Come live in the moment
> but do not build a house
> be at home yet remain homeless
> for the holy ground of the here is fluid
> it is not for residing but living
> The estate of the now is prime real and priceless

the only thing you have to pay
is attention

Inventing instant rhymes is a verbal tightrope that puts Brown straight into that realm, which he calls UTE, or Unfamiliar Territory Explored, the tripwire for all optimal experiences. "There's fear, doubt, but at the same time here comes courage, here comes joy," he told me later, describing the improvisational moment when he's most alive.

Known as the Flow Master for phrases that pour like liquid, he uses his poetry to help closed-off kids in Los Angeles high schools discover their own voices, breaking them out of the shells of coolness and posturing through what he calls "transflowmation." When he's got a performance rolling, picking rhymes out of the air, stumbling and righting himself into a new direction on the fly, "it's a combination of magic, surrender, and bliss, the experience of being lost and found at the same time."

Not surprisingly, the Flow Master knows his flow, the high point of direct experience. Being lost and found simultaneously is precisely what peak experience evokes. What's lost is the ego and anxieties from tenses other than the one you're in, here and now. What's found is the complete alignment of what you think with what you're doing and more. The Japanese painter Hakuin put it this way: "If you forget yourself, you become the universe."

These moments of forgetting and cosmic connection are similar to the spiritual release and realization of satori in Zen Buddhism or the Hindu moksha. There is a euphoric oneness and completeness to joy. Alan Watts described it well. "In those moments the significance of the world seems to be the world, and what is going on now. We do not look any further, because the scheme of things seems to justify itself at every moment of its unfoldment." Watts goes on to say that these moments are "particularly characteristic of music and dancing, of belonging with one's fellow man, and of the carrying out of some significant pattern of life . . . [that's] meaningful."

That's the bliss your passions can unlock. "There's elation and euphoria. It's all very intense, but inside it's also very peaceful," reports Chris Joosse, a whitewater kayaker in Tacoma, Washington, whose flow moments are literal, slashing through frothing rapids.

Considering all the less-than-stellar times you have to put up with during the course of a life span, is it too much to ask that you bask in as many optimal moments as possible? In these concentrated doses of energized involvement, you have more vitality and alertness, you tap more of yourself and your potential, and you reach the pinnacle of engagement and satisfaction. It "comes as close as anything that can be imagined to what we know as happiness," maintains Mihaly Csikszentmihalyi, the famed scholar and author, who a couple of decades ago identified the phenomenon of flow. "Only direct control of experience, the ability to derive moment-by-moment enjoyment from everything we do, can overcome the obstacles to fulfillment," says Csikszentmihalyi.

It leads us to the essential law of optimal life. It's not the money. It's not the popularity. It's not what's on the business card. It's the experience.

Repeat it. Emblazon it on the inside of your front door, so that every time you walk outside you're reminded where your best life is. Experience is the route to vibrant living. Follow it, and you'll unleash vitality you haven't felt since middle school. All you need is an acquaintance with a few skills—the ability to direct attention, pursue competence, problem solve, and match challenges with your abilities—to optimize your experiential chances.

# Are You Experienced?

Chances are, you're a head case. Most of us are these days, spending the vast chunk of our time stuck in the brain lock of cogitation and analysis. The rest of the body has almost become superfluous. But as fun as it is to weigh and mull, knowing is not the same as doing. You can't feel the rush of flying like a bird by thinking about being in a hang glider. You have to do it.

Malcolm Jones, who runs a hang-gliding company in Florida called Wallaby Ranch, has watched hundreds of landlubbers over the years transformed by their first out-of-terrestrial-body experience in the skies. "It's like they're two feet taller," he says. "It's very emotional for many people. I had a ninety-four-year-old woman cry in my arms when she got down, she was so happy."

The word *experience* comes from the Latin term *experientia*, which means "the act of trying." Giving it a go for the sake of it

---

### Condor for a Day

Much has changed since the days when the first step to hang gliding was jumping off a cliff. That was a bit of an impediment. At Wallaby Ranch, on the edge of the Everglades, the hang gliders come equipped with wheels, which make it easy for anyone to get airborne, from kids to senior citizens to the disabled. A small plane with a line attached tows the wheeled glider aloft, and then you're in the clouds, floating over the Everglades. A flight instructor is aboard to pilot the craft. It's as close to a magic carpet ride as you'll ever get, a moment in literal flow. See the gliders in action at www.youtube.com/watch?v=9wufka5Ooo8. For more information, go to www.wallaby.com or call 800-Wallaby.

is the essence of experience. Think of it as your life lab, in which the attempting is what matters. It's about what you figure out, encounter, discover, and feel, one moment at a time.

If you look at what experience does for you, you can't help but conclude that you were born to try new things. Experience delivers all of the essentials of engaged living. You are:

- Alive to the moment
- In the experience unconditionally
- A participant, not a spectator
- Liberated from your ego
- Satisfying your core needs
- Connected with the novelty and the challenge that your brain wants
- Owning your own time

Your core needs love experiences. The interactive process builds autonomy, competence, and relatedness as nothing else can. "People talk about their experiences as though they are integral to their identity and who they are in life," says Van Boven.

Your brain neurons love experiences, which deliver the stimulation they like in the form of surprise, spontaneity, and challenge. Your body loves experiences, because they produce the energizing physical sensations of vitality and elation. And your memory *really* loves experiences.

Interactive pursuits set off multiple neuron firings. When neurons fire together, they release a nerve-growth stimulant called brain-derived neurotrophic factor, or BDNF, which wires them together for future use. The fusion of firings that results from experiences produces moments that stick in your memory. This makes your full involvement in an activity an unmatched tool for learning. Humans are thought to retain 90 percent of what we do but only 20 percent of what we hear and 30 percent of what we see—which may explain why we retain so much ability to remain on our keisters.

Memories play another key role. They operate as an ongoing status report on your satisfaction. "The more positive and novel the recent experiences one can recall, the higher one will rate one's happiness," say researchers Kennon Sheldon and Sonja Lyubomirsky. Recent taken-for-granted experiences don't have any effect on your happiness, and negative ones undermine it. Studies show that remembering positive life events, such as engaging leisure activities, is a proven route to increased happiness.

····················· A C T I V A T E ·····················

### Total Recall

Your memory banks can tell you a lot about where you're getting the most engaging bang for your buck. Let's do a comparison test developed by Leaf Van Boven that gives you a chance to weigh the impact of your discretionary purchases. Think about three experiences you've had that made you happy. Now think about three material possessions that made you happy. Compare the two sets. Which contributes more to your satisfaction in life? Why?

····································································

## Aikido Gets Your Attention

It's raining men. And one woman. The bodies are falling in Karl Grignon's Shoshin Aikido studio in an old warehouse section of Montreal, Quebec. They tumble to the green mat in quick flips and slow-mo somersaults, a sweaty ballet of ducking heads and rolling backs as hands and feet slap and thud to the deck. I can see that you need good semicircular canal function for a semblance of balance in this Japanese martial art, because you spend a lot of time upside down.

"Pull and invite them in," instructs Grignon to five pairs of students, each clad in the traditional garb of baggy black pants and white robelike top. One of each pair lunges at the other in a simulated attack, while the defender uses the aggressor's actions to turn the energies to the defender's advantage and throw the person to the floor. Aikido (which means "the way of harmony with the life force of *ki*"), descended from jujitsu, and is more about a state of mind than combat. It's noncompetitive; there are no tournaments. The goal is to master the ego that drives rigidity and find ways to work with the conflicts that come your way. The practice uses intensely focused movements to increase awareness. This makes aikido a perfect training ground for the life intelligence skill of directing attention, which is essential to optimal engagement.

You need to fully focus on what you're doing in order to have an absorbing experience. That's harder to do these days because you are being bombarded by so many attention thieves—the onslaught of interruptions from e-mail, texts, cell calls, instant messages. Aikido shuts off the ADD festival by making you target your concentration on what's in front of your face.

"You really learn how to pay attention and see things," says Gabriel Guzman, thirty-one, a computer programmer who breaks away from the tumbling to fill me in on his passion, which he indulges in five to seven times a week. Through alert, calm body postures, Guzman tries to adapt his movements to whatever comes at him. In six years of doing aikido, he's learned how to concentrate on his experience and not on himself, which has given someone who had "always been introverted" confidence and self-assurance.

Guzman's girlfriend, Erica Gipson, twenty-seven, her cheeks flame red from the workout, has also seen her concentration soar from aikido, which she's been doing daily for three years. The focus on physical actions to the exclusion of self-dialogue has helped her see that "Ego is the biggest roadblock to improvement and movement. I used to get stressed out easily," she tells me. "I had a really hard time with criticism. Aikido helped me get more removed from that. I don't get caught up in it anymore."

Aikido focuses your awareness on all of the physical space around you, to the sides, behind, and in front, leaving no room for distraction. Students aim for a state known in the Zen tradition from which the practice springs as no-mind, a brain emptied of ego chatter. "No-mind is beautiful," says Grignon. "We have the ability to be natural, without the self-consciousness, but when we let the ego in, we lose."

As soon as the ego appears—Am I doing it well enough? He's more talented than I am. How will I look?—you are no longer in the experience. But in aikido, "everything just flows when you're on the mat," says Laurent McComber, a Montreal native and architect. "The ritual helps to shut down everyday preoccupations. Movements are repeated many times, paying attention to every detail."

What's great about active play pursuits such as aikido, dancing, or basketball is that they do the job of focusing for you. They force you to concentrate on the rules of the game and the action, so there's no space for anything else. Play for the sake of it, and you are naturally extracted from mental mayhem, because total awareness is directed to the moment of experience. "Every time I come in here, it frees my mind," says McComber, the father of one- and three-year-olds.

You can improve concentration on your experience by consciously directing your attention beforehand. College students who were prone to high test anxiety performed much better when they were given attention-directing instructions before the exam, such as "Don't let yourself get distracted from the task" or "Think only about the anagrams," reports one study. Making a conscious decision to focus brings the target forward from all of the competing information.

But you already have a focusing mantra, right? Any time that impatience, fear, excuses, or ego get in the way of the moment, you know what to tell yourself. It's the experience.

......................... ACTIVATE .........................

## Developing Presence

The quality of your attention is indispensable for optimal experience. This means directing more of it to where you are. Often, though, you're diverted by a future or past brain-lock, in a futile effort to predict what's ahead or relive what's already happened. To give you an idea of the kind of presence you need to really be where you are, here's an exercise you can do with a friend or a family member. It makes for a fun dinner game. The one and only rule is that you can speak only in the present tense. All other tenses are banned. See how long you can stay in the verbal moment. For more tools to increase your attention to the moment at hand, try these options:

*Focusing Strategies*

1. *Cue your attention to the activity at hand with an advance focusing phrase.* "I am a laser." "Don't miss a detail." Repeat it verbally or in your mind several times before the activity gets under way.

2. *Revisit your motivation.* Remind yourself of the internal goal behind the activity. Why do you want to pay attention? This will provide a sense of purpose that tells your brain it's important to be alert.

3. *Focus on a target.* The key to improving your concentration is having a target to train it on. Researchers

say that the best technique for this is meditation. You concentrate on the breath flowing in and out, coming back to the breath each time your thoughts stray. Using other targets can help as well. Try counting backward from 100, focusing on each number as you go.

4. *Listen intently*. Especially when you're learning a new pursuit, you need to be all ears. The tendency is to space out and drift into other tenses. Don't do it. Lock onto the instructions.

5. *Bring positive affect*. A positive mood can pump up your alertness; a negative frame of mind can shut down your receptivity. Bring a good dose of positive spirit to the task, and it will energize you, making you more engaged.

6. *Unplug*. Optimal experience is a no-interruption zone. Impound all e-devices for the duration of the activity. Mastery and enjoyment depend on how effective you are at leaving everything behind, except the action you're engaged in.

............................................................

## The Playing Field of Experience

There are countless interactions you can have with your world, but not all will be meaningful or engaging enough to vault you into a memorable experience. You can have an encounter with a doorknob, but chances are you won't be too involved with it, unless you're a locksmith. Staring at a stone isn't going to budge the experience meter, unless you're a fossil collector or a poet. Or maybe it's a very big stone, and you're climbing it—that's an experience.

The critical element in whether an experience is engaging is how absorbed you are in it. The more absorbed in the moment

## Don't Keep Up with the Joneses

The idea behind keeping up with the Joneses and having to buy material items to do so is that we supposedly admire the Joneses. But researchers have found that we don't admire them at all. The University of Colorado's Leaf Van Boven and his colleagues Margaret C. Campbell and Cornell University's Thomas Gilkovich reported in a 2009 study that subjects found materialistic people to be more selfish and self-centered than those who make experiential purchases. People from a variety of demographic backgrounds found the materially oriented to be less socially desirable, while they were keenly interested in the doings of experiential people.

So if you want to be admired, forget the designer labels and have more experiences. "Pursuing experiences reflects into some fairly widely shared values about being self-actualized, being part of meaningful social relations, challenging yourself, becoming a better person," says Van Boven. "Most agree those are good goals to have." What happens when it gets out that there's a stigma to the Joneses? Perhaps people will begin to make choices that are closer to producing happiness, hopes Van Boven.

you are, the more optimal your engagement becomes. In other words, you find what you're doing more interesting than yourself and your problems. This is actually possible. All sorts of activities can unleash flow: sailing, composing music, golf, kayaking, dancing, walking in nature, even reading and work when you're completely absorbed. Experiences come in all shapes and sizes and vary in engagement level, challenge, and intensity, but all have one thing in common: You're a participant, not a statue with hair. Let's look at the main genres.

*The World of Experience*

- *Off-the-shelf entertainment experiences.* You're probably quite familiar with these. You can have an experience by going to a restaurant, a theme park, an arts festival, or even to a theatrical retail outlet with a hands-on approach to its wares. You're not buying a product but an interaction that can liven up your taste buds or fun quotient. Some marketers have touted the "experience economy," in which people buy the memory of an experience instead of a product. The skill/challenge bar is low here, so it won't be an optimal experience, but there is plenty of enjoyment to be had from an experience at any level that charges you up. You can get pretty near celestial space at a great concert. Music is a more interactive experience than most off-the-shelf options, engaging your imagination and soul, and, with the best artistry, inspiring a sense of connection to something outside yourself, a flow hallmark (the merging of self with surroundings). I have a very long list of musicians and genres, from Coltrane to Steely Dan and samba to Latin jazz and African rhythms, that take me deep into rhapsodic musical experiences. The artists making the music, of course, have a much more intense and challenging experience, which sends them into flow.

- *Low-skill, high-environment experiences.* Some experiences have more to do with where you are, such as travel and hiking. When you're somewhere you've never been before or you're surrounded by natural spectacles, every minute and everything in it can be an experience. Two legs and the courage to leave the well-trammeled track are all you need to set off experiences that evoke your sense of possibility and arouse one of the best vehicles for exiting the thought factory and being fully where you are—wonder. Vacations are a great way to immerse yourself in a horizon-to-horizon experience.

- *High-skill interior experiences.* Highly focused mental engagement can lead to the peak of direct experience. The same rule applies here for flow as it does for engaging physical activities. Your thoughts and what you're doing are the same. Your mental energies are completely absorbed in moving the chess pieces, tracking stars with a telescope, or creating a vase on a potter's wheel. Few things can absorb you as artistic pursuits can. If you're skilled enough to engage deeply in your art or craft, you definitely know what flow is. Pursuits like these are a direct route to the authentic self, so you'll find plenty to satisfy your core needs for autonomy and competence.

- *High-skill interactive experiences.* You need to have some level of skill to indulge in the top end of direct experience. The sweet spot of flow is where your skills meet a challenge, although highly fulfilling experiences can also incite moments of flow. Once you have enough facility to fence or play hockey or a musical instrument without complete exasperation, you can generate flow activity by aiming for a level of challenge that is slightly above your skills.

The higher forms of direct experience are triggered when the activity clicks with your authentic core. You might have fun slinging horseshoes or zoning out to a video game, but they won't do much for you on the fulfillment front. Fulfilling activities connect with your real identity in some way, allowing you to express yourself, feel competence, and experience self-realization.

According to Csikszentmihalyi, meaningful involvement in flow depends on

- Focused attention on an achievable goal.
- A choice that gives purpose to your action.
- Inner harmony from meeting the challenge.

All four categories of experience provide you with plenty of opportunities to lift up your life, get out of the onlooker column, and feel the magic of participating here and now in your world.

························· A C T I V A T E ·························

### Dig Deeper

The best experiences go the deepest, resonating with your interests, building your competence, or providing a meaningful moment. Identify an activity that you could do for each of the four categories in the World of Experience list that would fulfill you the most. What would allow you to express who you really are? What could challenge you to put your competence to the test? What could allow you to feel more realized?
·······································································

## The Mastery of Competence

The surest path to moments of euphoric activation is something most adults are allergic to: learning new skills. The burning desire to figure out something you don't know how to do is a major experiential skill. The knack that motivates this is the pursuit of competence, the drive to challenge yourself to improve. It's a self-sustaining tool that keeps you motivated through the learning curve until you have the skills to really enjoy what you're doing.

People with life intelligence are motivated to stick with it until they get better, whatever their level of talent. You don't have to be a philharmonic genius to enjoy playing the piano. "One does not have to be best or first, or to get an 'A' to feel competent; one need only take on a meaningful personal challenge and give it one's best," says the University of Rochester's Edward Deci.

Pursuit of competence is a built-in self-propulsion agent. Each little thing you do less badly than you did before helps fuel a sense of forward progress, which encourages you to keep going no matter how much of a greenhorn you might feel. Developing competence requires patience and doggedness, inspired by determination as well as your intrinsic motive. The learning itself has to be the goal, so that you keep at it when ego and frustration threaten a flake-out. Remember, you can't satisfy your core need for competence unless you stick with it. The guiding motivation with this skill is mastery, a desire to improve your ability for the sake of it. Mastery is a powerful engine for life satisfaction and the skills that are the prerequisites for flow and optimal experience. The quest surrounds you with the stuff brain neurons live for—novelty and challenge.

People with life intelligence pursue competence so intently, they don't let their ego and self-sabotage get in the way. They don't fall for distractions such as the arbitrary deadline, the fantasy that they're going to be functional/good/perfect by such and such date. That sets you up for dejection when you don't meet these random expectations picked out of thin air. That's the performance yardstick again. It craves results so badly that it turns you into the boss you'd never work for. The clock is ticking! Get those skills by the appointed time, or you're going to fire yourself. Mastery is not a drive-thru; it's a process. The arbitrary deadline is none other than runaway time urgency, happy to strangle you in the act of living. Let the skill, and the experience, unfold at its own pace.

•••••••••••••••••••••• ACTIVATE ••••••••••••••••••••••

## Court Is Not in Session

What you need more than anything else to fuel pursuit of competence is the desire to learn. You want to get better for the intrinsic challenge of improving yourself, growth. That urge usually is no match, though, for the performance identity and its main weapon in sidelining your pursuit—judgment. The verdicts erupt fast and furiously—you're hopeless, you're not getting anywhere, you have two left feet, and on and on. To stay on the path, you'll need to shut down the judicial proceedings. You are not in court, and learning, not to mention living, are judgment-free zones. Remember, the experience is all that matters. To get off the verdict treadmill, for a week keep track of all the judgments you make about yourself and others. Put each on paper—"I blew it on that," "I should have done it this way," "You've got to be kidding with that hairdo"—and after each determine where it came from and what good it's doing you. The only verdict you need to be concerned about is the shortness of life.

••••••••••••••••••••••••••••••••••••••••••••••••••••••

## ~ Chris Joosse: Upstream with a Problem

The main attractions of your life often show up on the route to somewhere else. After a rafting trip with a friend, a guide asked Chris Joosse if he wanted to take a kayaking lesson.

Joosse, a Tacoma, Washington, software test developer for Microsoft, was open and unrushed enough to give it a try. It turned out that paddling a kayak was quite a bit more complex than navigating a canoe, which he had done growing up in Alaska, and that appealed to the engineer in him.

"It was a fascinating process. Oh, here's this thing I can work on and get better at," he recalls. "It's all a process of working on a problem, then working on another problem. As soon as I learned how to roll a kayak, that opened up new vistas of possibility. That meant I could run that other rapid that I wouldn't be able to if I couldn't recover right away. It just made possible doing more and more complicated, more and more challenging, more and more complex rapids."

## Adventures to Go

Travel is a great way to inject experiences into your life. You can explore on your own or buy an adventure experience from a host of outfitters who can help you go where you never have before. Trek, raft, cycle, dive, climb, visit other cultures—you can go from the humdrum to an extraordinary life in the span of a plane flight. The accent is on participation and exploration close to the ground, which are hallmarks of the experiential process. Raft the Snake River, island hop in Fiji, or trek in the Himalayas, and you'll come back different from when you left—fully alive. Check out OARS, www.oars.com (Grand Canyon rafting, Idaho whitewater, multisport trips from California to Peru); Trek America, www.trekamerica.com (Yosemite, Alaska, Death Valley, and Las Vegas); Wildland Adventures, www.wildland.com (family adventures, Costa Rica, and Tanzania); Go South Adventures, www.go-south-adventures.com (Galapagos Islands, Patagonia, and the Amazon); and Geographic Expeditions, www.geoex.com (Tibet, India, Vietnam, and Angkor Wat).

At the high end of experience—flow—a problem is a good thing. Confronting it leads to optimal experience as your abilities meet the challenge. With numerous techniques to master and each river posing new navigational obstacles, kayaking offers plenty of challenges. This gives Joosse a chance to exercise the life intelligence skill of problem solving, the ability to figure out challenges in an experiential context, as they come at you in an activity or a novel environment. The basic concept is being able to improvise, something that brain researchers tell us is a powerful inducer of conditions that lead to flow.

Using MRI scans, Johns Hopkins physician Charles Limb found that when jazz musicians played improvisational riffs, the part of their brains connected with less inhibition and self-monitoring, the prefrontal cortex, lit up, and they slipped into the dissociated state that accompanies flow. This didn't happen when they played standard tunes. Indulge in activities that offer impromptu challenges, from sports to chess, to outdoor adventures, and you activate heightened awareness and responsiveness.

"There's this intense focus. You're right here, right now," says Joosse, whose passion for kayaking grew so quickly that by the end of his first year, he had Class 5 river skills, which is the most difficult category of rapids (Class 1 being the easiest) and offers up a very intense gauntlet of problems, "a dangerous edge between apprehension and euphoria," as Joosse puts it.

He learned the hard way that one of the prime levers of flow is balancing skills to the challenge. If the demands are above your abilities, you feel only anxiety, not flow. Joosse once took on a creek over flood stage, which required skills he didn't have, and he wound up in a kayak-eating whirlpool that he barely got out of alive. His friends estimated that he was underwater for forty-five seconds. Chastened, Joosse went back to Class 3 for six months and worked his way up. The lesson here is, know your skills and take your time.

In a dozen years of kayaking, Joosse has gotten to know the flow experience intimately amid the roar of raging currents, backwashes, holes, hidden "pillow" rocks, and fallen trees. He and his fellow paddlers case their runs thoroughly beforehand, mapping out what's runnable and what's not. Joosse admits that it may seem hard to believe, but this is "the most profoundly peaceful thing" he does, despite "the bombs going off around me" in the form of rapids, currents, and drop-offs.

Sometimes *he's* the bomb. He's logged several first descents, including a couple of waterfalls, with paddling buddies. On one of them, he sailed off the edge of sixty-foot Skookum Falls in British Columbia. What do you think about when you're free-falling like a piece of bark while being blasted by the equivalent of a brigade of fire hoses? "I remember how beautiful it was," says Joosse, a contributing editor at paddling portal Playak.com. He aimed the nose of his craft at the most foamy water to cushion the blow, but he wound up overrotated and exploded out of his craft on impact. He got to the surface, swam to the edge of the river, and celebrated with his friends, who videotaped it.

Another problem solved. Maybe the biggest accomplishment Joose has gotten from kayaking has been on the personal side. He got to come out of the shadows and discover himself as a leader of kayak expeditions and an expert in water rescue. The boost in social skills from his hobby made him feel more confident. "It took getting out of my context of regular living so that it could come up as a lesson," he says. Score another one for the core.

## Ride the Moment

I've felt it many times on a long run, when my body and breath merge in a rhythm that feels instinctive and synchronous.

Surfers know the feeling well, as they move across a wave without doing the moving. Maximal and yet effortless effort at the same time. Immersed, yet connected to all. That's flow.

"Everything just goes into slow motion and your body does everything automatically," says Ally Sycip, twenty-eight, an artist and a surfer in Hermosa Beach, California, describing the liquid car pool of nature and human in the wave lane. "I think it's the best feeling in the world. My happiness is at the one hundred percent level, satisfaction at the one hundred percent level. It's like you're connected to the ocean."

"My brain, which is usually extremely loud, goes quiet," says climber Sara Lingafelter, when she's in the flow zone. "The chatter stops. The must-do's, the missed doings, the doubts and wonderings and self-criticism and second-guessing stop." On a recent climb at Red Rock, Nevada, she moved through it all "with just a few moments of stress. I don't know how long we were on the face that day—it had to be eight or nine hours—but just imagine eight solid hours of peace and calm and confidence."

The test of flow has traditionally been the point where your skills meet a challenge or are just slightly below it. But some researchers say that personally fulfilling experiences can also get you to a state of flow. I've had many flow experiences while traveling, which isn't a motor skills-to-challenge event. My sense is that flow arises when all my faculties are firing to the max in a self-realizing, interactive moment. I think that there are various intensities of flow, any of them being splendid when they make ego and the usual drumbeat of worries scram in the face of fun and challenge.

"There's something deeper going on than absorption," says Gary Ellis, who has done several studies on optimal experience and heads the department of parks, recreation, and tourism sciences at Texas A&M. In one, "the connection with self," the degree to which people felt personally fulfilled by the activity, was the best predictor of flow, which echoes the research on passion by Robert Vallerand. I can see this in the Flow Master's poetry, the rhapsody of the choir singers you met in the last chapter, and my passion for travel, which fulfills something in me that goes way back. At ten years of age, I was tracing maps of other countries and sending requests for brochures to the chambers of commerce of exotic places such as New London, Connecticut.

A third of Americans have never had a flow experience, according to one Gallup poll. Many others have them rarely. It takes a big shift from reflex habits to self-determination to get to flow. The whole dynamic requires intense immersion and a sidelining of the usual thought parade. If you want to know what it feels like when you're in flow, here's how some research subjects have described the experience of absorption:

- I am so involved in what I am doing, I don't see myself as separate from what I'm doing.
- My mind isn't wandering.
- During the activity, there were times when things were going so well, I felt as if I could do almost anything.
- I forgot my worries during the activity I was involved in.

Scientists have done voluminous research on flow, but little of it is household knowledge. It's hard to slip into peak experience if you don't know the characteristics, so let's review the traditional ingredients.

*The High-Water Marks of Flow*

1. *A balance of skills with challenge.* Stretch your abilities to the utmost to meet a challenge, and you're in line for flow. Just what might that challenge be? Csikszentmihalyi says it can be "any action humans are capable of responding to." Optimal experience occurs when high skills meet high demands. No challenge

means no flow. You can't keep playing tennis with the third-grader. You have to keep the ratio between your skills and the challenge the same or with the challenge just slightly above.

All ages can get there. In one study, seniors over the age of seventy reported experiencing flow in everything from playing sports and working to personal projects. The majority of thru-hikers on the Appalachian Trail were shown to have flow experiences daily as they hiked in the backcountry. There are a lot of ways to get life to flow, as long as you challenge yourself.

2. *Clear goals and immediate feedback*. Rules, goals, and performance techniques help focus your thoughts on specific demands, which prevents your attention from drifting. The clear directions also offer another crucial element of flow: immediate feedback. You know when you shoot the basketball whether you've done it well or not. That sense of proficiency plays off the challenge to incite flow. Choose pursuits that let you see tangible progress, and the odds of flow improve.

3. *Merging of action and awareness*. Your thoughts and movements blend together in this hallmark of flow. Your engagement in the activity is so complete that the usual mental tape loop of projects to do, conflicts to ruminate on, and insecurities to fret over is shut down. Harmony lives where thought and deed are unified.

4. *Loss of self-consciousness*. If you're thinking about how well you're doing an activity or what someone else thinks of you, you are not in flow. Self-consciousness is still at the helm and is draining your focus. The more you can dig deeply into the activity and lose yourself in it, the more you can slip into that state beyond ego that Karl Grignon teaches his aikido students.

5. *Altered sense of time*. Total absorption removes another obstacle that undermines the experience of where you are: time

consciousness. When Amy Doran, the kite flier we met earlier, sent her kite aloft and didn't land it until seven hours later, she was deep in flow. Increase the level of absorption, and time and pretty much everything else will get out of your way.

6. *Paradox of control.* This is one of the most intriguing aspects of optimal experience. As you handle the demands of an activity, this stokes a sense of control over the universe, a feeling that you can take on anything. But it comes—and here's the paradox—from an absence of fear of losing control. You surrender to what's thrown at you and don't try to fight it, but instead flow with it. By not trying to control the outcome, you wind up controlling the moment with your competency. It's a classic illustration of the Taoist notion of wu-wei, doing by nondoing.

## Accept No Substitutes

The universe of potential enjoyment, expansion, and gratification is contained within every instant you are alive to it. Accept no external substitutes. The real path to a vital life is where it's always been: in the moment of internal activation through experience, in Brown's estate of the now. All that you have to do is

- Pay attention to your experience.
- Pursue competence without regard to where it's going.
- Stand in and solve problems.
- Let your skills stretch to meet the challenges.
- Get so absorbed in your experience that nothing else matters.

# 7

## Play Is Where You Live

It is a happy talent to know how to play.
— *Ralph Waldo Emerson*

The nun walked over to me on the playground and leaned down, and her stern, ghostly expression broadened into a rare grin. "Your face is redder than anyone else's," she said. Later, I looked in a bathroom mirror. She wasn't kidding. Any self-respecting tomato would be envious. It was no mystery where the color came from, though. I had the reddest face in the second grade from playing during every recess as if was my last.

I didn't know it at the time, but my flaming mug was a testament to the burning need to play that adulthood diverts but doesn't extinguish. Back then, nothing could get in the way of my total abandon to dodgeball, tetherball, or, especially, kickball. There's a reason that soccer is the world's most popular sport. Kicking is gratifying at some cathartic, steam-releasing level. By fourth grade I could occasionally boot a ball off or over the rectory wall. Then someone had to go interrupt the padre to get the ball back.

Even today, I occasionally dream of a kickball rolling at me in slow motion. I approach, plant, strike it squarely, and launch it high over that wall again. Of course, with dreams also being the repository of epic humiliation (is that so we feel grateful afterward?), sometimes I miss the ball completely. Needless to say, I was very pumped to learn that my kickball days weren't confined to shuteye. In fact, there is a thriving kickball league for adults, the World Adult Kickball Association, or WAKA, which has teams across the United States.

Clearly, I had some unfinished business, so I joined up with a WAKA outfit at a dusty baseball diamond in a West Hollywood park. There was something about the team's name, Menace to Sobriety, that let me know this was a different brand of kickball than Sister Mary's. I was relieved to find that the team appeared sober, at least at game time. Team captain Ariana Mayman, a blond, ponytailed first baseman, preached kickball as if it were a lost gospel. "What's great about kickball is that anyone can play," she said, wearing a maroon bandanna to match the color of the team T-shirt. "We have this expression: 'It's just kickball.'"

Yet in the guise of this child's game, there's a lot more going on than meets the eye. Before kickball, Mayman was like many urbanites, adrift in urban sprawl, having trouble meeting people. Now she needs a social secretary. She says that she's made hundreds of friends through the bouncing red ball. She met all three of her roommates through kickball. Her boyfriend is on another kickball team.

"My life has been dramatically changed by kickball," says Mayman, a marketing coordinator for a music company. "In a city like Los Angeles, it's easy to feel very small and alone. Kickball gives you the confidence to walk up to anyone, anywhere, and feel comfortable having a conversation."

That was the idea behind the kickball revival, when some newly minted college grads started WAKA in Washington, D.C., as a way for people to connect around a symbol of the original playtime. Launched in 1998, the group now claims leagues in twenty-seven states and England. Most of the participants are in their twenties and early thirties. The average age on my team is twenty-five.

Researchers say that the social element is a major factor in the life satisfaction delivered by active play pursuits. Play solves the eternal quest for an opening line between strangers, providing an instant common bond. The evidence of that was all around me, with a super-revved crew who high-fived and cracked one-liners. Kickball is like baseball with a big rubber ball, except that you play five innings instead of nine; you kick, instead of bat, the ball; and you can throw someone out by hitting the runner with the ball. The league rules also stipulate that there have to be four women out of the eleven players on the field at any given time.

A flurry of singles got us off to a three-run lead against our orange-shirted opponents, who should have been awarded a couple of runs for their name alone: Your Mom. We never looked back. I made it into the game a few innings later. Sporting my official Menace T-shirt, I jogged out to left field, amazed to be in this child's game again. I tried to remember the last time I had played kickball—fifth grade?—but my body was way ahead of my mind, crouching into ready position. I was as alive and free to catch or kick a ball as I was at nine. Why didn't I do it more often?

I got to the plate the next inning. The pitcher served up a mean twister-ball I didn't recall from the old days. The ball was larger, softer, heavier, more unwieldy than the sphere of my youth. The first pitch bounced way out of the strike zone. My teammates yelled, "Good eye!" as I let another pitch go wide. Finally, I booted a spinner off the side of my foot to the third baseman, who threw the ball up the first base line.

The first baseman tried to tag me, but I dodged him and made it to the bag untouched. The ump called me out, though, for going out of the base path. It wasn't exactly like in my dream, but the old instincts were still there, and so was the fun. My team went on to vanquish Your Mom and from there to a local sports bar, where, loosened by play and libations, these former strangers would find plenty of common ground.

Play itself is a kind of truth serum, lowering your guard and liberating the scripted self to reveal the still-enthused, red-faced second-grader inside. It's a life-giving resource right in front of you, but it's held at bay by the performance reflex and the adult mind. You can awaken it again with the law of optimal fun: play is where you live.

With a flip of the mental switch to the play mind, you're out of the box of obligatory existence and into a self-chosen state that resets authentic life. You are not an automaton anymore. There's no age limit on enjoyment, but it can't be accessed with the usual office equipment. You have to play with skills that may have been on a long hiatus: eagerness, playfulness, positive affect, an ability to suspend reality, and social initiative. Learn how you can resuscitate these talents and discover the building blocks of enjoyment, including the fun pyramid, which is as crucial to your quality of life as the food pyramid is to your physical health. Listen closely, and you might be able to hear the bell. Recess is on.

## The Hokey Pokey *Is* What It's All About

When you're a kid, you need permission from your parents to play. When you're an adult, you need permission from yourself. Parents are an easier mark. That's because most of us can't see fit to do something that doesn't have a purpose. We learn that productive adults must do things that have a point, a logical outcome.

This has made play for grownups one of the last remaining taboos, an irrational deviation from gainful obligation.

Anthropologist Gregory Bateson believed that most of the ills of the modern world came from a bad case of too much purposefulness. The fixation with making everything productive and rational cuts us off from the world of the spontaneous that is home to real knowledge. Wisdom, Bateson believed, is to be found in the realms outside of intentionality, in the inner reaches of art, expression, and religion.

## Playing on the Job

Salespeople the world over know that the art of the deal happens outside the office—over lunch or on the golf course—at play, when people have a chance to get to know each other beyond their business cards. You cut to the core in play, making the usual boundaries drop away.

Playfulness can seriously upgrade your work. In one study in Taiwan, known for its intense work culture, playfulness at work increased job performance, innovation, and satisfaction.

Play does amazing things for creativity. It has an ability to loosen the mental set, breaking up old associations that keep us stuck and lubricating new ideas. Surveys show that people get their best ideas for the job, not at work, straining until their temple veins bulge, but when they're at play—running, playing tennis, even taking a lunchtime walk. There's a reason for this: Motion keeps the logical left brain occupied with controlling your movements, so that the more creative right brain can wander.

Sociologist A. L. Kroeber once said, "Play is responsible for all the discoveries of pure science and fine art." What we need at work, not only at home, to break up the day and brain-lock is the injection of regular doses of energizing play.

"That is the domain of play," says psychologist and cultural explorer Bradford Keeney, recalling the words of his mentor Bateson. "We just became too serious. And then we regarded anything without a conscious purpose as problematic, to be corrected, alleviated. The whole culture is suffering from over-conscious intentionality, overseriousness, overemphasis on productivity and work. We've forgotten that the whole picture requires a dance between leisure and work."

Why would evolution select something as pointless as play to survive into the twenty-first century? It turns out that play is not so useless after all. Play, for instance, increases exploratory and risk-taking behavior. Marc Bekoff at the University of Colorado has studied play in a variety of social carnivores—from dogs to wolves—and says that play is a kind of rehearsal hall. It allows you to try things out without repercussions. It's only play. Scientists have also found a big social upside to playing around. Walter Freeman at UC-Berkeley argues that music and dance evolved to bond people in groups, which improved trust and allowed them to work together and build securities.

Anything that greases the relational wheels as play does has a lot going for it with the social animal. People who have healthy social lives are happier and live longer, because their core need for relatedness is regularly satisfied. Studies have shown that participating in enjoyable social activities—specifically, doing things that are pleasant and fun—is a strong predictor of increased daily well-being.

Play also pays off in big health dividends. It's a proven stress buffer, reducing strain and burnout, boosting your immune system, and pumping up vitality and energy. The positive emotions that play evokes are essential to the mental and physical renewal process. Participating in recreational activities has been

connected to increased positive mood and experiencing pleasure, both of which come absolutely free with the experience.

"When I'm on my bike, I'm at my happiest," says Linda Imle, a
computer technician in Fairbanks, Alaska. "Being in the moment
outside, I'm at peace with myself, at peace with the world."

When a forty-year-old goes headfirst down a water slide, that
person is not forty anymore. A few decades have been knocked
off, because something inside has come alive again. It should
be pretty obvious that the animating spark of play is the fast
track to happiness, which is a good evolutionary reason to keep
it around through the millennia. There is no quicker transport
to the experiential realm and full engagement than through
play, which brings together all the elements you want for the
optimal moment.

1.  Play is 100 percent experience.
2.  It's done for the intrinsic pleasure, for the participation.
3.  With no judgment or outcomes needed, play grounds
    you in the now.

The "Hokey-Pokey" really is what it's all about. It's all
there in the children's song that was aerobic before its
time—fun, bonding, skills, challenge, risk, learning, and the
experiential magic of turning yourself around. When you put
your foot in, your hands, your head, you put your core self
into the life circle in the form of autonomy, competence,
and relatedness, which are all met in the unconditional act
of play.

This might be the biggest thing that play does for you. It's a
restorative. Play brings you back to life—your life.

"Adults need to play because so much of our life is utilitarian,"
the University of South Alabama's Catherine O'Keefe explained

to me. "We need to reconnect with the things of our lives that ground us in who we really are and why we like our lives."

In a world of constant upheaval, you can be staggered by a feeling of groundlessness from time to time. It can seem as if there's nothing to hang on to. When you're free-falling, play is there to catch you, restoring your perspective and reminding you that you're still capable of enjoyment.

Play is not a character defect; it's the builder of character. Studies show that it's more congruent with your personality than what you do at work. When you're engaged in activities of personal expressiveness, ones that are self-chosen and that advance your life goals, you're operating from the "true self," says Alan Waterman of the College of New Jersey. That leads to optimal psychological functioning, in other words, happiness. We're talking about something that is far from tangential to your existence here. Play scholar John Neulinger called passionate play pursuits none other than the "central life interest."

The life force can't be felt unless you are awake to it. This is the service that play provides, yanking grownups out of their purposeful sleepwalk to reveal the animating spirit within. Isn't it time to give yourself permission to come out and play?

Here's your permission slip:

---

**The Play Okay**
(Your name here) _____ has my permission to take part in recess to celebrate the freedom of self-determined enjoyment.

_____
*Your signature*

---

## Hit Reset

When you get confused, it helps to go back to the beginning. That's what play does. It's the reset button, slicing through grownup complexity to the heart of where you come from, the interests and the spirit that were there before all of the gunk got piled on. What are the elements of that core self? What's different about you when you're at play, in interests and attitudes, than when you're in the work mind? See if you can identify five ways that you are different during play than when you're at work. From now on, use the change from work clothes to civilian clothes as a reset button to turn on the core qualities on your list.

••••••••••••••••••••••••••••••••••••••••••••••••••••••••••

# Playfulness: The Skill of Irrational Exuberance

Sounding like a cross between a hysterical hyena and orgasmic moaning, the cuica is a musical instrument that seems to have been invented for a Monty Python gag. Yelping away in the rhythm section of samba music, this Brazilian percussion device appears to exist for no purpose other than sheer whimsy. Its cheeky bedlam is an exhortation to let go of all futile attempts to keep a straight face and roll with the human comedy. And it couldn't come from any land other than Brazil.

When the national personalities were handed out, Brazil got an extra helping in the levity department. Brazilians have more than their share of intractable problems, but many have managed to master the ability to shift dark clouds, something that samba and their famed Carnaval celebration embody to the last note and sequin. After a few days in Rio de Janeiro, I find myself catching the exuberance, adopting the twinkling eye, grinning for no reason, and embracing perfect strangers as if they were long-lost friends. The spirit comes courtesy of a skill that Brazilians dominate as much as they do soccer: playfulness and its sidekick, positive affect, the look of obvious good vibes on your mug and in your body language. When you have it, humans are drawn to you by all of the mirroring synchrony built into the neural circuitry. They want in. Forget the Porsche and the little black dress; the strongest attraction in the world is the glow of someone having obvious fun.

When I was traveling in Thailand once, I had an American tourist and her husband come up to me and ask, "Excuse me. We couldn't help but notice you seem to be having a good time. Could we just ask what it is you're doing so we can do it?" That's positive affect, something easy to exude when I'm traveling, but hard to summon in the workaday world without frequent doses of play.

"Playfulness throws off a kind of charisma; adults, children and even lab rats are drawn to spend more time with those who have had abundant practice playing," notes Daniel Goleman in *Social Intelligence*. Part of what makes this state so attractive is the sensation at its core, joy, which is both a trigger and an outcome of playfulness. "Joy creates the urge to play and be playful in the broadest sense of the word," says the University of North Carolina's Barbara Frederickson, author of *Positivity* and a leading researcher in the study of positive emotions.

Playfulness begets more playfulness, which explains a theory I have about Brazilians. There's a kind of tipping point of playfulness for a given place or culture, when the vibe is so widespread that it turns enough mirror neurons to send a majority of the population into the positive affect column. It plays out on the beaches of Rio in a ritual that symbolizes the local joie de vivre. At the end of a sunny day on the sand in Ipanema and Copacabana, beachgoers have been known to applaud the sun as it sets. Being awake to joy makes you appreciate what brings it to your midst.

Most of us, though, have a different outlook. We have been harangued since grade school to get serious, look serious, be serious, as if life was a penal colony or a monastery. Shifting out of that rut is problematic unless you can suspend the stranglehold of the ultralogical mind-set. Play is also blocked by negative mood states. "The play circuitry defers to bad feelings—anxiety, anger, sadness—all of which suppress playfulness," points out Goleman.

---

### Pick Your Playground

Don't throw up your hands and say that there's nothing to do. Plenty of resources are out there to get you into the game, the class, the sport, or the outing you want to do. One of the most overlooked sources is the county parks system. Yes, there are still parks, hundreds of them, which offer a range of activities at a price that's right for all ages, including people with disabilities. You can find everything from table tennis to geocaching, swimming, yoga, baseball, and dancing. Do a Google search of your city and county parks and recreation Web sites for activity schedules. For a list of county parks across the United States, try www.nacpro.org/county_parks/county_parks.shtml.

Other playgrounds include college gyms and extension programs (from dancing to badminton) and league activities sponsored by recreational organizations. Search out the association Web site for the activity you want to do, such as the World Adult Kickball Association (www.kickball.com) and the Ultimate Players Association (for Frisbee football; www.upa.org/ultimate), both of which list leagues in your area.

On the other hand, playfulness predisposes you to seek out and savor enjoyment, helping you develop the capacity for pleasure. Extroverts have an edge when it comes to loosening things up, but anyone can increase playfulness. You just have to switch off autopilot and consciously apply new behavior—the ability to transform your environment. "You take what's there and turn it into something else. Just because it's amusing," says Lynn Barnett-Morris of the University of Illinois, who has studied the playful personality.

The skill you need for that is the knack of suspending reality, which, ironically, allows you to be more real. You put aside the momentary mood of boredom or irritation and leap into an alternate universe that houses your authentic identity. Switching over to the play side is no different from pushing the buttons on your remote to watch a movie, which requires you to suspend your belief to enjoy it. Look at your play in the same way—you're flipping on another movie, except that you're starring in it.

The positive emotions triggered by playfulness, humor, and leisure activities actually help you get more control over the suspended reality. They disrupt the stressors that keep negativity in place. You shut off the funky moods when you play.

Barnett's research has pinpointed four main components of the playful attitude:

- *Gregariousness.* This isn't extroversion but an ability, based on self-confidence, to not care so much about what others think. You can move in and out of social situations. You're comfortable with yourself and aren't caught up in social pretenses or people's responses.

  *How to put it into play*: The secret to gregariousness is simple. You don't wait for people or situations to come your way. You initiate. Start the conversation, reach out, with no need to have anything reciprocated.

- *A comedic quality*. This is another element that calls for you to initiate and not hold back a moment of whimsy. "It's the idea of being motivated to entertain yourself and sometimes other people," says Barnett-Morris. "Being able to take situations and turn them around for pleasure. Some people make funny faces, others joke. But it's also things you do to amuse yourself when no one else is looking or listening. It's really self-entertainment."

  *How to put it into play*: The comedic requires time to detour from the expected, to go off on a tangent. You want to be in a whimsical ready state, looking for associations that can spin a comment or a behavior around. It's as much about listening as it is delivering witticisms. Things that don't add up, contradictions, exaggerations, and self-deprecation are good areas to mine. Act for the fun and not the laughs, and you don't have to hold off humor for fear that it won't get enough of a response. Do it to do it.

- *Spontaneity*. Playful people jump into the unpredictable and impulsive, content to try something new for whatever they get out of it. They don't live or die for the reaction of others. This comes from a confidence "that I'm going to take a risk here and be fine," says Barnett-Morris.

  *How to put it into play*: Being more spontaneous is a matter of turning down the self-editing and following up on comedic impulses. Be less wedded to linear conversations and more open to sidetracks. Try things for a humorous effect. Turn a handshake into arm-wrestling. Wear your shoes on the wrong feet or your shirt backward. If you see the tetherball hanging there, jump out of the control line and smack it.

- *Amiability*. Geniality is a great springboard to playfulness. People who are amicable and social are already in the spirit of playful interaction. Because the friendly cues are written on your face and your demeanor with positive affect, playful types will seek you out.

*How to put it into play*: Amiability emanates from unconditional receptivity. Protective walls keep it at bay. Place the palm of your hand in front of your face and wipe downward. As you do, change your expression from defensive to expressive and upbeat. It's a rehearsal for the way that play makes you feel. Changing demeanor shifts your experience—whether you feel it or not initially. I can guarantee a vastly more fun time at salsa class when I make a conscious effort to go in with positive affect on my face and in my voice. The more you throw yourself into the participation, the easier this is to do.

## Square One for Fun

In 2009, decathlon champ Dan O'Brien set a Guinness record for the fastest game of hopscotch, leaping to a finish in 1:21:63 at the age of forty-two. It reminded grownups that the games we walk away from still have something to offer—in the case of speed hopscotch, quite a workout, plus balance and a return home.

The tradition dates back to the Romans and a time when manly soldiers played hopscotch on a court more than a hundred feet in length. Over the centuries, it spread to kids around the world and landed on your sidewalk or school playground in the nine- or ten-square format. As you'll recall, the idea is to put your marker down in square one, then hop on one foot to the first box, then when you get to the next row of two boxes, you straddle the line between the boxes, and so on. The point is to land on all of the squares without touching a line or losing your balance.

Recently, I saw a man who looked to be in his forties walking down the sidewalk on my street. It could have been any of us doing the adult shuffle, head-down, lost in thought. Except suddenly he broke into a series of hops, straddles, and jumps. Local kids had chalked in a hopscotch pattern on the cement, and he leapt right in. After his last hop, he straightened himself out and continued walking with a big grin on his face. He didn't look back once to check if anyone was watching. For a moment, anyway, the day had come to life for him and for me, through play.

You can animate your day, too, with a time-honored hop in your step. Get some chalk, or buy a plastic hopscotch mat online that you can use in your house. Use it to transition from the work mind to the play mind and as a symbol of the balance you're about to discover.

•••••••••••••••••••••• ACTIVATE ••••••••••••••••••••••

## Ignite Your Life with Eagerness

Another key to playfulness is a basic life intelligence skill that adults have long since abandoned: eagerness, energized readiness to embrace the moment as if there were no other. Eagerness propels play and increases the jubilation that results from it. Shutting eagerness down because you don't want to look naive or set yourself up for rejection cuts off the entire joy brigade. Set the stage for playfulness by rediscovering the energizing agent of eagerness. Identify something that would really excite you—maybe sitting in the first row at a concert of your favorite musician or a vacation in the South Seas. Now visualize that it's coming true next week. Feel the enthusiasm and excitement, and freeze-frame an image of that state. Bring that energy to your next outing, and you'll have a head start on playfulness.

# The Real Law of Attraction

"Yes!" Kathy Smolik and I both blurted it out at the same time, after we'd shocked ourselves by completing a new salsa sequence right off the bat. We were at Gabriel Gamboa's Arthur Murray Dance Studio, an oasis of life in a sterile office park in Leesburg, Virginia. I'd found the studio in a tiny ad in a tourist magazine in my hotel room. Kathy and I had known each other for a grand total of a couple of minutes, but that was enough to have indisputable, fist-pumping fun together. Where did this sudden effervescence come from?

It turns out that there were quite a few factors leading to the "instant" fun of a couple of strangers: the readiness to have it, a playful state, the surprise of doing something we'd never done before, the social connection of teamwork, and the elation of the act itself. Spinning and twisting the body in a symmetrical way is delightful, in and of itself. One study found that what people are really attracted to in good dancers is symmetry, the harmony of a fluid body. Harmony is at the root of play on so many fronts—you and your true identity, you and other people, thought and action. No wonder it feels so good.

But there's another item that got Kathy and me off to a rousing start, something I have found to be one of the absolute keys to the universe: positive affect. We both had it activated in the form of eagerness, openness, smiles. We knew we were going to have fun, and we had the body language that would guarantee it.

It's amazing what can happen when you've got the spell of visible vibrancy going. I remember once boarding a plane to Africa for a story I was writing. My photographer and I were so cranked up about the trip that it showed, and a flight attendant got caught up in our excitement. After a brief chitchat about the adventure, she offered a free upgrade to business class. Those kinds of things don't happen when you're cool. That's something I was not a stranger to earlier in life. Cool, I discovered, curbed my natural enthusiasm. Eagerness is off-limits when you're cool, because it goes way past the bounds of indifference that are supposed to indicate you have seen it all. Research shows that it's the opposite of coolness—an overt, genuine, positive mood without concerns for how you come off that others are drawn to. People with positive affect, an upbeat outlook that shows up in their demeanor, are more likely to be happier and healthier, live longer, and meet their goals.

If you didn't know the term before, I'm sure you know people with positive affect, folks who can turn the mood of others around instantly with a quip, a touch of the arm, a whispered crack, a beaming smile. The scientific literature is loaded with testaments to the powers of positive affect. Researchers Sonja Lyubomirsky, Ed Diener, and Laura King make the case that this "hallmark of well-being" may be the trigger of a host of traits and outcomes that are associated with happiness, including—drum roll—success. "Chronically happy people are in general more successful. . . . Their success is in large part a consequence of their happiness and frequent experience of positive affect." This tonic extends your health. The state increases your immune function, while negative affect lowers it by boosting the level of the stress hormone cortisol.

There is a predictive property to positive affect. When you start out on the positive side of the ledger, you don't have as far to go to be playful, to connect with someone, to enjoy yourself, to jump into something new. The green light is on for more positive things to happen. Positive affect tells the world that you came to play, that you are engaged, and it makes you want to do just that. People who are animated by positive emotions are more inclined "to approach, rather than to avoid," say Lyubomirsky and colleagues.

Some people are always well stocked in positive affect. It can be 105 degrees in the shade with 90 percent humidity, and they are upbeat. They are lucky. The rest of us have to develop this knack, which gives you the ability to counter the cynicism and frustrations that we fall prey to in a difficult world. The kind of spirit we are looking for here is not a blind, Pollyanna, power-of-positive-thinking stupor. The goal is a state of vitality and problem-solving acumen that can push through the setbacks and the moods that sideline you. You can develop positive affect as a skill by understanding its key components: optimism, expressive body language, sociability, and energy. Let's dig into the ingredients of visible vibrancy:

1. *Buoyant optimism.* The baseline of positive affect is an optimistic attitude, a belief that gets translated into a genuine, hopeful demeanor. Every day we cycle multiple times through negative and positive moods, but some people are more adept at accentuating the upside, while pessimists can find a downside to every silver lining. The difference lies in what the University of Pennsylvania's Martin Seligman dubbed "explanatory style," the story you tell yourself about negative events. That story is usually supplied by the fear-doubt-inadequacy script of the primitive emotional brain, the amygdala, which makes you see negative events as permanent, pervasive, and personal. When you buy the calamitous tale of the three Ps, as Seligman calls them, it leads to pessimism. You can reverse the story by viewing the situation as temporary, specific, and nonpersonal. It's all about disputing and challenging stress-fueled pessimism with the real story.

2. *Expressive body language*. Leave the frozen face at home. Animate. You don't have to be an infomercial host, but you need to bring the signs of an amiable spirit—punctuating the conversation with more smiles or laughs; listening intently; demonstrating surprise or enjoyment, instead of world-weariness; making eye contact—and ask for nothing in return. An animated body language is a contagious piece of activation, connecting with the mirror neurons of other people.

3. *Physical vitality*. Good vibes tend to emanate from people who exude energy and vitality. It's not surprising, because fatigue and exhaustion aren't usually a springboard to congeniality. Diet, exercise, personal energy, interest, passion—all are important in projecting the physical signals of engagement. Bring eagerness and enthusiasm to the mix, and it all comes together.

4. *Sociability*. Positive affect communicates to others that you are open to relate and enjoy. You're not there under protest. You're not there to watch. You're interested in people. The sociability that spins off from this frame of mind is a nonjudgmental one, something that others can pick up on. You are friendly to all and not ready to zing someone who makes a blunder. Bring a light spirit, and leave the critiques and baggage at home.

·················· ACTIVATE ··················

## Priming Positive Affect

I've always marveled at how Vin Scully, the virtuoso voice of the Los Angeles Dodgers, can bring that upbeat, sunny delivery to every broadcast, game after game. One of his secrets: he primes positive affect before he goes to work by listening to his favorite classical music and opera. That's a great strategy, as is the whole idea of getting your psyche in tune with your destination. Before you head out for a life opportunity, take a few minutes to set the stage for a change in mood from the negative states that tend to gang up on you when you are about to exit productive mode. Use music, exercise, or anything else that gets you in the right state. I use samba to fire me up. Another strategy, once you begin your activity, is to crank up the positive affect, even if you don't feel like it at first. I like to challenge the caveman brain and its killjoy moods by making it my conscious mission to bring extra energy, conversation, or smiles than I normally would. You will feel as if you're acting, but that's okay, because within a couple of minutes, you'll be fully engaged. Action vanquishes the funks and negative mood states we let get in the way of our lives.

............................................................

# The Architecture of Fun

We all have plenty of information on the various requirements of good nutritional health or physical conditioning, but the mechanics of soul-stirring fun have been a mystery, no doubt because the topic has been considered beyond the pale of triviality. Now that you know how crucial this life-stirring resource is—for health, friendships, joy, competence, and all-around bliss—it's important to understand the building blocks of fun, so that you can indulge it more often. I have distilled the key components into the first official fun pyramid, which breaks down the elements of play into the essential enjoyment vitamins.

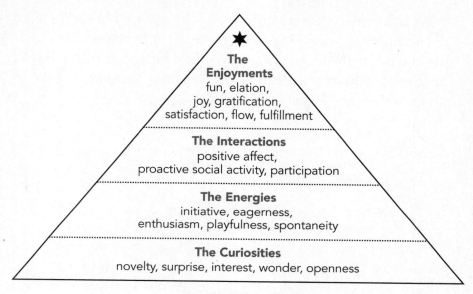

**The Enjoyments**
fun, elation,
joy, gratification,
satisfaction, flow, fulfillment

**The Interactions**
positive affect,
proactive social activity, participation

**The Energies**
initiative, eagerness,
enthusiasm, playfulness, spontaneity

**The Curiosities**
novelty, surprise, interest, wonder, openness

## The Fun Pyramid

The foundation of fun, the Curiosities group, gets everything going with novelty, surprise, interest, wonder, and openness, which locate the potential fun opportunities. Follow the interest, and you need the fortification of the next group, the Energies, the spark plugs that activate further investigation—initiative, eagerness, enthusiasm, playfulness, joy, spontaneity—to drive the effort. Redondo Beach, California, surfer Ally Sycip is well fueled in this department. "I crave the water," he says. "Some nights I can't even sleep thinking about the next day of surfing. I want to be in the water that bad."

The next tier, the Interactions, ignites the transformative component that comes from participation, positive affect, and proactive social activity. "It's really deep," says choir singer Felicia Kelly, talking about the social connection she's found in her passion. "I was going to leave Los Angeles, but I can't now because of the choir. I've met people who will be my friends for the rest of my life."

It all comes together at the top of the pyramid in the form of the Enjoyments, which range from sweet bursts of elation, joy, and fun to the long-lasting glow of satisfaction, gratification, flow, and fulfillment. These rewards are as nutritious as the best proteins or grains—food for the soul.

•••••••••••••••••••••••••• ACTIVATE ••••••••••••••••••••••••••

## Take Your Multi-Enjoyment Vitamins

The cycle of fun has more to it than we think. It's a process of research and growth that moves you from initial interest to activation and beyond. Take a close look at the fun pyramid and identify which of the four nutrient groups could make the biggest difference in triggering the other elements of fun for you. Is it at the beginning, the Curiosities? Could you be doing better at the Interactions stage to get to the top of the pyramid more often? On a scale of 1 to 5, with 5 being the best, rate the current state of each of your groups—Curiosities, Energies, Interactions, and Enjoyments. Which groups do you need to put more effort into?

••••••••••••••••••••••••••••••••••••••••••••••••••••••••••••••

## The Virtual Recess

What about digital play? The best experiential bang for the buck is definitely Wii. The virtual reality device simulates activities from bowling to tennis and gets your whole body moving, not only your fingers, as you act out the activity on the screen with the Wiimote device. Wii bowling and tennis are so good at re-creating the serve or the bowling action that your arm may be sore the next day. In Nintendo's latest edition of Wii Sports

Resort, you can play archery and give wakeboarding a go. After you try it virtually, it may whet your appetite for the real thing. Wii has turned out to be a hit on a circuit that's way beyond the video game world: nursing homes. Residents at the Erickson Retirement Communities in Chicago now stage regular Wii bowling contests. Patients who may be able to move only one arm can be back in the active world, at play with a Wiimote in their hands.

## ⌒ Kim Travis Has Game

Kim Travis must have the record for the most frequent flyer miles racked up en route to a weekly softball game. For six years, every Thursday the actress and theater owner commuted more than three thousand miles round trip from Austin, Texas, where she was taking care of her ill mother, for softball games with the Actor's Equity team each spring and summer in New York's Central Park. After leaving on a six a.m. flight, she would be on the field in uniform in the Big Apple by game time at three-thirty p.m. And she wasn't even playing. She's managed the team for eight years.

It's a long way to go to chew out an ump. Travis loves softball, but the jet-setting was all about one thing: the people. "Most of us have been playing together for years," she says. "There's not one person on that team who doesn't love the others. We're a family now."

The team includes people like first-baseman Bill Johnson, "who looks like everybody's dad" and appears in various commercials. There's Greg Solata, pitcher, outfielder, theater owner, and former regular on the television series *Kate & Allie*. Jason Robards's son Sam Robards plays first and third. Catcher Wendy Worth has a dance school. "They were all there for me when my mother was ill," says Travis, whose mother lost her battle with cancer.

Travis, who used to play second base on the Actor's Equity team, is the only female coach in the very competitive thirty-six-team Broadway Show League, which was founded in 1953. The division includes teams from shows such as *The Lion King*, plus producers' and union teams, all doing battle on Central Park's iconic sandlot fields. Al Pacino, Kevin Spacey, and Sam Waterston are some of the players who have taken the plate there over the years. But it's not all marquee names. Teams field a mix of actors, stagehands, and crews in one of the great spin-offs of play—the chance to meet folks from all walks of life and get out of their social rut.

Travis has been hooked on softball since she broke in as a shortstop for the team in 1984. "It's hard to put into words the release I get from it," she says. "It's not just exercise or being outside. If you ask anyone on my team what their favorite day of the week is, it's Thursday. The issues of the day just completely go away once the game starts."

In a profession that is notorious for rejection and uncertainty, softball gives Travis and her team a badly needed shot of stability and support. "It's a homecoming every year when the season starts."

## The Social Core

Time and again, life enthusiasts tell me that the people they meet in their play pursuits are as big a draw as the avocation itself. I can't think of a way to find better friends faster than by diving into a hobby with other people. A special bond develops from shared passions that forges friendships based on mutual fun, not on what you do for a living. Improving your ability to be socially proactive, to jump in and swim with strangers, is an important skill that can reap a bounty of satisfaction for your core need for relatedness.

So much of friendship comes from shared interests, and you get that immediately when you have a passion in common with someone. You don't have to be a social butterfly, because the activity itself brings everyone together. I've seen many painfully shy people come alive in salsa classes after they persist through the initial instruction and become more adept on the dance floor. They start to make eye contact more often. They initiate conversations and laugh more. The difficulty of approaching others fades. Each class provides a group ready to play, with everyone on an equal footing, the music and fun not just breaking the ice but destroying it.

You can send social fears back to their cages with small, practical adjustments in your behavior. Most of the following tips are part of the unwritten grab bag of signals that no one gets any training in. The reality is that introverts have the capability to be just as effective socially as extroverts are. When introverts played extroverts and vice versa in a study that used a role reversal, introverts were just as successful in creating a good impression on others as the naturally friendly folks were.

So, with a little acting and shoring up of your social skills, you can step right up to the relatedness bar. Start troubleshooting with this social behavior inventory from recreation and leisure educator Jean Mundy. Which areas do you need to improve on? How will you do it?

*The Social Tool Kit*
1. Initiating social interactions
2. Greeting skills: saying hello, matching the greeting to the person and the situation; nonverbal—eye contact, tone of voice, facial expression, posture

3. Listening/understanding

4. Responding skills: comebacks, verbal reinforcement of others, self-disclosure, sharing the interaction

5. Keeping a conversation going

6. Accepting and giving compliments

7. Being assertive

8. Making requests

9. Issuing invitations

10. Closing interactions

Social activities open the door wide to relationships, because fun itself is a social affair. "The feelings of fun only emerge in this social bond and require an equality condition among members," says sociologist Walter Podilchak.

For a few precious moments in time, the judging stops and the relating begins. And that's important at a time when more Americans are living alone than ever before. The solution lies where it was when there was always someone to have fun with: on the playground.

•••••••••••••••••••••••• ACTIVATE ••••••••••••••••••••••••

## Breaking the Ice

As is true with just about everything in life, the tricky part of being socially proactive is starting. The defensive reflex will trot out all sorts of reasons to avoid contact with new people, and your job is to not latch onto any of those automatic thoughts. Recreational activities give you the perfect opportunity to get past social awkwardness with a host of conversation starters from your shared experience. You don't have to be creative. Walking over with a handshake and introducing yourself will get the ball rolling—"My name is . . . I have no idea what I'm doing." Asking for help is always a good ice breaker. You'll meet a lot of people easily in beginner classes out of your mutual cluelessness. Not knowing is a fantastic facilitator of friendship. When you have to reach out, you are more open and approachable. Be friendly, no matter what the response. Don't let your mirror neurons get manipulated by the folks with negative affect. Act unconditionally. What are three questions you could ask to initiate conversations? Now take the two most thorny issues for you from the Social Tool Kit list, and create an action step for each.

........................................................................

# Boost Your Play Quotient

Adulthood builds a thick rhino hide over the eagerness that leads to play. The premium is on suspicion, protection, responsibilities, production—not a fertile ground for purposeless diversion. But the evidence says you'll be healthier, happier, and even more effective at work if you break the taboo against recess. Activate your birthright to be fully alive by boosting your play quotient. It's a process of loosening up your mind and muscles as you relax into who you are. You can increase your play frequency and enjoyment with these attitudes and aptitudes:

- *Shift to play mind.* This is the essential tool of a high play quotient: being able to suspend reality and switch from resistant, performance mode to random acts of fun and nonproductivity with the play mind. You learn that you can shift from one state to another and return to the duty mind-set after refueling without any violation of the penal code.

- *Enable enthusiasm.* It's okay to be excited about your life, even if you're a grownup. Allow the enthusiasm that normally fades with hard knocks to flourish. You are now writing a new history.

- *Get red-faced.* Kids aren't worried about being too intense. They don't hold anything back. You can't, either. There's no way to half-play your way to optimal enjoyment. You're either in it fully or you're not going to feel optimal fun.

- *Slim that ego.* Don't let responsibilities or status leave you too consumed or highfalutin' to break away to do something as pedestrian as play. Be on the lookout for when you are taking yourself and your life far too seriously. You are one of six billion and counting.

- *Loosen up.* The more structured your life, the harder it is to play, say researchers. To loosen things up, avoid over-scheduling and rigid ideas about what you do and don't do and when you do them. Leave open time on your calendar, and be ready to take advantage of impromptu events by doing things you normally wouldn't.

The bounce of play and life is inside all of us. You just have to give it permission to resurface, something you can do when you're minding the lessons of this chapter:

- Don't hold back your eagerness.
- Let your backbone slip into playfulness.
- Invent the world you really want to live in by suspending reality.
- Change your experience from head down to life up with positive affect.
- Meet a whole new family of friends by becoming socially proactive.

# 8

## You Are the Audience

Courage is resistance to fear, mastery of
fear—not absence of fear.
—*Mark Twain*

Every now and then something happens that's so freeing, it's like one of those dreams where you don't
need a plane to fly or clothes to wear, or both. I'm talking
about the sensation of being so immersed in your own fun
that you don't care if anyone is looking. The gaze of strangers
means absolutely squat. It's a rare experience, because most of
the time what people we don't know and will never see again
might think about us can overrule a lot of living.

What skill have you always wanted to learn but didn't because
you were afraid of looking foolish or awkward? Maybe just the
thought of performing in front of anyone else was enough to put
an end to the idea. Maybe what you wanted to do wasn't cool
enough. Or maybe it was just too embarrassing not being perfect
at something you didn't know how to do. This is the kind of logic
that rules when others are in charge of your life. Who are these
people with the power to chill your self-expression and cheat you

out of a lifelong passion? They're usually folks you don't know from Adam who are so wrapped up in their own self-consciousness that judging you is the furthest thing from their minds.

The stranglehold of social judgment can snuff out leisure skills in the making, and on a complete fallacy to boot: the belief that what others think can validate you. The science is clear that only one person's opinion counts on that topic: yours. What anyone else thinks about how you hit a tennis ball or play the guitar falls into the external approval column, which is ephemeral.

A lot of dreams get shelved because of concerns about the peanut gallery, and the performing arts are at the top of that list. I've journeyed to the seaside community of Carlsbad, north of San Diego, to join a group of folks who are determined to master one of these arts and not let the fear of messing up in front of others get in the way of what they want to do more than anything else: play music. I'm at a rehearsal of the North Coast New Horizons Band, a forty-piece unit that's part of a national effort to bring music skills to adults. It's the brainchild of Roy Ernst, a former music professor who believes that anyone at any age, even a grownup, can learn to play an instrument. New Horizons International has incubated 150 community bands around the United States, Canada, Australia, and Ireland. Initially, the bands were for people over the age of fifty, but many are now open to all ages of adults. You don't have to know how to play an instrument or have any musical experience. They'll teach you from scratch. If you've always wanted to learn an instrument, there are no excuses anymore.

In a hallway of the Museum of Music Making overlooking the Pacific, I meet Stuart Lease, a retired agriculture biologist wearing shorts and sporting a gray mustache. Lease had wanted to play an instrument since his college days but has only been taking lessons the last four years. He plays the euphonium, a small tuba, in the North Coast band and a banjo on his own. The reason it

## Join the Band

The fiction that only a child can learn an instrument was repeated so often that even educators believed it—but not Roy Ernst, who taught music at Eastman School of Music in Rochester, New York, for twenty-five years. Ernst knew the numbers. Only 15 to 20 percent of kids get music education in high school, leaving a whole lot of adults without a chance to ever develop musical skills. Rejecting the myth that adults couldn't learn music, Ernst started the New Horizons program in 1991. He discovered right away that anyone could play. One student took up clarinet lessons at eighty-nine. Ernst's concept is to put aspiring musicians together in a supportive environment with no competition and let them learn at their own speed. His motto is "Your best is good enough." Ernst created a template that can be duplicated in any city, including yours. All you need is a music instructor, a venue, and students. The New Horizons Web site provides a starter kit with all of the details on how to get a band going in your area or where to join an existing one. Band members pay $5 to $10 a week for instruction. For details, go to www.newhorizonsmusic.org/nhima.html.

took him so long to finally play music may have something to do with the fact that he is afflicted with a condition almost all of the band members here either have or have worked through: performance anxiety. "I feel that anxiety about other people watching," admits Lease. "I worry about mistakes or standing up in front of other people. It's stressful." He says that it took him four years to be able to play in front of his banjo teacher.

His wife, who also plays in the band, was so nervous at a rhythm workshop at last week's session that she's waiting in the car for an hour while Lease and the band members do another primer on the beat with instructor Allison Hargis. I join the group, sitting next to Lease in a semicircle of eight women and seven men, mostly sixty-something, each of us with a hand or field drum on which we will try to tap out the musical notation on a whiteboard. Part of the instruction here is that everyone learns how to read, as well as play, music. Although the group members can play instruments and read notation, the drums are new for them, so everyone's nerves are on edge.

"What we've proved is that our steady beat needs work," says Hargis, a teacher with the right sense of humor for this assignment. She's going to play a pattern, and then it's our job to identify it with the notes on the whiteboard.

We're all fine when we go through the beats together with Hargis. Then comes the spotlight. Each of us has to play one of the bars of music, and Hargis will identify which one we've played. Which bar should I do? Even though I have nothing at stake here—I obviously haven't been in the class and don't know what I'm doing—I still feel the tension of having to perform it "right" and not make a mistake. Where does this relentless need to do things perfectly, even things we've never done before, come from? Add sixteen people, and you have scrutiny. With scrutiny comes judgment. Or does it? The class is completely noncompetitive. Most of the time, judgment comes from us, from serial mind- and face-reading. When we are worried about what others think or racked about the results, we miss the nature of education. Learning a new skill is essentially a series of mistakes that lessen with familiarity. If you're not making mistakes, you're not learning anything.

A couple of students drum their beats confidently, but it's white-knuckle time for most. Lease is shifting around in his chair, but he gets through it. Now it's my turn. I muster a tentative and choppy rendition and wind up missing an eighth note. I'm pleased to say that after Hargis mentions it, I'm able to laugh it off. It just doesn't matter. I remember my mantra: It's the experience!

Music is the great leveler. There's a lawyer in the class, a gynecologist, and social workers, but they all wind up feeling like they're ten years old when they try to learn one of the most challenging avocational skills. Bob Edwards, an attorney in crisp slacks and a dress shirt, decided to buy a saxophone after his son started to take sax lessons. Playing the alto is unfinished business for a "failed sixth-grade player," who "didn't get it" back then. He's determined now, but even this accomplished attorney who is used to performing confidently before courtroom juries allows that he has grappled with the tension of playing in front of others. "The first time I played with the group my mouth was completely dry," he says. "I'm less worried now. I've gotten used to playing. It's like anything else. It's not being afraid to step off the edge."

Another thing that reduces the anxiety level is realizing that the perceived judges are actually friendly and are all in the same boat of trying to improve their talent and enjoy a social outlet. "The camaraderie is great," says Colleen Foster, who switched from flute to tuba for a new challenge. "Everyone is so supportive."

It's time for the music to commence. Hargis takes her conducting stick, and about twenty horn and woodwind players start to blow. From the back, I see gray heads and bald pates, but what I hear is something quite different—youthful exuberance, as they take off on a series of marching songs. These intrepid life enthusiasts aren't buying the age limit on living. They're not letting the fear of what others think stunt their growth. The more they push through the judgment barrier, the more they can see that progress is personal.

The real lesson here every week is the law of optimal expression: you are the audience. It doesn't matter what's in anyone else's head, only what's in yours. Play for your organic core, where the gratification equipment lives, and you will be motivated more by the desire to express yourself than by the fear of failure. In this chapter, you'll discover the life intelligence skills that it takes to exit onlooker mode and do what you always wanted to—reframing performance anxiety; being willing to act foolish; believing in your own choices, known as locus of control; and ignoring social comparisons, including the self-consciousness of acting cool. Why hold yourself back in a jubilant moment? That makes about as much sense as swearing off laughing. You have the freedom right now to live as if no one's watching.

## The Only Thing You Have to Fear Is Being an Onlooker

The band launches into an irresistible dance tune. Your body begins to stir. People in the bar are getting up and shaking it, some with rhythm, some spectacularly without, and they couldn't care less. Your legs ache to get out there, but you can't. You're grounded by eyes unseen, comments unheard, and the strange life-denial of self-consciousness. The thought of getting up in front of others is too mortifying for you to move. Yet there's no crowd police permitting only professionals to take the floor. It's only the ego police holding you back. Guess who's in charge of that?

This scenario has grounded me more than once over the years, but I came to see that I could contest the illogic of sitting on my aliveness. The problem wasn't with me dancing but with all of those who weren't. They were blowing it, passing up a chance to celebrate release from the survival game. As I learned about direct experience, I discovered that the whole notion that I was performing was itself bogus. I was in an experience, not a performance. I was doing it to do it, for myself, for fun.

The performance identity reduces life to a constant audition. It's a fragile existence when you're on a catwalk every day, held hostage to an image gleaned from stray comments and out-and-out guesswork about what's in other people's heads. It would be nice if all of the allowances we made for others' unknown thoughts were an investment in anything other than pointless angst, but no. They are the wrong audience. As psychologist and self-esteem pioneer Nathaniel Branden has written, "Self-esteem is what you think and feel about yourself, not what someone else thinks about you."

You are the audience. What will do more for your esteem, stewing about what people think or increasing your competence? The answer seems obvious, but the performance yardstick blinds us to the paradoxical nature of the results fixation. Worrying about not messing up causes you to do just that, because your mind is not on where you are but on what disaster might strike. Expression is lost in the mirror.

We have it all wrong about mistakes. They are the essence of the universe. The planets exist because the gases that formed after the Big Bang were a billionth off, says physicist Stephen Hawking. Humans exist because we're also a mistake, the result of a series of mutations on the evolutionary tree. Mistakes are the necessary path that moves us forward. If you're not making them, you're not moving, trying, or being the mistaken species that you are.

I like Pema Chödrön's description of the straitjacket that holds us to perfection. "Being preoccupied in our self-image is like being deaf and blind," she says. "It's like standing in the middle of a vast field of wildflowers with a black hood over your head. It's like coming upon a tree of singing birds while wearing earplugs."

Opening your ears to the song of life requires that you remove the earplugs, the performance yardsticks. Life intelligence practitioners leave the judging to superior courts and Olympic panels. "In the beginning you're so awful it's going to defeat you unless you get past it," says Wade Lindsay, an attorney I met at a pottery class at the Jill Hinckley Studio in Washington, D.C. "You have to stay focused on the process, not the results. The world doesn't come to an end because of a bad pot."

The culprit behind performance anxiety is fear of negative evaluation. Like all fears, it's triggered by false beliefs and projected worst-case scenarios—being a klutz, not getting it, making mistakes, looking foolish, winding up on YouTube—because it's coming from the home of panic, the amygdala. So the real evaluator is you. It's the stories you tell yourself that either feed the anxiety or let you push through it.

Negative self-talk is one of the biggest factors in triggering the fear of negative evaluations that keeps you from living; garbage such as, "I'm going to blow it," "I'll look ridiculous," "I'm not very good." The panicked brain fixates on catastrophe, overestimating the probability of disaster and underestimating your ability to handle it. You can just sit there and buy these outlandish fantasies, which keep you in onlooker mode, or you do what Colleen Foster of the North Coast New Horizons Band did. You argue back. "I wanted to be a musician," she told me, "so I had to just push through the fear."

Taking action defeats fear's fantasy scenarios. As these diligent musicians have done, get yourself physically on the scene, then start to chip away at the anxiety. Acting despite the fear lets your body prove to your mind that you can get through it. You will see that the fear is exaggerated. As you improve, you build confidence with the real audience, you, and that shuts down the false alarms of the caveman brain. Life fulfillment, to a large extent, is the direct result of how you push back against reflex fear to take on the challenges that provide you with gratification.

The performance headlock gripped my friend Ran Klarin when he took up painting. He began oil painting to express himself, a need that had been stifled in a career as a secondary education administrator. But when a feedback session at an art retreat resulted in pretty much no feedback for his work, he was stung. "It was like, I must be lousy. Nobody likes my stuff," he remembers. But then he got mad. He argued back and decided that he would keep painting until he had a show.

Clarified intentions tend to clear a path. A local merchant asked Klarin whether he knew any artists who could exhibit at a monthly art walk in Venice, California. He thought about it, then realized that *he* was an artist. He got the show but was afraid that nobody would like his work or even show up. But at the opening, the exhibit was buzzing with supporters, who gave him plenty of positive feedback about his canvases. He even sold one.

"The fear was the fear of not being liked and appreciated," Klarin says. "The reality of that night showed me that I was liked and appreciated. I also realized that what matters was whether *I* like my work—not anyone else."

As with all anxieties, stage jitters thrive on a false tale of doom. So the key to beating them is the life intelligence skill of reframing performance anxiety. You turn the stress signals into signs of excitement, not of impending disaster. When you feel your heart racing and that grabbing in the pit of your stomach, reframe the emotional responses as positive and natural. "Successful musicians see a bout of nerves before a performance as normal, something that's part of the process of public expression," report Glenn Wilson and David Roland. They interpret the body's preperformance early warning system as a shot of adrenaline to be used to increase focus.

It's all in the spin. It's your choice: irrational panic or a feeling of intense alertness; running away from the fear or straight at it, which defangs it. Every time the fear of being evaluated comes up, imagine that tomorrow is your last day. That's how puny the judgment of others is in the scheme of things. Here are some tools researchers have found that can turn the fear around:

*Trumping Performance Anxiety*

- *Realistic self-appraisal.* The best way to beat the negative self-talk that fuels performance anxiety is to transform it into positive self-talk. In one study, people who used self-comments such as, "I'm bound to make a few mistakes, but so does everybody," were able to turn anxiety into reinforcement.

- *Mental rehearsal.* Visualize yourself in the activity the way you would like to be. Mental rehearsal provides a neuromuscular programming that makes the live event feel more familiar and therefore less stressful. Act it out over and over.

- *Pre-performance rituals.* Put together a few rituals before the event that relax and prepare you. They can include closing your eyes, centering yourself, and repeating positive phrases, such as, "I'm the audience," and "It's the experience."

- *Relaxation techniques.* Calm your nerves with one of the many relaxation techniques available, from progressive relaxation to yoga breathing, to meditation.

- *Dispute the distortion.* Paralyzing fear is fueled by a vague panic that you won't be able to survive a mistake. Your survivability might be in question if you're stuck in a rowboat in the Pacific for two months, but performing in front of others is quite survivable. Call out the fear and specify it so you can dispute it with the facts.

- *Flow, not flaw.* Focus on the experience of the moment, the flow, and there are no flaws.

## Perfection Is a Mistake

The main perpetrator of performance anxiety is the illusory expectation of perfection. It's a myth that makes about as much sense to chase as the fountain of youth. Flaws are your lot as a fallible human, and an absurd reason to hold back your life. You can't learn or enjoy what you're learning if your motivation is not to make a mistake. You're not in the experience then, only a future calamity. Besides, people don't like folks who are trying too hard to be flawless. It comes off as too calculated, inauthentic, not human enough. Let's get more comfortable with the essential nature of learning: imperfection. Your lesson: Make a couple of small mistakes on purpose in front of others this week. You'll start to see that the results are survivable, no big deal, mere stumbles on the road of the experiment of life.

· · · · · · · · · · · · · · · · · · · · · · · · · · · · · · · · · · · · · · · · · · · · · · · · · · · · · ·

# Fools Have More Fun

It would be foolish not to use everything at your disposal to get the most out of your time on this planet, including being foolish, something that's supposed to be an infraction of the adult operating code. Yet that's precisely what you need more of to move yourself into new skills and thrills: more spontaneity, more vulnerability, more ridiculousness.

Kids aren't afraid of being fools. They'll plunge right in, oblivious to how they might look. Kids have more fun, because they're not afraid to be foolish. Adults have the weight of history locking us into rigid behavior that doesn't allow for doing

---

## Life List: The Poor Man's South Pacific

You might think you can't put a South Seas experience on your life list. It's too expensive. You're wrong. The Cook Islands, between Tahiti and Tonga, are affordable (they cater to budget-minded New Zealanders and Australians, so they're not strewn with five-star resorts) and uncrowded and have one of the world's most remarkable lagoons on the island of Aitutaki, a seven- by nine-mile oval of shimmering turquoise formed by a sunken volcano that I did a quadruple-take on when I saw it from the air. A fifty-minute flight from the main Cook Island of Rarotonga, Aitutaki fit my South Seas fantasy to the hilt. You can indulge in the foolish behavior of play via kayaking, snorkeling (you'll see butterfly fish, damsels, the odd green turtle, giant clams, and trigger fish), and join in on the great local dancing and singing. Air New Zealand gets you there on an overnight flight from Los Angeles.

---

things out of character, imperfectly, or unadultlike. We also get typecast by our own self-inflicted code of conduct, which is held in place by habit and by others we fear will call us on any deviation from the norm.

"We're constantly aware of what our societal norms say, what the expectations are, how to behave," says the University of Illinois's Lynn Barnett-Morris. "With adult play, it seems to be so pervasive, worrying about what other people think of you or worrying that you're not going to get a certain kind of payoff, or you're going to be thought lesser than, or you're going to be thought to be unproductive or you're not a hard worker or serious."

What you think other people are thinking is pretty iffy evidence for life denial. On top of that, it's futile because (1) no amount of external approval can produce self-worth, and (2) we're lousy at mind-reading. "People do not view themselves as others actually see them but rather view themselves as they think others view them (through biased processing)," report Dianne M. Tice and Harry M. Wallace of Case Western Reserve University.

Acting foolish flies in the face of everything you were raised to be—serious, purposeful, controlled—which is why it's a very unexpected life intelligence skill. There's absolutely nothing of import and no point to foolishness, so it can't help but put you into the intrinsic mode of living for the moment. It automatically removes the security blanket, forcing a new trajectory. Foolishness is really just a state of active not-knowing, a basic stop on the way to play and learning. As Shakespeare noted, "The wise man knows himself to be a fool."

Foolishness feels squirmy, because it's silly and not productive and makes you vulnerable. But it's precisely that vulnerability that shuts down the adult force field that keeps out your life. Foolishness short-circuits the left-brain rationality that tells you that grownups don't do things in front of others that they don't do well. That shows just how truly foolish adults are, because it's in the irrational slipstream where bumbling about and feeling out of your depth meet that you tend to find central life forces that the logical brain has been keeping from you.

## Richard Weinberg Steps Out

There's something about playful physical movement that really rattles grownups. Richard Weinberg was having dinner with his wife one night at a Chicago restaurant, when suddenly the tables disappeared and the salsa dancing commenced. Before long, his wife was on the floor being twirled by one of the waiters and trying to drag Weinberg out to join her. No way was he going to make a spectacle of himself. "I was scared to death," he told me. "I didn't know how to do salsa."

Like many of his gender, the entertainment producer and real estate investor didn't want anything to do with public displays of gyration. "I was afraid I was going to look foolish. Swiveling my hips like that? There was fear of how I would look out there."

But the next day, Weinberg had a change of heart. Maybe dancing wasn't so foolish. His wife had so much fun he decided to take a lesson at a top local studio, Chicago Dance. Suddenly, everything changed. In three months, he was a salsa fanatic, taking lessons seven days a week. Five years later, at age fifty-five, Weinberg competes in fourteen different dance categories—rumba, cha-cha, tango, waltz, salsa, and foxtrot among them—at events around the country, and his competition partner is a professional dancer and the owner of Chicago Dance, Tommye Giacchino. It's a phenomenal transformation, something Weinberg marvels at. Before he started dancing, he had a successful business career and thought that maybe he'd done it all. Little did he know that his real life was just beginning, as his dancing busted through the false ceiling.

"It wasn't that I was not living. I wasn't focused on *really* living," says Weinberg. "Now I'm looking twenty or thirty years down the road. Dancing has completely changed my outlook. I love it!"

Weinberg quickly got past the fear he'd felt that night at the restaurant once he started to take lessons. His focus shifted from others' eyeballs to gaining skills and the exhilaration they delivered to the real audience: himself. "Nobody else really cares what you're doing," he says. "They all have plenty of other things on their minds—themselves."

## The Mambo

One of the many dances born in the rhythm cauldron of Cuba, the mambo first appeared in Havana in the 1940s. It was introduced by bandleader Perez Prado, who popularized the mambo rhythm, a mix of Cuban and American jazz influences invented by bassist and composer Israel Cachao Lopez, who was playing mambo up until his death in 2008 at the age of eighty-nine. Mambo would become a building block for a lot of modern Cuban music, including *son* and salsa. It replaced the rumba as the favorite Latin dance style in the 1950s and was later eclipsed by the cha-cha. The lively modern version of the mambo puts hips to the test and minds to rest. Check out the basic steps with this YouTube video to get an idea of the fun in store: www.youtube.com/watch?v=aeu30QZUV68&feature=related. You're most likely to find mambo lessons in a ballroom dance class.

As Weinberg learned, feeling foolish in the service of fun is not a bad thing. It's a signal that you are about to leave the world of the android. Don't let the awkwardness of operating outside your element put you on the defensive. The wise fool goes on the offensive, rushing right in.

**ACTIVATE**

## Go Where You've Never Gone Before

We all have set points of propriety beyond which we dare not go. Foolishness requires that you go beyond them anyway until you feel like you're over-the-top. What you're doing is increasing your range of physical and emotional motion. You'll feel as if you're acting.

But as public speakers and people trying to learn a language can tell you, the more over-the-top you feel, the more your audience likes it and the more effective you are. Practice what you would consider to be going overboard in speech, body movement, or personal expression at home, and get used to that feeling. That way, it won't seem so out there when you deploy it in public. What kind of over-the-top behavior could help you break through to a richer life? Identify it and start expanding your range of expression.

........................................................

## The Life Learner

Grownups could have a lot more fun if it wasn't for the adult ego. Its need to know it all has typecast beginners as lowly greenhorns, amateurs, rookies. All the language we use for "beginning" is loaded against ourselves, because our brains don't want what we already know. They want to learn new stuff. That's convenient, because the sooner you can get in step with your gray matter and see yourself as the life learner you are, the sooner you can focus on your internal audience through the intrinsic path. It's no longer about outside opinions then but about the learning experience. You're not trying to impress others or avoid looking clueless. You can relax into the role of novice, a liberating role in which you're free to release the ego that's starving your core needs.

"The general skill is one of saying, 'I'm a beginner. I don't have to be good at this right now. I'm just going to try it,'" says psychologist Tim Kasser of Knox College. Tell yourself that "my experience suggests I don't know what I'm doing, so I'm not going to judge myself and say I'll never be able to do it."

Cultivate a beginner's mind-set by giving yourself permission to be a lifelong learner. Look beyond the humble pie to the skills you're acquiring. The learner never has to get neurotic about not being number one. The beginner's frame of mind frees you to always be in the process of engaging novelty and challenge, which keeps your brain, and you, happy.

*Beginner's Starter Kit*

- Remember, it's only play.
- Focus on what you learn, not on what you haven't learned.
- Reaching out is not a weakness; it's a part of the learning process. Ask questions, be curious.
- Focus on little improvements, not on what you don't know.
- Have no timetable for mastery.

## Cool Kills

In tennis, it's called an unforced error. You manage to miss the point all by yourself. In the stunting of life, it's known as being cool—you lose the point in this case because of a slavish attention to appearances. There have always been fashionistas and the vogue of the moment—the coolest hunter-gatherer baskets, the hottest togas, people who wanted to be as stoic as a Spartan hero—but no doubt we have the dubious privilege to be living at the zenith of allowing others to determine our worth by how we look or act.

Cool kills the quality of your life, putting your core needs in the deep freeze by making you play to the wrong audience. Being cool is supposed to make you irresistibly confident in your blasé-ness, but it does the opposite. It feeds insecurity with the false belief that popularity, attractiveness, or the right gear is needed to make you feel worthy. Tim Kasser at Knox College and Richard

Ryan at the University of Rochester have shown that image and possessions are lousy at creating self-worth and happiness, because they leave your self-worth up to the fickle opinions of others, which can change on a dime. Real self-worth comes from the self-acceptance that informs intrinsic goals, says Kasser, such as "I will follow my interests and curiosity wherever they take me."

The amount of money spent, eagerness held back, potential friends not approached, and passions spurned because of the pursuit of cool all add up to one helluva deficit in self-determination and happiness for many today. The absurd assumption of being cool is that you are an individual if you are copying somebody else and devoid of specialness if you are yourself. That keeps out life opportunities and passions that aren't on the hip list, as the zero-wattage cool personality keeps other people away.

Play destroys this virus and the judgmental attitude that transmits it. I love to look around at the first session of a samba or salsa class and take in the Noah's Ark of looks, ages, and types. It's a lesson in how wrong our snap judgments about others can be. A few sessions later, folks who appeared to be from other planets are comrades in the dance of getting a life. No longer are people holding back their enthusiasm—one of the worst side effects of coolness. How dumb is limiting your keenness for life? Popularity can't make you happy, but a cross-body pass to a butterfly sure can.

## Nellie Owen: Live As If No One's Watching

Nellie Owen grew up on a farm in Columbia, Missouri, where she loved to ride horses through the countryside. One night it all came to an end as her car hydroplaned in the rain. The accident would leave her without the use of her legs. At the age of twenty-two, she was confined to a wheelchair.

Her father didn't take it well. He didn't want to go out in public with her because of the way others stared. But Nellie was made of sturdier stuff. "I don't care what I look like. I don't care what other people think," she says. "I was a person before I got hurt, and I was after I got hurt."

The able-bodied have a lot to learn from people like Owen, such as the monumental triviality of what others think about the way we look or play. Owen went on to college and, despite the difficulties and the surgeries (some forty to date), graduated to work in cancer research and eventually in the veterinary field. To be around horses again, she volunteered her vet services at the Cedar Creek Therapeutic Riding Center in Columbia. Therapeutic riding can help increase range of motion, balance, and coordination for people who don't have the use of their legs. It also builds competence through riding skills and brings many social benefits to children who are mentally challenged. One day the owner asked Owen whether she'd like to have a go.

Owen was thrilled, but getting on the horse would take some strategy. There's no easy, or dignified, way to get an adult on a horse from a wheelchair. It took a hydraulic hoist to lift her atop the first horse she'd sat on in a couple of decades. She could not have cared less about the entrance. Once on board, "it was like I was walking again," she says. "The hip movement is like walking. I was euphoric."

As it has for thousands of riders, therapeutic riding transformed Owen's life. Before, when someone had asked her what she did for fun, she realized, "Not a damn thing." Now she rides every week, transcending time and her own body. "I'm up in the air, closer to God, and I'm feeling fabulous. It doesn't matter if I've got to spend two hours getting ready," she says. "This is what it's all about."

•••••••••••••••••••••• ACTIVATE ••••••••••••••••••••••

## Don't Get Frozen Out

The dictates of cool are held in place by the same dread that rules performance anxiety: negative evaluation. What if you didn't need other people's approval to validate what you're doing or wearing, because you're not looking for it? When intrinsic motivation is your guide, you shut down the outside interference. Remember, it's all about the experience. You're there for the fun, the challenge, to satisfy your core needs, to live. The basic need at the heart of coolness is a very prosaic one: to fit in. When it rears its head to freeze out an activity because it or you might be unhip, old hat, square, or too cool for school, imagine yourself encased in a full-size ice cube. Counter the cool instinct with some antifreeze, unconditional enthusiasm for the life you're grabbing from the forces of soulless detachment. When coolness threatens to chill your eagerness or fun, think ice cube and take your enthusiasm up a notch.

••••••••••••••••••••••••••••••••••••••••••••••••••••

### ⌒ Susan Dworski Is the Boss of Her Life

Living vibrantly has a lot to do with the ability to entertain yourself, to dig out interests and apply yourself to the skills of indulging them. You don't need permission from anyone. You know in your gut that this is what you want and that you are capable of handling it. This skill is known in the psychological trade as internal locus of control, which has nothing to do with defending yourself from a biblical plague. It's a belief that what you do and what happens to you depend on your choices. This essential tool of self-determination fuels your entrepreneurial and fun-preneurial endeavors.

A strong internal locus of control gives you the freedom to determine your own destiny. It's been shown to be a crucial factor in health (proactive patients recover better than helpless ones do), on the job (you perform better and earn more), in education (you learn more), and for leaders, including parents (you can make tough decisions). An external locus of control leaves you at the whim of others. An internal locus produces higher self-esteem and less stress, because you feel more control over the stressors.

Venice, California, graphic designer Susan Dworski is a poster woman for internal locus of control. She's taught herself everything from ceramics to weaving, watercolors, glassware, clothing design, sculpture, museum exhibit design, and now jewelry. One of the rarest talents in my experience, she writes (magazine articles, criticism, books) as well as she designs. It all seems perfectly normal to Dworski. "I see my whole life as an opportunity to express creativity," she says in her home studio. "I'm very passionate about a lot of things, kind of a serial hobbyist."

She took up jewelry making after a friend died and left her a trove of African beads and silver. It sat in her closet for years until she had a garage sale and found herself unable to part with the inheritance. Instead, she decided to turn the stash into jewelry to honor her friend. She didn't have any idea how to do this, but that was nothing new. "Everything I've ever done I've never done before," says Dworski. "You just figure it out. There are things to read, you talk to people. There's always information available."

A jewelry convention set off the sparks. Dworski bought some tools and started to craft necklaces from her Ethiopian silver—and she was off. She shows me drawers and bowls filled with her raw materials: semiprecious stones, brass, amber, and ethnic beads and artifacts from around the world. The finished works are in the garage: gorgeous jade creations, pieces with Tibetan or Afghan pendants. I'm not surprised that she now sells her creations at museum gift shops and jewelry shows (just to pay for her materials; she doesn't want to be in business, which would take the fun out of it). At one show, she watched as a lovely eighteen-year-old girl in a white peasant dress tried on one of her turquoise necklaces in a mirror. "Her face just lit up," Dworski says, still captivated by that moment. "It's really magic when you hit it right."

With an internal locus of control that is focused on what pleases her, Dworski isn't inhibited by what stops many people from trying. "I'm not afraid of failing. What is that? That's living up to somebody else's standard. Everything I do is play for me, so there's no judgment at all in this."

...................... ACTIVATE ......................

## Focus Your Locus

It's easier when you let others determine your path, but unfulfilling because it's not your path. An active internal locus of control shuts down the disapproval reflex that holds back your aliveness. What would you like to do that you put aside because of what others might think? Or because of beliefs stuck in external locus of control mode—that you don't have much choice in what happens in your life; you're too busy (being busy); you're too important, shy, uncoordinated, old? Identify an external belief that is keeping you from using your internal locus of control to self-determine the choices you want. How could you turn that belief around with an attitude based on an internal locus?

..............................................................................

# Life beyond Compare

Marooned on an island off the coast of Chile, Robinson Crusoe's real-life inspiration, Alexander Selkirk, had at least one thing he didn't have to worry about: social comparisons. He didn't have to fret about whether someone had a better grass hut than his or a more impressive beard.

Whether it's in the classroom, the office, or at play, egos have a relentless need to know how they're doing. Because objective standards are not always available, the usual cues come from measuring how we're doing compared to others. We compare our salaries to fellow employees' and how attractive our bodies or homes are with any number of idealized images from the media, yardsticks that don't exactly work in our favor. This plays right into the hands of the performance yardstick, which distracts you from who your real audience is.

The more dependent you are on external goals, the more you fall prey to social comparisons, which then pits your archery score against the next person's or your stick figures against the paintings of the best artist in the class. In one intriguing study, UC-Riverside researcher Sonja Lyubomirsky and Stanford's Lee Ross suggest that happier people are able to ignore negative social comparisons, possibly because they have more confidence in their own overall competence, whereas unhappy people dwell on unfavorable comparisons that make them unhappier. It's yet another reason to establish competencies, instead of contingencies of worth.

You can let others define you, or you can be self-determined by ignoring comparisons and going for the skills and the experience. That's what North Coast New Horizons band member Maggie McNeil did. She decided that enjoyment wasn't a competition. "I'll always play third clarinet, and that's fine with me," she said. "It's just a hobby and for socializing." The level of musicianship does not equal the level of amusement.

•••••••••••••••••••••••••• ACTIVATE ••••••••••••••••••••••••

### Comparison Detox

Social comparisons bring you nothing but grief, because there's always someone who has more money or a bigger house, is more stylish, dances better, has better hair days, and so on. Only you can create self-worth, by taking care of your needs for competence and autonomy. Whenever comparisons crop up, become aware of them and dismiss them. This will take some practice. Keep track of all of the comparisons that arise in one day: he's got a bigger house; she's a better speaker; he's more talented; I'm tougher; she's got better teeth. Write them down, so that you can see how inane this stuff is. You'll be amazed at how often this noise goes off. You don't have to attach yourself to these neuron burps. Treat them as the comedy they are. Train yourself to laugh every time a comparison pops up. You know that an optimal life is incomparable.

••••••••••••••••••••••••••••••••••••••••••••••••••••••••••

# Call Your Tune

The name of the game of life is self-determination, and no one but you has anything to do with that. You are the audience. All of the roadblocks that curb your full expression in front of others—from performance anxiety to trying to act cool, to making social comparisons—come from trying to play with the work/performance mind on. You're not in output mode. You are not performing. You're experiencing the act of your own life, and that's a no-judgment zone. Turn off the performance identity. Turn on the play mind. Activate unconditionality by deploying these strategies against everyone who would cramp your maximum expression:

- Beat performance anxiety by disputing distortions with positive self-talk and realistic self-appraisal.
- Use intentional foolishness to disrupt the seriousness that fuels the fear of not being perfect.
- Kill cool by following the enthusiasm of your real self.
- Be the boss of your life by deploying an internal locus of control.
- Vanquish social comparisons by living a life beyond compare.

# 9

## Passions Take
## Persistence

Persistence is the foundation of all
actions.
—*Lao Tzu*

The path less traveled is not a metaphor for Chris Shaffer. It's his hobby—and your obstacle course, if you're hiking with him. I am, so I get on my hands and semi-crawl through a gap under a fallen tree before battling a jungle of branches on our off-trail bushwhack in the wilderness of the Los Padres National Forest outside Ventura, California. Shaffer's passion is waterfalls, and nothing gets in his way when he thinks there's a possibility of finding one tumbling off a ledge somewhere in the backcountry. The outdoor writer discovered and named more than a hundred waterfalls in California by his mid-twenties, something that would have been no big deal in 1845. Today we're in search of one of his favorites, Potrero John, a gusher he found and named after numerous forest service personnel told him it wasn't there.

For three-quarters of the hike, there's no trail. We bash through brambles and boulders on a slope along a creek. "We're going to cross the stream and head into that thicket hugging the cliff," says Shaffer, for whom obstacles are the natural path to discovery.

I'm feeling more respect by the minute for the unsung trail builders of the land, not to mention explorers such as John Muir, who crisscrossed vast tracts of wilderness without trails or Vibram soles. We boulder-hop across the stream, and when I get to the other side, I come down hard on a log that was only pretending to be stationary. It rolls and I fall, landing with my shin on the bark of another log. It's primal scream time, but I can't dally. A thundering waterfall awaits somewhere.

Another couple of hours of bushwhacking later, we get to a ridge, and I can hear it first. The sound gets louder and louder, and then I see it booming through a carved chute, the biggest falls in the state south of Yosemite National Park. It's eighty feet high with some real propulsion behind it, pouring into a foaming pool. Shaffer has an ear-to-ear grin and is yelling something over the roar of the thundering water. "How many people have seen this?" he screams. We stand gaping at this glimpse behind the natural curtain.

Waterfalls by their nature do their act in steep terrain, mostly out of public view. If you are persistent, you can gain admission to their private shows. Over the years, I've learned that if you climb above one tier of falls, you often discover more of them higher up—and nobody's there to see them but you.

"It's like a secret hideaway. You can have a tranquil moment in here," says Shaffer, thirty. "If I wake up in the morning, and I'm in a bad mood, a waterfall seems to soothe me."

By that count, Shaffer has gotten a lot of stress relief during the last decade. The Chatsworth, California, resident started to hunt waterfalls in college, sometimes skipping classes to slip into the mountains for reconnaissance trips. He learned how to scour topographic maps for places where elevation and water coincide: the conditions that can indicate a possible waterfall. The night before one of his explorations he says he "can't sleep. I'm like a kid still. I'm, like, wow, that water's going to be raging. We're going to find something really exciting."

And he has—even in Yosemite, famed for its spectacular cascades, Shaffer has located and named a few more, such as Three Chute Falls. Shaffer's passion for his self-made avocation, as often happens, has led to a vocation. He's authored the *Definitive Guide to the Waterfalls of Southern and Central California* and three other guidebooks.

Besides the call of the falls, there's something else that keeps Shaffer coming back for more adventure, a skill that's crucial for life activation: a bias for action. He doesn't overthink his next foray, talk himself out of it because he doesn't want to drive, decide that he is too tired, or worry that something might happen. He goes with the impulse to act. "I have to go out and discover something," he says. "There's always something new. No waterfall is the same. Every time you head into a canyon, there's that mystique, that sense of adventure, of journeying to a place few people have been.

"I don't own a Nintendo. I don't own an Xbox," the waterfall hunter says. "I'd rather be out here. People are missing life. You only live once. If I were to die today, I could say I lived to the fullest."

Is that something *you* could say at age thirty? Maybe it's time to awaken the life hunter within you by picking up on the proactive skills of the final law of optimal life: passions take persistence. In this chapter, you'll get the tools that will keep you engaged in the best of life, talents such as a bias for action, tolerating the ambiguity of the learning curve, and deploying the discipline of commitment. The road to the fullest life is one that you have to keep activating.

## Nature's Ionic Breeze

If you've ever stood in the presence of a thundering waterfall, you no doubt have felt a twinge of wonder. There's something spellbinding about these vertical rivers. The sights and sounds of falling water provide a quick pick-me-up from the loop of the nattering mind. Now some researchers think they know why: negative ions.

Waterfalls may be the place to go for an attitude adjustment, elevating your mood without a prescription. Air molecules in highly humidified environments retain negative ions, and humans seem to like it that way. Ocean waves, caves, and especially waterfalls are hubs for negative air ions, which researchers have found can elevate mood. Michael Terwin, the director of the clinical chronobiological program at New York State Psychological Institute in New York City, says that exposure to high concentrations of negative air ions has an antidepressant effect, brightening your mood.

Standing in front of one of my favorite gushers recently, Mist Falls in California's Kings Canyon National Park, I reveled in that ion rush, as a flash flood of whitewater kicked up a cloudburst of spray a football field long. I felt better already in the ionic mist.

## The Magic's in the Movement

Passions don't come from sticking your toe in the water and turning back, but from plunging all of the way in—and staying in. They're driven by the inclination to keep moving and growing, which is the mandate of your core needs. Even your physiology is designed for movement. You were built, down to your big toes, to tread far and wide as a hunter-gatherer. Motion is the direct route to emotion (from the French word *emouvir*, which means "to stir up"), to the life you can feel. Movement opens you up to experience, challenge, friends, and discoveries—to the vast universe beyond the solitaire game on your phone.

Most of us today, though, are about as active as lawn ornaments, frozen in front of digital screens and disconnected from this activating resource. The life intelligence tool that gets you back into animate mode is a bias for action, a bent to move that propels you to where the progress and fun are. People equipped with this acumen are driven by two resources that promote activation: self-belief and the physical energy of vitality. I really like the definition of vitality that self-determination theory cofounder Richard Ryan uses. He describes it as a state of "having energy available to the self." In other words, vitality is a storehouse for the authentic identity, which makes it a great engine for fueling your core needs. For people who have it, it's pretty potent stuff, associated with higher self-actualization and esteem, and it serves as a bulwark against anxiety and depression.

Vitality is an item that's in short supply these days, thanks to the performance identity, unbounded e-tools and schedules, time urgency, and stress. Stress causes you to withdraw from the very things that fuel vitality—exercise, relaxation, and recreation—and fixates your brain on perceived crises and the mental block of busyness. It's a self-reinforcing loop that puts a vise grip on your vitality. You're down, and all you can think about is how down you are. That's where a bias for action comes in. It impels you toward recreational action, no matter what. You go with the movement. You leap before you look.

Jump into an engaging leisure activity, and you release the stranglehold of stress and restore your vitality reserves. This increases your enthusiasm and readiness for spontaneity, which primes you for more action. Aerobic exercise, feelings of competence, love and intimacy, and contact with nature are some of the things that can increase vitality, says Ryan. I certainly buy that last one. Natural spectacles infuse the soul and the body with the renewing spirit of splendor.

"Negativity and neutrality constrain your experience of the world," says Barbara Frederickson. "Positivity does just the opposite. It draws you out to explore, to mix it up with the world in unexpected ways."

The more positive experiences you have, the more energized you are. You increase your energy potential when you

---

## Wonder Lust

When did you last feel a moment of jaw-dropping wonder? If it's been too long, you're probably an adult. Wonder is a mother lode of vitality that can restore the jaded modern in an instant. Goethe called the feeling of wonder "the highest man could attain." That elevating mix of awe and humility, inspired by the marvels and the inexplicabilities of the planet, has the power to evoke the enthusiasm that we usually edit out of adult expression. In effect, we revert back to being kids for a moment, and guess what? That childhood vitality comes rushing back in. Develop wonder lust, and you will do wonders for wondrous experiences your aliveness. The place to go for wondrous experiences is wherever your mind can latch onto images and concepts that make you feel small in comparison. When the ego is put in its place by the size of the world, you suddenly have room for amazement, elation, and curiosity. Pump up your vitality with scenes of grandeur or mysteries of the universe. The smaller you feel, the higher your spirits, making vitality soar.

do things you choose for the sake of them, says Ryan. Intrinsic motivation promotes autonomy and competence, which also fuel your ability to be proactive. You're much more prone to act with an intrinsic frame of mind because you don't let excuses about the outcome get in the way—"I won't get anything out of it," "I might look clueless." Wanting to know the end before you've gotten to the beginning makes zero sense, whether it's a movie or your life.

The act of self-mobilizing is energizing, in and of itself, and can change your attitude within minutes. Make the leap, and you'll be vitalized.

······· ACTIVATE ·······

## Accentuate the Positive

Because a positive frame of mind is a trigger for the buoyant spirit that fuels vitality, it's well worth your while to stay in that frame. Researchers have found that one of the most effective ways to do that is to build your reserves of gratitude. In our culture of "getting," the focus is on the opposite of that: on what you're *not* getting. This breeds a feeling of victimhood, cynicism, and a sense that the glass is always half-empty. You can counter this negative loop, though, by focusing on gratefulness with an exercise proven to boost optimism. Every night before you go to sleep, think of three good things that happened to you that day, and come up with a reason why they happened. I can vouch for the effectiveness of this practice. Since I've been doing it, it's increased my positive mood and, even better, made me conscious of when something good happens during the day. Normally, we miss the small kindnesses. Now when I have a nice conversation with someone or a driver lets me go in front of him, I notice it and think, That's going on the good list tonight.

.....................................................................................

# The Glue of Stick-to-it-iveness

Whether you can keep persevering on the activation path depends on a snap calculation that you can handle it. This comes from self-belief, which is usually under the thumb of the performance identity. Self-belief is a sense that you can figure it out as you go along, even if you've never done it. Without some anchoring belief in your ability to take things on, the best times of your life can be over before they begin, short-circuited by snap judgments that the outcome would be too hard or take too long.

The performance identity can't cope with less than stellar results, and so it pushes to abort the effort. Yes, that taskmaster is a quitter if it doesn't get the results it wants when it wants them. Luckily, you can outflank it by arming yourself with a few motivation tools. Here are some options you can use to boost self-belief:

- *You can because you have.* Remind yourself that you can handle it because you've tackled other challenges. Think of a time when you took on something you'd never done before and kept at it. What comes to mind? It was difficult, but you persisted. What kept you going then? Use that experience to boost your staying power. If you don't have an experience similar to the one you're in, use an example from another realm. It's the same concept: sticking with something until you've built up your capability and skills.

- *Use your imagination*. Create mental imagery of yourself doing well at an activity. Visualize yourself on the volleyball court, serving the ball smoothly, setting effectively, and enjoying yourself. Locking in images of yourself being up to the task can get you through the early stages to a level of competence that's self-sustaining.

- *Find role models*. Identify others who have learned a similar pursuit or friends who have stuck with a goal and who can inspire you to keep going. If you're taking a beginning-level class, get to know more advanced students and find out how they got through the learning curve. I did that when I first took salsa lessons. People assured me that they were as clueless as me in the beginning. Keep showing up, they said, and it will happen.

## David Lee Thinks He Can, So He Does

Humans accomplish what they think they can. There's no better example of the power of mind over matter than David Lee. Momentary exasperation pales beside the challenges that have come Lee's way. A motorcycle accident at the age of twenty put an end to any notion that the next day was a given for him. Lee's injuries were so critical, he was declared dead at one point.

The accident in 1990 caused major frontal lobe and spinal injuries that took away the use of his legs, affected his speech, and shattered his dreams. "I thought I had the world at my feet," he says today from his home in Cardiff, California. "I thought I was going to make lots of money. I was sad. It was tough to realize I was in a chair for the rest of my life. It was like, Where do I go from here?"

At an age when most young people are just gaining their independence, Lee had lost his and had plenty of time to think about it, staring at a hospital ceiling for months on end. Besides breaking his back, he had serious head trauma, a fractured brain stem, and an injury to his right frontal lobe. Among his multiple surgeries, doctors had to close a flap that was exposed in Lee's brain. Lee's family was a constant source of support, pushing him to see that he wasn't done yet. Despite the devastating reality, he listened.

After a long and grueling course of rehab, Lee decided to rejoin the world again. He focused on what he could do, instead of on what he couldn't, and it led him to consider wheelchair racing. He had been a skier before the accident and craved an active outlet. In his first race, a 10K, he finished last. That didn't discourage him, though. He loved the challenge and the people he met through racing. He trained harder and wound up doing a marathon. It would be the first of forty during the next nine years, eight of which he won.

The source of Lee's tenacious spirit? He believes in himself. "I know I can do it, so I do it," he says. "There's no question of not doing it. I always complete my goal."

Few have had as much get in the way of their goals as Lee has. While training in San Diego in 1999 for an Ironman race in New Zealand, incredibly, it happened all over again. This time a car made an illegal turn and T-boned Lee. He fractured his L1 and L2 lumbar vertebrae at the base of his back and lost a kidney. "One kidney was not going to keep me down," Lee jokes. "No big deal."

But it was not a fender bender. Lee had to have a lot more surgery and more rehab. He managed to fight his way back to racing again, but then his spine collapsed because of an undiagnosed injury from the latest accident. The surgery to repair that problem failed, and he had to undergo another operation. He was in a body cast for ten months. "I was thinking, How could this be happening?" he recalls.

Again, he had to summon up the will to start over again with rehab. But not only did he meet that challenge, he took on another one: hand-cycling. The damage to his spine from the second accident made it impossible for him to do the wheel-pushing motion that was needed in wheelchair racing, so he switched to hand-cycling. He knew the routine. Start from scratch. Build strength. Keep getting out there. Keep pushing. He tried out for the U.S. Paralympic team and made it, competing in the Beijing Paralympic Games in 2008.

Lee came in second in what has been called the toughest race in the sport: the 270-mile Sadler Challenge in Alaska. "I can't tell you how gratifying it is to watch people's faces as I fly by them on the road. It is a freedom from the confines of my wheelchair that's similar to flying."

Today Lee works as a personal trainer, creating fitness programs for people who want to get in shape or lose weight. No doubt, they get a huge dose of inspiration along the way from a man who won't say die and a lesson on why you shouldn't either. "I appreciate every day," says Lee. "Every day I pray, thank God, for every minute. I was dead in 1990 and almost dead in 1999. I feel very blessed. Every moment is a gift."

When your spirit flags, I have two words for you: David Lee.

## The Tenacity of Tolerating Ambiguity

Persistence requires that you operate in the shade of the palette that defines the human adventure: grayness. We want definition, but there is none, at least not at the outset of a new learning experience, relationship, or job. You have to feel your way through, keep your mind open, and push through the fog.

If by the third archery lesson you're hitting more hay bale than target and you have no long-term goal motivation, the tendency is to bolt. The skill that helps see you through the bumpy stages is an acumen known in the entrepreneurial trade as tolerating ambiguity, a talent for living with uncertainty.

It's a skill that ought to be required for all humans, because uncertainty is our lot. Developing passions requires that you surrender to the unknowable: how long it's going to take, how you'll figure it out, how much fun you'll get out of it when you can really do it. The jury, yourself, needs to be out for a while, on your skills and the entire activity. Withholding judgment on your capabilities is an exercise in the art of self-regulation—controlling moods and delaying gratification so that you can accomplish a longer-term goal.

Doing a hobby with one eye on the clock is a habit of the performance identity—it wants a result. You can defeat this impulse by internalizing your intrinsic reason for doing the activity. Focus on the value and the meaning inherent in gaining the skill, doing the practice, and training your attention, and you can tolerate the vagaries. Focus on the process, not on the finish line.

Everything that's enjoyable about a passion—from discovering it to honing it—takes place over time. It's the repeated effort that builds the satisfaction of progress and the social relationships that make it all worthwhile. You can't put a stopwatch on talent or friendship. To keep thriving amid the initial uncertainty, you'll need to elude a gauntlet of false alarms coming from the performance chip. There is a frustration barrier for almost any occasion or state of mind. How you push through barriers like these will determine whether you bail or rally:

## Happy Feet

When you resist the drive-by instinct and linger in the experience, amazing things unfold. On a bushwalk in Zimbabwe, I was watching a group of elephants get ready for a swim in the Zambezi River, when something made me do a double-take. One of the bigger males came down an embankment to the waterline, and before he entered the water, he stopped, picked up one of his huge feet, and dipped it side to side. He looked like he was trying to bust a move. Then the next elephant stepped up and did the same footwork before wading in and hosing himself off with his huge trunk. I had stumbled onto some kind of *Soul Train* line dance for tuskers. I asked around later and found out that it's called "happy feet." Elephants love water, so the anticipation of taking a dip sets off a dance. We think of delight as a human trait, but here it was, and I noticed it only because I persisted in hanging around and paying attention.

### Managing Frustration Barriers

- *It's not working.* If you fixate on the possibility of failure, it usually means that your motivation not to fail is stronger than your motivation to learn or have fun. Change your purpose from trying not to fail to discovering what you can learn today. Learning is the process of failing less and less until you have acquired knowledge and skills.

- *It's taking forever.* This barrier is widespread in a time-urgent world. But the timetable, or choosing not to have one, is completely in your hands. See this barrier as an attempt by the performance identity to get results. Remember, you're playing. No results are needed.

- *This is hard; it's supposed to be play.* You can't feel satisfied and competent unless you do something difficult. Forget about what is supposed to happen, and let the road to fulfillment meander as it will.

- *Feel like bolting.* This is a very common response by the ego when the adult can't get something right away. It's part impatience, part performance yardstick. Don't give in to the instinct to bolt. The solution: linger. Lingering is the fastener of friendship and the essential tool of getting to know anyone or anything. Make it your goal to linger as long as possible, as often as possible.

- *I'm the only one not getting it.* In my experience, if you're not understanding it, plenty of others aren't either. Keep the focus on the learning, not on what others are doing. Comparisons are a life-killer. They do zero for you.

- *It feels awkward.* Feeling socially comfortable in a new activity takes time. Choir singer Sheila Gross says that it took her a little while to feel at home with a group she now considers family. Have you walked away from people or an activity too soon in the past?

## ACTIVATE

## Expect Hard

We don't expect play to be hard, yet that's the contradictory nature of leisure activities. You have to gain facility to have fun. Adults are used to being in control. Being clueless doesn't fit that expectation. I'd like you to create a new mental association, one in which difficulty is not a sign of ineptness but instead a signal that you are taking care of your core needs. Your core requires things to be hard, or there's no payoff in the form of satisfaction. Expect it to be hard, and you won't be thrown off your hunt for a gratifying life. At the same time, make sure that you start at a level that's not too difficult, or competency can seem too unachievable. Instead of just falling for a frustration barrier when it hits, identify the ones that tend to come up for you. What's one action you can take to keep persisting when each of those barriers wants to sideline you?

## You Won't Get to It Later

If you look too long before you leap, you are liable to fall prey to one of the biggest contributors to a missing life: procrastination. There are plenty of temptations to choose from—"I'll just have a few Mallomars"; "Maybe I'll have more energy next week"; "I have to check e-mail." But you can put the brakes on future flake-outs, with a change in priorities.

Researchers say that you're more likely to procrastinate if an activity ranks low on the "importance and meaning" scale, the slot that most of our off-hours tend to fall into. You can stop postponing life by upgrading the importance of that time. Remember, it's the small positive experiences that constitute the bulk of life's positive experiences. See each R&R moment as an investment in your life portfolio. Remember, you're working to live. What's more meaningful than that?

Another key to getting and staying activated is cutting down on the number of distractions that can divert your best intentions at any moment. Impulsivity is a big factor in procrastination and missing out on your life. Turning off e-mail software and all alerts, shutting off the phone, and not going on the Internet are all good moves to keep the delaying reflexes down.

You need all the help you can get in this department, because humans weren't designed to resist the easier or quicker path. We were built for instant gratification. We pick what's in front of us, instead of a longer-term goal, because we are not good at forecasting future rewards. It comes from a time when the order of the day for the species was grabbing what we could on the savanna the instant it was available. Here are a few tools that can help you fight off the distractions and the inertia that fuel procrastination:

*Forging Tenacity*

- *Be one move ahead of your ego.* You can outflank threats to your staying power by anticipating them with a technique called an implementation intention, which will help you stick to your goals. Developed by Peter Gollwitzer of New York University, the tool plays off the lower brain's automatic tendency to process events with a cause/effect dynamic. You combat specific temptations to bail with "If, then" statements of intention: "*If* I get frustrated, *then* I will focus on the learning." Or, "If I feel awkward around others, then I will initiate more, not less, conversation." Implementation intentions keep you conscious, so that you don't fall prey to old habits of bolting or procrastination.

- *Keep your eyes on the prize.* Instead of letting your emotions of the moment—exasperation, fatigue—dictate your decisions, connect regularly with your goal. Researchers have found that it's harder to self-regulate and stay focused if you don't monitor your progress relative to your ultimate goal—say, competence or fun. When you waver, check in with how far you've come and your long-term goal.

- *Reframe loaded appraisals.* Your core needs for autonomy and competence require you to take on something that is beyond your comfort zone. Yet you can undermine that effort when you use language that harps on difficulty. Words like "too hard" or "impossible" set you up for failure and an early exit from a pursuit that could be a lifelong delight. Reframe your self-talk so that "a problem" becomes "a challenge"; so that "stress" becomes "excitement"; and so that it's the effort, not the result, that is important.

Delaying gratification and eliminating the self-sabotage of judgment liberate you from reflex mode and ensure that you, not the performance identity, do the deciding.

....................  ACTIVATE  .......................

## Your Missing Person Report

It's easy to delay life, because each postponement and procrastination doesn't seem like a big deal at the time— but it adds up. This week keep track of every time you don't act on a life opportunity. You didn't get together with your friends? Put it on the list. Tabled that beach outing because of traffic? Mark it down. Procrastinating on starting a new hobby? Get it on paper. Keep this list going for as long as it takes you to see all of the missing life that mounts up when we're caught up in default tasks that seem more important or distracting. This is not a list you'll want to pull out in your golden years.

....................................................

# The Art of the Rally

The mind might be willing, but the flesh is glued to the sofa. There will be many reasons to bail on the road to competence, all of them appearing to be a better choice than frustration or public ineptness. We expect our fun to deliver a payback in the zero-point-one seconds of a Google search, and as a result wind up with off-hours that leave us as sated as an entree of melba toast.

Patience is the author of proficiency. At my first orienteering race, a handful of us were led to a ridge overlooking the rolling hills outside San Jose, California. The starter called my name. I was off. No, I wasn't. I looked at the topographical map with its wavy lines and numbered circles, which indicated where I would have to locate hidden control boxes, and I didn't have the faintest idea what direction that first box was in. It felt like the time I got lost in the grocery store at age four. It took me twelve minutes to find my prize behind a cluster of oaks on a hillside opposite where I first started looking and another ten minutes to find the second control—and I'd thought I was good with maps. I told myself, "It's the experience," and kept going. After the third control, I started to get the hang of it, and my times all went down during the final six controls.

You can override the momentary mind freezes, fears, and perceptions of external obstacles that make you want to flake by using the little-known key to persistence: the rally. Instead of falling for automatic killjoys—fatigue, stress, inertia—you build in a counterpunch. You're not going for that first reaction. You're rallying. You transcend the alibis by summoning your commitment to live without excuses and ego.

The next time your body wants to veg when it's time to take care of your core needs at a class or on a weekend getaway, rally. When the gloom of a bad day says that you're not in the mood to go out, rally. Within five minutes of arriving at your destination, you'll be glad you did. I know I always am. The mind can come up with any number of alibis: too exhausted, too hungry, the spouse won't like it (whose life is it anyway?). Rally!

•••••••••••••••••••••••• ACTIVATE ••••••••••••••••••••••••

### Rally Practice

What if all that was standing between you and a passion that could transform your life was trying it one more time? Without the ability to rally, you would bolt, and a thrilling new skill and a crew of potential lifelong friends would never happen. The rally says that you're not going to roll over for comfort defaults and fears. Make the ability to rally a counter to any alibi. Let's get started. Identify three frequent reasons you bail out on pastimes and social activities. After you write them down, repeat them out loud a couple of times. Feel free to steam about how these things can hijack your life. Now rally to counter each of them. What will you say? How about: "I can rally!" What physical actions will you take to defeat the flake-out? How about standing up, putting your keys in your hand, and pumping your fist? Repeat whenever you need to rally.

•••••••••••••••••••••••••••••••••••••••••••••••••••••••••••

## Eager in the Face of Setbacks

The image of a high achiever is of someone who is indomitable in a world of wimps. The reality, though, is quite different. Researchers have found that having strong external performance goals actually undercuts persistence. The reason: any setbacks will shake the self-image of people who are ruled by performance standards. Yet people who have intrinsic goals are able to find enjoyment even in activities that they don't do well.

In one study, Stanford's Carol Dweck found that students who were oriented to the intrinsic goal of learning, instead of to the performance yardstick of doing well, were able to get enjoyment out of the challenge even when their performance wasn't good. They remained eager in the face of difficulty. How useful could that be for your arteries, not to mention your perseverance? Meanwhile, externally motivated students said that they wouldn't be interested in a subject that they didn't do well in. What if that subject was life?

We return to our anthem of doing it to do it. The skill of the intrinsic approach helps you stay more determined, because your goal is the process of learning. Dweck also found that when

## Take a Leap

Getting into the habit of taking action requires practice. You can get your body used to physical liftoff with a tool that puts a bounce into each and every day: a personal trampoline. It's small enough to fit in any home, but it can launch you into an orbit of active living. You can bounce for fun and fitness simultaneously. A number of core workouts can be done on the device, as well as basic jogging and jumping jacks. When you come home after a day at the grind, you can bounce back with a quick hop aboard the trampoline. Check out the Urban Rebounder Trampoline Workout System. It comes with a stabilizing bar and a DVD with three workouts.

a task has a high degree of difficulty, learning goals promote better results than the results mind-set.

# The Long Haul of Commitment

It's a given that long-term endeavors we take seriously require more effort to get right. Relationships and careers demand enduring dedication and the discipline of commitment. But strangely, it's a concept that is seldom associated with the ultimate ongoing effort: living. Why not make a commitment to your life—a commitment to live?

People with life intelligence understand that the things that make life most worth living take the skill of dedication. The idea of committing to play seems almost illicit, so we usually don't apply a lot of staying power when we indulge the nonprofessional side. We take a quick bite and are on our way. No one is holding us to it, and that's the problem. Someone has to, or it's not going to happen.

That someone is you, via a commitment to indulge your living as intently as how you make it. Immersion in your pursuits reveals the deeper gratifications of competence and fulfillment you can never feel with hit-and-run appearances on the play circuit.

•••••••••••••••••••••• ACTIVATE ••••••••••••••••••••••

## The Commitment Compact

It's hard to stay committed to something nebulous. To build the discipline you need to support activation, you have to know what you're dedicating yourself to. Identify what it is about your pursuit that you are committing to and why. Why is it important to you? Determine the purpose of a life opportunity and the void it can fill.

How long will you be willing to stick to it? Put a brief agreement on paper. State why you're committing and what goal you're committing to. Post this commitment on your refrigerator and on your life résumé. Refer back to it when your spirit wavers.

······························································

## Ian Glazer: Less Bad Is Good

The performance yardstick doesn't lend itself to any experiential pastimes, let alone to Eastern practices such as tai chi chuan, which take years to learn and are rooted in the opposite framework—getting rid of the ego that creates yardsticks. Ian Glazer, a ten-year practitioner of classical tai chi chuan, might feel as if he knows how to do it in another twenty years. He approaches his learning process with Zen-like humility and humor, for the long haul.

"Just know that you're going to be bad, and you'll be a little less bad tomorrow," says Glazer, a technical analyst at a research firm in Washington, D.C. "You have to really push yourself through, getting a little better each time. Don't think too much about why you are doing this. You don't get mastery in a day."

Glazer is a process guy, so he was a prime candidate for the slow, hard practice of the brand of tai chi that is taught at the Great River Taoist Center. It's not the slow-mo exercise routine you see people doing in public parks. Great River is one of the few places in the country that teaches tai chi as a martial art, before "it got watered down," says instructor Scott Rodell. When Glazer started to take classes, he was amazed by the ability of senior citizens in his class to deflect his moves and push him to the ground. He wanted to have that flexibility and strength. He started to come to class one day a week, then two, then three and four days.

His passion for the practice took off when he was introduced to the arcane skill of Chinese swordsmanship, which added more athleticism and focus to his practice. There's nothing like a three-foot blade coming at you to upgrade your attention. Glazer practices with bamboo swords, but at tournaments, people use the real thing. "There's a risk," he admits, but he's never been injured.

Glazer has been able to stick with the rigorous training because of behaviors that encourage self-discipline and dedication to the goal. The benefits of commitment have come back to him many times over. "It washes away the gunk in my life," says Glazer. "It's really invigorating. I'll be doing it for a long time. There are masters eighty years old doing this practice."

The training at the root of tai chi and many other practices from the East builds commitment through the realization that you're not trying to get somewhere where you will have *it*. In the Taoist way of thinking, you already have it and can't *not* have it. That means you can relax to be 100 percent where you are. You're already there. This makes it much more likely that you'll want to stay there and not bolt.

The practice is the way for people like Glazer and anyone who takes the intrinsic approach. Every stretch, every exercise, every mistake, every slip is part of their life practice, which will always have a new trick for them to learn.

 ACTIVATE

## Stay in School

Too often, we want to be as good as the instructor or the pro, ASAP, but we forget that it took years, if not decades, to attain that skill level. Wanting to have that ability instantly leads to frustration and a quick exit from what could be a vital outlet. Instead, make practice your practice. Think of an activity you would like to do or a skill you would like to learn. Now make your objective the practice of the activity itself. What intrinsic goals could support the act of practice?

## You Can't Hurry Life

Life opportunities are no different from those in the business sphere. Dally and they will disappear. When you're vitalized with readiness and persistence, you can take advantage of the opportunities before you get sidetracked by overthinking or inertia. It's the steady, determined pursuit of competence that yields the passion, a process that runs counter to all of the impatient twitching of time-urgent bodies. Rushing your way to a vibrant life is like trying to finish your cake without tasting it. There's no stopwatch for competence or enjoyment. Settle in and enjoy the ride with these life-sustaining skills:

- Seize life opportunities with a bias for action by increasing vitality and self-belief.
- Push through the frustrations of the learning curve with the tenacity of tolerating ambiguity.
- Use intrinsic motivation to stay eager in the face of setbacks.
- Don't give up; rally!
- Develop the discipline to live what you love by being committed to the practice, not to the result.

# 10

## Seven Days to Your Life

> The more a person is able to direct his life consciously, the more he can use the time for constructive benefits. The more conformist and unfree he is, the more time is the master. He serves time.
>
> —*Rollo May, psychologist and author*

Life is like a muscle. Use it, and its vitality grows stronger. Ignore it, and it atrophies. Only a shriveled existence is possible when you're not conscious about how you use your time. Without a daily practice of time ownership—living as if you own your free time—autopilot and inertia are in command. The universe of exhilaration waiting for you vanishes in preoccupation and the belief it creates that you are too busy or worn down to shift to a lighter space.

Stress constricts thought, fixating it on problems and crises, a mental state incompatible with having a good time. The result is a kind of learned helplessness, a belief that there's nothing you can do except take the pounding. That was Annie, the woman I mentioned at the beginning of the book who hadn't had a vacation in seven years. For many people, a wall of fatalism closes off active living by keeping out choice and self-determination. It's a mirage, a haze of fear-fueled resignation. You remain sidelined by this initial state as long as you are in a defensive posture.

But the excuses—too much work, no money, parenting responsibilities (most of the life intelligence practitioners in these pages have kids)—don't fly when you own your time. You're on the offense then. You are no longer in serving-time mode, oblivious to why you're breathing. I'd like to bring back Hope Afloat dragon boat paddler Cindy Roberts here to help us grasp what we need to be using our breathing for and why there's no time to waste. She once floated through time, believing, as many of us, that there was always more of it. After her battle with cancer, her priorities changed completely. "Live it now! Don't put things off!" she says today. "Enjoy every moment in the here and now."

Roberts reminds us of the mandate at the heart of optimal living:

My off-hours are mine.
The nights are mine.
The weekends are mine.
My vacations are mine.

How you spend those hours determines whether you look back later on the richness of experiences that thrilled or elated you—or with regret. We're led to believe that the big choices we make will determine a happy life—the professions we go into, where we live, the awards we win—but it's actually the hundreds and thousands of small decisions to engage with friends, fun, passions, challenges, service, and adventures that add up to a sense of having fully lived. The memories leave no doubt about it. The cumulative effect of many small satisfactions leads to happiness, as the positive outweighs the negative—the three-to-one ratio that tips you into the positive column. Blowing off the little things blows off the bulk of your living time, so taking them more seriously would be a very smart thing to do.

Let's get started, then, with a proactive plan to activate the fullest experience of this planet. The way forward is life optimizing, enhancing active living skills and beefing up quality free time for the richest life possible. The "Optimal Life" program will give you the tools to mobilize the most gratifying and exhilarating experiences and get you off the sidelines to stay.

The program (which you can also experience in person via workshops and optimal-life training at dontmissyourlife.net) provides you with the essential components of life intelligence, equipping you with the skills of full engagement, intrinsic motivation, and experiential enjoyment. Each day in the seven-day plan represents one of the laws of optimal life and provides lessons to put the aptitudes of that experiential rule into practice. Feel free to go at your own pace. When you've finished with one day's activities, move on to the next.

You'll also find tips to help you stay on track with your life goals throughout the year with an easy-reference support system, a five-step checklist that can get you out the door before the sofa changes your mind. And finally, you don't want to leave any dreams on the table simply because they've never spilled out of your head and onto a page before. You can start making them real now.

Everything starts with time, that elusive dimension portioned out sparingly to humans and particularly to those who don't own and manage their allotment skillfully. It's one of the oldest nuggets of time management: you have to take time to make time. You have to step back from the frenzy of hurry-worry and things that must be done to carve out space for your life.

# Optimal Life: Live to the Core

## Day 1: Worth Is an Inside Job

*Mobilize time ownership.* The first step on the path to optimal living is dedicating yourself to a new relationship with time. Make sure that you sign the deed to time ownership in chapter 1. Photocopy it, and paste it on your wall or refrigerator. You now own the time of your life. You will no longer *fill* free time with rote busyness, mindless cell phone twiddling, or Web surfing. Real worth comes from *fulfilling* time; your new mission. Repeat the time ownership manifesto:

- I agree to use my time as if my happiness depends on it, which it does.
- I agree to seek out engaging activities for no other reason than the often delirious experience of them.
- I agree to never turn down an opportunity to live it up.

*Shut off the performance mind.* The performance mind follows you home and on vacation, pressing you to get your fun done, if you don't shut it off. To do that, you have to be able to separate the two functions of work and life. The work side is output, the life side input. The better you can get at seeing your leisure time as input, the more you'll enjoy it, because you won't feel the need to get a performance result ASAP. I'd like you to take three actions today that are about input. It could be doing a favor for a neighbor, talking to a family member, or riding a bike. Do each of them as pure inputs, with no timetable or need to get anything done. How different does that feel from your normal behavior during the day? How difficult is it to be in input mode? Any time you leave the office, visualize yourself flipping a light switch from output to input.

*Play your Life Card*. Finish the Life Card exercise in chapter 2. Create a business card for your life, identifying yourself by a passion, something you'd like to do or used to do, or by an interest that looks intriguing—gourmet chef, fossil hunter, fanatic birder. If you have several identities outside the job, all the better. Print up your new identity on an actual business card as a reminder of who you really are. You can get one produced cheaply at vistaprint .com. Refer to the card when your life disappears.

*Shut off time urgency*. Stop defining yourself and determining your value by how busy you are. Recognize nonstop busyness for what it is: an excessive need to be validated by performance. From now on, whenever you're asked how you are, never say busy. Take an extra couple of minutes for small talk today with someone, no matter how much of a rush you're in. Use this as a braking device. What's going on in your colleagues' or neighbors' lives?

*Create your free-time budget*. Use the free-time budget in chapter 1 to identify how your time is being spent over the course of the week and which slots are open for engaging activities. Where do you have a spare hour or two? What are the best weeknight and weekend times to slip in some fun? What time drain can you reduce or eliminate to make time for your life? Tally up the days and the hours when you can clear some free time. When are your openings? Which days? What hours? Now go to the passion finder in chapter 3 and identify a few activities that you could do in the evenings after work. What pursuit will you commit to for at least six weeks? Which time slot will it fit into?

*Disconnect from your e-overlords*. The more caught up in electronic interruptions you are, the less time you have for your life and the less attention you have for the full engagement of direct experience. Interruptions scramble a part of your brain that controls attention and along with it impulse control. Use, but don't become a hostage to, e-mail checking, Twitter, or your Facebook page. I'd like you to start implementing some interruption management. If you have your e-mail on autopilot, checking every five minutes, that adds up to ninety-six interruptions over the course of the day. Try to cut your e-mail checking to four times a day (the most effective schedule, according to researchers)—when you get to work, before lunch, after lunch, and before you go home. Don't check your work e-mail at night or on the weekend. Take back more time for your life by cutting your social media and Web time. Start with a 25 percent reduction, and once you see that the world won't come to an end, cut it some more. Between better e-management at work and Web control at home, you will free up time to live instead of just clicking. .

## Day 2: Safe Is Sorry

*Take out regret insurance.* Imagine yourself in your final years looking back on your life. Will you feel you lived it fully or that you missed it? Will you be able to say, as Erik Erikson put it at the beginning of this book, that you got what you came here for? That it was a good time? What fears stand in the way of making the answer the one you want: maximum life? Spell out those fears on paper. Look at those words. Get irate at the prospect that they could shut out the life you want. Thoughts, and that's all that fears are, aren't real; only experience is. Identify the main discomfort zone that's holding back something you want to do or experience. What's at the root of the fear? Avoidance is not a strategy for living fully. What step can you take toward the momentary discomfort, beyond which is the aliveness? What's the next step?

*Opt out of stress sabotage.* Stress closes down the brain's receptivity to what's new or playful and fixates the mind on problems, but you can opt out of this default. It's not work or the negative event that's causing your stress. It's your reaction, the story you tell yourself about it, that fuels the stress response. The emotional alarm system of your brain, the amygdala, reacts to a perception that you can't cope by triggering a false story of panic and fear. Unless it's a life-or-death situation, it's a false alarm. Tell yourself a different story, and the stress can't bite. Take a minute to identify a stressor that's keeping you in an anxious or negative frame of mind and unable to enjoy life. Now pinpoint the false belief behind it. Dispute it with a different story—"It's not life or death," "It's temporary," "It's a false alarm," "Stay neutral," or make up your own phrase. Say it repeatedly, bring in the facts of the situation to counter the emotion—and you will stop fear and its ban on enjoyment in its tracks. What regular stress-reduction activity—going to the gym, yoga, running, meditation, tennis—can you do to keep the tension at bay? When will you start?

*Build risk-taking skills.* You now know that your brain neurons don't want comfort; they want to discover and engage. You do that by trying new things through the skill of risk-taking. You get better at this when you practice taking risks. What three risks could you take that might open up your life? Chart out two action steps for each risk.

*Initiate to participate.* High-quality living time depends on your willingness to do the legwork to ferret out engaging activities. This requires frequent use of the skill of initiating. Put together a master list of sources for activities in your area—daily, weekly newspapers, Web sites, schedules for sports and recreational events at parks and social centers, college extension and Learning Tree/Learning Annex courses, entertainment listings for clubs and concerts, volunteer programs, and travel opportunities. Check your source list each weekend for the upcoming week's possibilities. What five sources will be on your list for checking every week?

*Search out novelty*. Habit keeps the life-giving spice of novelty at bay. Pump up the life intelligence skill of novelty-seeking, and you will be drawn outside the bubble. You can start to open things up today by going on a novelty scavenger hunt. Ask people you meet today to tell you one thing you didn't know and to recommend an activity they've had fun doing that you might, too. At the end of the day, take a look at what you've uncovered and choose one of the items to explore further. What's the next step to get the pursuit going?

## Day 3: Expect No Payoff (and You Get One)

*Act without regard to outcome*. External expectations keep optimal living at bay by demanding that your play produce a result. The most vibrant and fulfilling times come when you use the skill of intrinsic motivation, acting for no gain. Since this is such a crucial tool to transform you life, I'd like you to spend the entire day acting intrinsically. Don't expect praise, recognition, or a leg up from anything you do today—no external rewards whatsoever. Act for the inherent interest, challenge, or learning. Offer a gift to someone completely anonymously. Participate in an experience that has no purpose other than fun. What can you do just for the enjoyment? Shift your notion of success from the external reward that doesn't stick and makes you want more to the authentic success that comes from acting for an internal goal that satisfies your core. Keep reminding yourself that real success is in the living.

*Go for the gratifications*. Make a list of all the activities you do in your free time. Identify which ones are pleasures, the chocolate bars of life that provide a short-term delight but don't stick with you, and which are gratifications: experiences that engage and expand you and provide lasting satisfaction. What gives you the most gratification? Why?

*Shut off the force field.* If you're always in control, nothing new gets in. The life intelligence skill of openness creates the receptivity that allows gratifying experiences to come your way. Identify the force fields of control that keep you from seizing more fun. What's in your way? Judgment? Jadedness? Starting conversations? Initiating activities with others? What one change in your behavior could you make to open yourself unconditionally to more people and activities?

*Follow the curiosity.* Locate your passions by boosting your curiosity skills. The two key components of curiosity are exploration and absorption. Practice both of these aspects to improve your radar for intriguing pursuits and to heighten the ability to lose yourself in your interests. Identify an interest or an experience you'd like to know more about. What intrigues you? Why? Exploration is an interrogatory process. Prepare a list of five questions that can satisfy your curiosity about that pursuit. Now research it, and find the answers to each question. You can use the Web or talk to experts. After you've dug into the topic and learned more, determine which part of it you were most absorbed in. What really held your interest?

*Let affinities be your guide.* We all have affinities in our play, preferences for certain kinds of activities. Try to identify some of these right now, to let your inner inclinations lead the way. What types of activities do you like most? Sports? Social activities? Creative outlets? Competitive pursuits? Do you prefer your pastimes indoors or outdoors? Do you like structured or unstructured activities? Individual or group? Physical or mental activities?

*Spread the net.* Choose five activities you will try within the next six months. Go to the passion finder in chapter 3 and identify the pursuits you'd like to explore. Remember, the more things you try, the better your chances of finding a passion and making some great new friends. Don't spend too long analyzing. Make your selections, book the classes or lessons, and jump in.

*Cross-train your life.* Just as in the sports world, mixing up your R&R activities will help you keep your interest level high and overdoing it in check. Call it cross-playing. Try to find a blend of physical, social, and expressive pursuits that can keep brain and body challenged and invigorated. What would be a good mix for you? Make a list of activities that could keep you cross-played physically, socially, and creatively.

## Day 4: It's the Experience

*Ride the moment.* The best times happen when you are fully involved in your experience. This means allowing yourself to let go and be absorbed in the participant moment. Close your eyes and visualize yourself on a raft shooting down a mountain river. Notice everything in your experience—the feel of the inflatable raft, the jostling and bucking of the current, how fast you're going or not, the wind on your face, the cliff wall, the rocks in the river, the water splashing on your legs, the sounds of the shrieks and the laughs. Identify an activity that could bring you a high level of absorption like that. What skills would you need to have to participate? What first step will you take toward getting these tools and being completely immersed in that experience?

*Direct your attention.* The life intelligence skill of directing attention is essential for optimal learning or absorption. Lock your eyeballs on the teacher, the movement, the game. You strengthen your concentration by training focus on a target. Researchers say that one of the most effective ways to do this is with meditation. Sit down in a quiet place, let your body relax, and focus attention on your breath. Concentrate on the outflow of your breath and then on the inflow, nothing else. Do it for fifteen minutes every day. Another tool: Count backward from 100, moving from one number to the next without spacing out or drifting to another thought. When you're finished, do it again, this time counting every fourth number.

*Make practice your practice.* Passions and mastery are born from determined practice. Make the practice of learning a new skill an end in itself. See yourself as a lifelong learner. Take something you would like to do better and practice it fifteen minutes a day for the next week. Each time you practice, consider that you are practicing life. What phrase could you tell yourself at the beginning of each practice session or when it gets frustrating, to remind yourself that your real practice is life? Use that phrase before each practice as well, to remind yourself that you're not here to get it over with.

*Pursue competence.* The skill that makes you persist long enough at an activity to unleash your passion is the pursuit of competence. It's a determination to get better, to stay on the road of mastery. Impatience and the performance yardstick, however, can get in the way. Jot down three frustration barriers that cause you to drop things when you don't see instant results. Think of the last time you tried to learn a new skill. What stopped you? How could you counter that obstacle and pursue a new skill for the sake of it? Instead of measuring yourself by the external standard of how good you are at it, switch this around and aspire to being a little less bad than the time before. Stay with the internal goal: learning, having fun, discovering a potential passion.

*Match your skills with the challenge.* The peak of direct experience, flow, is found where skills and challenge meet. You stretch your abilities to the limit until you are fully involved, mentally and physically, which is the definition of living to the fullest. Choose one activity in which you have felt flow—complete absorption that allows you to lose yourself in the experience. Write down five words that describe the feeling of absorption you get from it.

## Day 5: Play Is Where You Live

*Alter the script.* Suspend the adult and work mind and slip into an alternate, nonpurposeful reality. Do something today that has no purpose but fun—play a Wii game, shoot baskets, jump on a mini-trampoline. Write down how your mood and thoughts are different after playing from how they were before. What changed? Why?

*Incite playfulness.* One of the chief predictors of the life intelligence skill of playfulness is spontaneity. Find two things you can do today to ad lib some fun. Slow down so that you can josh, rib, and uncork a humorous comeback. Use your impromptu imagination. Take a handshake and turn it into a mock arm-wrestling contest or a dance. Tell the coffee house server you'd like 443 lattes to go. Walk a block sideways down a crowded street. After you've done a couple of playful actions, rate how hard that was on a scale of 1 to 5, with 1 being easy and 5 being hard. Also on a scale of 1 to 5, 5 being most playful, how playful did you feel?

*Initiate prosocial activity.* Don't let shyness, inertia, or going out alone get in the way of one of the best benefits of an active leisure life: the social component. Who could you invite to join you in a new activity? If you don't have a candidate, invite yourself. What social block is preventing you from getting out there with others? How much life has this kept you from experiencing? What would be a better way to respond to the fear? The best way around the social barrier is to simply join a local activity group. Meeting people is easy when you all have a common interest. If there's a local Audubon Society or Sierra Club in your neighborhood, get together for a hike or an environmental outing. Check out the running stores, bike shops, and gyms. Many bike stores have weekend group rides. Are there triathlon or dragon boat clubs in your region, where you can pick up training and camaraderie? Online, check out meetup .com for get-togethers on everything from philosophy to films, and reach out to social media friends to see what events are going on. Do a Web search for sports clubs or associations in your city. One of my favorite places to find play partners is the local junior college. On Sundays at Santa Monica College, you can play pick-up games of badminton and table tennis, no matter what level your talent is. For more, go to www.dontmissyour life.net.

*Be eager to play*. Kids play one way, all-out, and you need to do this as well, to enjoy optimal living. Eagerness intensifies your immersion and makes you more likely to seek out play in the first place. What gets you really excited? What does that feel like? Create a phrase that describes the feeling you get when you're really looking forward to something. Refer back to that phrase before you go out to play.

*Unleash the real law of attraction: positive affect*. Increase the odds of attracting good times and people who want to share them with you by using the skill of positive affect. Ditch your usual assortment of grim facial expressions—the harried rusher, the uptight professional, the "don't mess with me" stoneface— and the grunts that go with them. Stand in front of a mirror and build your range of expressions. Start by practicing an expression for listening intently. Now demonstrate surprise, moving actual facial muscles in the process. Practice raising your eyebrows and opening your eyes wide to demonstrate enthusiasm. Most important, work on your smile. Nothing transmits positive affect and your openness to play better than a regular smile. But it can't be a fake one. Work on a quick-flash smile to use in conversation to punctuate your sentences. Now create a look of general bemusement that can give others the message that you are available for enjoyment. Now brace yourself for a surge of attention—and fun.

## Day 6: You Are the Audience

*Flip the fear of evaluation.* Take a moment and think of a pursuit you'd like to try but have some anxiety about being judged at—say, singing or dancing in public. Now imagine you're out there involved in the activity. What fears or thoughts pop up? What self-talk comes with them? Be a reporter and take notes on that interior monologue. That voice belongs to your inner taskmaster, the performance identity. Now take your real identity back by challenging the tales of doom. Turn the self-talk around to something positive and realistic. "Everybody makes mistakes, and if I do, it's not life or death." Or "I'm just here to have fun, not win an award." Or, "It's the experience." Or, "This is the living I'm making for myself." Keep a journal and track when the negative self-talk erupts and transform it with constructive self-talk.

*Fool around.* Fun and games often require a shift from grownup importance to outright foolishness. Take a stab at something you don't have a clue about—do salsaerobics at the gym, play your kid's video game, paint a canvas. After, write down how you felt while out of your realm. Was it survivable?

When you do something out of character, your age, or style demographic, don't cringe. Smile when you fail. You're on the way to knowing. What activity can you try that would make you feel completely out of your element? Sign up for it for a couple of weeks to expand your range of playful behavior.

*Make sure you are getting all of the life vitamins on the fun pyramid.* Besides the food pyramid, you need to pay attention to the fun pyramid, or you're a less healthy, and certainly, a much more dull boy or girl. Locate the fun pyramid in chapter 7 and identify where your biggest fun nutrient deficiencies lie. Are you too preoccupied to miss the foundation of fun, the Curiosities—novelty, wonder, spontaneity? Maybe you're missing out because you're not stocked up on the catalyzing power of the Energies, such as eagerness or enthusiasm, or the relating skills of the Interactions—social proactivity, positive affect, or participation. Make a list of the fun vitamins you need to fortify yourself with and create an action step for each.

*Do something uncool.* Don't let what's cool cramp your eagerness or which interests you pursue with whom. Optimal living is not a popularity contest. Start the deprogramming process by being uncool today. Do something that is out of fashion, unhip, not sanctioned by your usual social circle. It can be anything from using a passé cell phone to wearing an out-of-date shirt or dress to square dancing. Check out people's reactions. How does that feel? Notice how controlling the coolness yardstick is; it's the opposite of the autonomy that your core wants.

*Trust your gut.* The stronger your internal locus of control, the more you can self-determine the activities your core demands. Identify a pursuit you'd like to indulge that other people wouldn't approve of. Now work on remaining steadfast in your decision to pursue it or any other activity that the nay-sayers disapprove of. Have a friend play the role of a person who is blasé or disapprove of what you're doing. This friend will be the designated stoneface. Practice being enthusiastic about your interest or goal while your friend is unimpressed. Stay enthused while the friend sits impassively. Train yourself to override the disapproval on others' faces and stick to your choices no matter what the reaction. They don't know what you need to feel alive. Only you do.

## Day 7: Passions Take Persistence

*Build a bias for action.* To stay in the thick of optimal life, you'll need to resist and outwit the forces of procrastination. Go with the action, not analysis, or negative moods and the couch will win. Create a built-in response to overcome alibis and cold feet. Use an implementation intention to bolster your bias for action. Repeat ten times, "If I start to flake on a life opportunity, then I will choose action, no matter what."

*Push through uncertainty.* It can seem as if you're going nowhere in the initial stages of pursuing a challenging goal, but becoming skilled at how to tolerate ambiguity can get you through. You need patience and intrinsic goals to build this talent. Visualize yourself tackling something you've always wanted to learn—a foreign language, a musical instrument, a martial art. Imagine that you have achieved some mastery at it and are having the time of your life doing it. Create a picture of yourself in that place. How good does it feel to have this talent to use any time you like? Now imagine that you don't have that skill and the gratification that goes with it because you didn't have the patience to learn it or were too concerned about getting a result right away. What intrinsic goal could keep you persevering through the ambiguity. Fun? Learning? Challenge? Leave the timetable at the office.

*Master the rally.* Rallying is the ability to internalize stick-to-it-iveness. You don't even think about not bouncing back from fatigue, a grim mood, a bad day, bad hair. The rally is as automatic as brushing your teeth. Start building the rally ethic today. Whatever the excuse or obstacle, tell yourself, "I can rally!" Tell this to others, too, when you're at low wattage: "But I can rally!" Saying aloud what you'll do predicts the action. Hang "Rally'" signs around your house, in your car, and at work. Make the rally automatic. You don't even think about not rallying. Get more rally support at www.dontmiss yourlife.net.

*Lock in commitment.* Thinking that you're going to do something is no lock that it's going to happen. A tangible agreement can make the goal more real and binding. Sign a commitment agreement that holds you to a pursuit or a project for a certain period of time. Start with a six-week deal, in which you agree to commit to the activity for that period of time. After the term ends, renew the contract to a longer term, perhaps a year. If you're not feeling it, try something else. Make a copy of the commitment contract below and fill in the blanks.

---

**The Commitment Contract**
I hereby agree to throw myself into life opportunities with full dedication. I commit to learn, practice, and stick with (fill in activity here) _____ for ____ months. I will rally at every whiff of an excuse and not bail.

_____
*Signature and date*

# Keep the Bucket Filled

Now put together a list of your biggest dreams, the things you want to experience while you're still kicking. You are allowed to do these things, but they won't happen if you don't get them down on paper. Put together your life list. It will give you life assurance, which is a lot better than life insurance, because you'll actually be around to take advantage of it. Start with ten items. What do you want to see, learn, try, feel, and do just for the experience of it? Here are some of the bucket list items that people in my seminars have come up with:

Sail the South Seas
Hike the Appalachian Trail
See the Northern Lights
Learn Spanish
Run a marathon
Go on a safari
Play an instrument
Orbit the earth
Start a program for the needy
Dive the Great Barrier Reef

What's on your wish list? Keep a rotating top-ten ranking, and as new ideas come up that you want to prioritize, put them at the top of your list. Don't just list them; take your top five and add two action steps below each one. The ideas become real only when you're moving forward on them. Don't worry if the ideas seem outlandish. That's what dreams are—at first.

# Act As If Your Life Depends on It

For the vast chunk of our lives, time seems limitless. We drift through the temporal ether unconcerned about the availability of a resource we've always had. We stop paying attention to the wonders in our midst—a guardian peak, morning birdsong—and don't reflect on other wonders that might be out there. We think we can always get to it later. No, you can't always get to it later.

All of the life intelligence skills in the world are moot if you don't do something with them. Only action can make your intentions real. Whatever you want to do, it all comes down to plunging in. You can make that happen with some activation insurance. All you have to do is follow the five-step list here and you're guaranteed to be in the thick of full engagement.

*The Activation Guarantee*

1. *Make the time.* Clear the space, move stuff around, eliminate the too-busy mental block, and carve out a time slot for your activity.

2. *Calendar it.* Make it official by entering the activity into your cell phone, on your calendar, or on a very large Post-it. Set a reminder notice in the task function of your e-mail software. You're not going to let this life opportunity slip by.

3. *Commit.* Confirm in writing that you will follow through on the activity with the commitment agreement. Have a friend witness it to hold you to it.

4. *Activate no matter what.* Initiate, initiate, initiate. Make this your constant affirmation. Put one foot in front of the other, until you are immersed in the activity. Keep moving.

5. *Rally.* Fight for your life. If you start to flake, rally your self-determination. Remember, this is where you live. Reach out to the rally page at dontmissyourlife.net.

## ⌒ The Real World

For the last year, I've had the pleasure of inhabiting a parallel universe that the world of doom, scandal, stress, and misery would have you believe doesn't exist—a world of joy and elation, of soul-stirring experiences and ear-eating grins. I've played, danced, paddled, kicked, volleyed, and flown as high as a kite with people as enthused as they want to be, folks from all walks of life, incomes, and ages, living their best lives in the middle of the worst economic meltdown since the Depression.

They wouldn't let fear ground their passions while they waited for some better day. That would be absurd, when the thing that you like most in the world is standing right in front of you, with the power to slay all dragons in an instant. I can see Nao Kumagai pumping his fist at the badminton net. I hear the whoops of Kathy King and the Hope Afloat dragon boat team, as they cross the finish line in first place, doing what all of their doctors said they couldn't. I feel the goose bumps rise with the harmonies of my choir mates Felicia Kelly, Sheila Gross, and company. I hear hand cyclist David Lee telling me, "Quitting is not an option. I don't even think about it."

I can't help but think how different this planet would be if everyone had a passion. If everyone was as eager to be alive as Reynaldo, the seventy-year-old samba lover who can dance nonstop for three hours. If everyone had something to look forward to each week. If we self-determined our identities through the enthusiasms that define our truest nature. If the "dessert" of play became a main course. If everyone had a bounce in their step.

It's in that spring that you find the swing, and that's everything, as Duke Ellington famously said. That's what your passions bring. They add the verve, the spark, the soul, the reason to get up in the morning.

Without life in your life, it doesn't mean much. I would be bereft without the trails of Cedar Grove in Kings Canyon National Park, a campground my family has been visiting since I was two years old. I would be wonderless without all of the folks and experiences that have come my way through the adventure of travel—snorkeling the translucent lagoon of Aitutaki Island in the Cooks; meeting new friends in a stilt longhouse in the highlands of Burma; drinking in the awe in the spray of the "smoke that thunders," Victoria Falls.

Without samba, I'd be grounded, cut off from this animating force of fun and consolation that tells me that no matter what the struggles and the headlines, I can feel delirious joy, whenever I please. That's easy to forget in the daily fray, but play brings you back to life—and to the bounce that's still inside you. Follow it to the heart of what you live for.

# Notes

## Introduction

4    *As a* New York Times *story*  Stephanie Rosenbloom, "But Are You Happy?" *New York Times*, August 7, 2010.

## 1. The Life Force

18    *This agent of aliveness has been shown to increase*  Kennon M. Sheldon and Sonja Lyubomirsky, "Is It Possible to Become Happier? (And If So, How?)," *Social and Personality Psychology Compass* 1 (2007): 5.

23    *"The power to achieve leisure"*  Josef Pieper, *Leisure: The Basis of Culture* (Indianapolis: Liberty Fund, 1998), 32.

26    *"the tipping point"*  Barbara Frederickson, *Positivity* (New York: Crown, 2009), 32.

28    *Reduce stress by buffering setbacks*  Dennis Coleman and Seppo Iso-Ahola, "Leisure and Health: The Role of Social Support and Self-Determination," *Journal of Leisure Research* 25 (1993): 111–128.

28    *Increase life satisfaction*  M. London, R. Crandall, and D. Fistgibbons, "The Psychological Structure of Leisure," *Journal of Leisure Research* 9, no. 4 (1977): 252–263.

29    *Enhance social support*  Laurence Chalip, D. R. Thomas, and J. Voyle, *Sport, Recreation and Well-Being* (Palmerston North, New Zealand: Dunmore Press, 1992).

29    *Improve mood*  I. L. McCann and D. Holmes, "Influence of Aerobic Exercise on Depression," *Journal of Personality and Social Psychology* 46, no. 5 (1984).

29    *Help develop risk-taking skills*  Alan Ewart and Steve Hollenhorst, "Testing the Adventure Model: Empirical Support for a Model of Risk Recreation Participation," *Journal of Leisure Research* 21, no. 2 (1989): 124–139.

29    *Physical exercise*  Norman Doidge, *The Brain That Changes Itself* (New York: Penguin Books, 2007), 254–255.

29    *High-quality leisure activities*  Seppo Iso-Ahola, "Leisure Lifestyle and Health," *Leisure and Mental Health* (Park City, UT: Family Development Resources, 1994).

30 *Half of your potential happiness is hereditary* Kennon M. Sheldon and Sonja Lyubomirsky, "Is It Possible to Become Happier? (And If So, How?)," *Social and Personality Psychology Compass* 1 (2007): 1–17.

30 *A landmark study* Alan Krueger, Daniel Kahneman, David Schkade, Norbert Schwarz, and Arthur Stone, "National Time Accounting: The Currency of Life," Working Papers, Princeton University (2008).

39 *"The release of dopamine"* Gregory Berns, *Satisfaction: The Science of Finding True Fulfillment* (New York: Henry Holt, 1997), 15, 244.

## 2. Worth Is an Inside Job

45 *"Intrinsic motivation is its own"* Edward Deci, *Why We Do What We Do: Understanding Self-Motivation* (New York: Penguin Books, 1995), 46.

47 *Chronic work weeks* Haiou Yang, Peter L. Schnall, Maritza Jauregui, Ta-Chen Su, and Dean Baker, "Work Hours and Self-Reported Hypertension among Working People in California," *Hypertension* 48, no. 4 (October 2006): 744–750.

47 *Productivity dives 25 percent* Circadian Technologies, Shiftware Practices survey (2005).

48 *"A more rational assessment"* Martha Davis, Elizabeth Robbins Eshelman, and Matthew McKay, *The Relaxation and Stress Handbook* (Oakland, CA: New Harbinger Publications, 2008), 141.

48 *A study of forty-nine of the Forbes 400* Ed Diener, Jeff Horwitz, and Robert A. Emmons, "Happiness of the Very Wealthy," *Social Indicators Research* 16, no. 3 (April 1985).

51 *In a study on workaholism* Ronald J. Burke, "Workaholism, Self-Esteem, and Motives for Money," *Psychological Reports* (April 2004): 457–463.

62 *"but when the results"* Alan Watts, *Become What You Are* (Boston: Shambhala, 2003), 24–25.

62 *Edward Deci conducted a study* Edward Deci, *Why We Do What We Do: Understanding Self-Motivation* (New York: Penguin Books, 1995), 25.

66 *Sheldon says you should ask* Kennon M. Sheldon, "The Self-Concordance Model of Healthy Goal Striving: When Personal Goals Correctly Represent the Person," in *Handbook of Self-Determination Research*, edited by Edward L. Deci and Richard M. Ryan (Rochester, NY: University of Rochester Press, 2002).

## 3. No Skills, No Thrills

80 *"Once the external stimulus is gone"* Martin Seligman, *Authentic Happiness* (New York: Free Press, 2002), 105.

92 *Passions take foreplay* Robert Vallerand, "On the Psychology of Passion: In Search of What Makes People's Lives Most Worth Living," *Canadian Psychology* 49, no. 1 (2007): 1–13.

92  *Vallerand and his colleagues have studied*  Robert Vallerand, Genevieve A. Mageau, et al., "Passion and Performance Attainment in Sport," *Psychology of Sport and Exercise* 9, no. 3 (May 2008): 373–392.

92  *This jibes well with research findings*  Sonja Lyubomirsky, Kennon M. Sheldon, and David Schkade, "Pursuing Happiness: The Architecture of Sustainable Change," *Review of General Psychology* 9, no. 2 (2005): 111–131.

93  *In a study of first-year music students*  G. A. Mageau, Robert Vallerand, J. Charest, S. J. Salvy, N. Lacaille, and T. Bouffard, "On the Development of Harmonious and Obsessive Passion: The Role of Autonomous Support, Activity Valuation, and Identity Processes," *Journal of Personality* 77, no. 3 (June 2007).

## 4. Safe Is Sorry

101  *The fascinating thing about regrets*  Marcel Zeelenberg, Eric van Dijk, et al., "The Inaction Effect in the Psychology of Regret," *Journal of Personality and Social Psychology* 82, no. 3 (March 2002): 314–327.

108  *One study found that the need for novelty*  Bianca Wittman, Nathaniel Daw, et al., "Striatal Activity Underlies Novelty-Based Choice in Humans," *Neuron* 58, no. 6 (2008): 967–973.

109  *"People so often stop growing"*  Tom Pyszczynski, Jeff Greenberg, and Jamie Goldenburg, "Freedom versus Fear: On the Defense, Growth, and Expansion of the Self," *Handbook of Self and Identity* (New York: Guilford, 2005), 329.

113  *People whose self-worth*  Pyszczynski, Greenberg, and Goldenburg, *Handbook of Self and Identity*, 332.

125  *Initiating is one key*  Sonja Lyubomirsky, Kennon M. Sheldon, and David Schkade, "Pursuing Happiness: The Architecture of Sustainable Change," *Review of General Psychology* 9, no. 2 (2005): 120.

## 5. Expect No Payoff (and You Get One)

133  *Singing can make us healthier and happier*  Robert Beck, Thomas Cesario, et al., "Choral Singing, Performance Perception, and Immune System Changes in Salivary Immunoglobulin A and Cortisol," *Music Perception* 18, no. 1 (2000): 87–106.

136  *The more importance placed on wealth aspirations*  Tim Kasser, M. Vansteenkiste, and J. R. Deckop, "The Ethical Problems of a Materialistic Value Orientation for Businesses (and Some Suggestions for Alternatives)," in *Human Resource Management Ethics*, edited by J. Deckop (Greenwich, CT: Information Age Publishing, 2006), 283–306.

136  *When self-esteem is based on external measures*  Jennifer Crocker, "The Costs of Seeking Self-Esteem," *Journal of Social Issues* 58 (2002): 597–615.

136  *The stronger the financial goal*  Carol Nickerson, Norbert Schwarz, et al., "Zeroing in on the Dark Side of the American Dream: A Closer Look at

the Negative Consequences of the Goal for Financial Success," *Psychological Science* 14, no. 6 (2003): 531–536.

136 *Higher extrinsic values*   Tim Kasser, *The High Price of Materialism* (Cambridge, MA: MIT Press, 2002).

136 *Focusing on extrinsic goals*   Bruno Frey and Felix Oberholzer-Gee, "The Cost of Price Incentives: An Empirical Analysis of Motivation Crowding-Out," *American Economic Review* (1997).

136 *Pursuit of extrinsic goals*   Jennifer Crocker, "Contingencies of Self-Worth: Implications for Self-Regulation and Psychological Vulnerability," *Self and Identity* 1 (2002): 143–149.

137 *External approval concerns lead*   Tim Kasser and Richard Ryan, "Further Examining the American Dream: Differential Correlates of Intrinsic and Extrinsic Goals," *Personality and Social Psychology Bulletin* 22, no. 3 (1996): 280–287.

137 *"People lose interest"*   Edward Deci, *Why We Do What We Do* (New York: Penguin Books, 1995), 29.

139 *These are known as negotiation strategies*   Anna Nadirova and Edgar Jackson, "How Do People Negotiate Constraints to Their Leisure? Results from an Empirical Study," abstracts of papers presented at the Ninth Canadian Congress on Leisure Research, 1999.

147 *To help you determine*   Kennon M. Sheldon, Tim Kasser, et al., "Personal Goals and Psychological Growth: Testing an Intervention to Enhance Goal Attainment and Personality Integration," *Journal of Personality* 70, no. 1 (2002): 14.

153 *Curiosity is the spark plug of interest*   Barbara Frederickson, "What Good Are Positive Emotions?" *Review of General Psychology* 2, no. 3 (September 1998): 305.

154 *"Curiosity motivates people to act"*   Todd Kashdan and Paul Silvia, "Curiosity and Interest: The Benefits of Thriving on Novelty and Challenge," in *Handbook of Positive Psychology*, edited by C. R. Snyder and Shane J. Lopez (New York: Oxford University Press, 2009), 367.

## 6. It's the Experience

163 *"In those moments"*   Alan Watts, *The Tao of Philosophy* (Boston: Tuttle Publishing, 2002), 66.

164 *"Only direct control of experience"*   Mihaly Csikszentmihalyi, *Flow* (New York: Basic Books, 1990), 8.

166 *When neurons fire together*   Norman Doidge, *The Brain That Changes Itself* (New York: Penguin Books, 2007), 80.

167 *"The more positive and novel"*   Kennon Sheldon and Sonja Lyubomirsky, "Is It Possible to Become Happier? (And If So, How?)," *Social and Personality Psychology Compass* 1 (2007): 8.

169 *College students who were prone*   I. G. Sarason and S. Turk, "Coping Strategies and Group Interaction: Their Function in Improving Performance of Anxious Individuals," University of Washington, 1983.

172  *The University of Colorado's Leaf Van Boven*    Leaf van Boven, Marga-
     ret C. Campbell, and Thomas Gilkovich, "Stigmatizing Materialism:
     On Stereotypes and Impressions of Materialistic and Experiential
     Pursuits," *Personality and Social Psychology Bulletin* 36, no. 4 (2010):
     551–563.

176  *You don't have to be a philharmonic genius*    Edward Deci, *Why We Do
     What We Do: Understanding Self-Motivation* (New York: Penguin Books,
     1995), 66.

179  *Using MRI scans*    Charles Limb and Allen Braun, "Neural Substrates
     of Spontaneous Musical Performance: An fMRI Study of Jazz Impro-
     visation," published online in *PLoS One* 3, no. 2 (2008), www.plosone
     .org/article/info:doi%2F10.1371%2Fjournal.pone.0001679.

183  *In one study, senior*    Amy Love Collins, Natalia Sarkisian, and Ellen
     Winner, "Flow and Happiness in Later Life: An Investigation into the
     Role of Daily and Weekly Flow Experiences," *Journal of Happiness Stud-
     ies* 10, no. 6 (December 2008).

183  *The majority of thru-hikers*    Allan Mills and Thomas S. Butler, "Flow
     Experiences among Appalachian Trail Thru-Hikers," *Proceedings of the
     2005 Northeastern Research Symposium*, edited by John Peden and Rudy
     Schuster (Newtown Square, PA: U.S. Dept of Agriculture, Forest Service,
     Northeastern Research Station, 2005).

## 7. Play Is Where You Live

189  *In one study in Taiwan*    Ping Yu, Jing-Jyi Wu, I-Heng Chen, and Ying-Tzu
     Lin, "Is Playfulness a Benefit to Work? Empirical Evidence of Profession-
     als in Taiwan," *International Journal of Technology Management* 39, no. 3/4
     (2007): 412–429.

190  *Walter Freeman at UC-Berkeley*    Walter Freeman, "A Neurobiological
     Role of Music in Social Bonding," in *The Origins of Music*, edited by N.
     Wallin, B. Merkur, and S. Brown (Cambridge, MA: MIT Press, 2000).

190  *Studies have shown*    Harry Reis, Kennon Sheldon, et al., "Daily Well-
     Being: The Role of Autonomy, Competence, and Relatedness," *Personality
     and Social Psychology Bulletin* 26, no. 4 (2000): 428.

190  *Participating in recreational activities*    Peter Hills and Michael Argyle,
     "Positive Moods Derived from Leisure and Their Relationship to Hap-
     piness and Personality," *Personality and Individual Differences* 25, no. 3
     (September 1998).

191  *experiencing pleasure*    T. DiLorenzo, D. Prue, and R. Scott, "A Concep-
     tual Critique of Leisure Assessment and Therapy: An Added Dimension
     to Behavioral Medicine," *Clinical Psychology Review* 7, no. 6 (1987):
     597–609.

192  *It's more congruent with your personality*    Robert Emmons, Ed Diener,
     and Randy Larsen, "Choice and Avoidance of Everyday Situations and
     Affect Congruence: Two Models of Reciprocal Interactionism," *Journal
     of Personality and Social Psychology* 51, no. 4 (1986): 815–826.

192 *When you're engaged in activities*   Alan Waterman, "Two Conceptions of Happiness: Contrasts of Personal Expressiveness (Eudaimonia) and Hedonic Enjoyment," *Journal of Personality and Social Psychology* 64, no. 4 (1993): 25.

194 *"Playfulness throws off"*   Daniel Goleman, *Social Intelligence* (New York, Bantam Dell, 2006), 180.

194 *"Joy creates the urge to play"*   Barbara Frederickson, "What Good Are Positive Emotions?" *Review of General Psychology* 2, no. 3 (September 1998): 305.

201 *Positive psychology leaders*   Sonja Lyubomirsky, Laura King, and Ed Diener, "The Benefits of Frequent Positive Affect: Does Happiness Lead to Success?" *Psychological Bulletin* 131, no. 6 (2005): 804.

210 *"The feelings of fun only emerge"*   Walter Podilchak, "Distinctions of Fun, Enjoyment and Leisure," *Leisure Studies* 10 (1991): 145.

## 8. You Are the Audience

220 *Negative self-talk is one of the biggest factors*   Richard Parncutt and Gary McPherson, eds., "Performance Anxiety," *The Science and Psychology of Music Performance* (Oxford: Oxford University Press, 2002), 47.

222 *In one study, people who used self-comments*   A. Steptoe and H. Fidler, "Stage Fright in Orchestral Musicians: A Study of Cognitive and Behavioral Strategies in Performance and Anxiety," *British Journal of Psychology* 78, no. 2 (1987): 241–249.

235 *In one intriguing study*   Sonja Lyubomirsky and Lee Ross, "Hedonic Consequences of Social Comparison: A Contrast of Happy and Unhappy People," *Journal of Personality and Social Psychology* 73, no. 6 (December 1997): 1154.

## 9. Passions Take Persistence

242 *I really like the definition of vitality*   Richard Ryan and Edward Deci, "From Ego Depletion to Vitality: Theory and Findings Concerning the Facilitation of Energy Available to the Self," *Social and Personality Psychology Compass* 2, no. 2 (2008).

243 *"Negativity and neutrality constrain your experience"*   Barbara Frederickson, *Positivity* (New York: Crown, 2009), 23.

253 *You can outflank threats to your staying power*   Peter Gollwitzer, "Strong Effects of Simple Plans," *American Psychologist* 54, no. 7 (1999): 493–503.

257 *In one study, Stanford's Carol Dweck*   Carol Dweck and L. Sorich, "Mastery-Oriented Thinking," in *Coping*, edited by C. R. Snyder (New York: Oxford University Press, 1999).

257 *Dweck also found that when a task has a high degree*   E. Elliot and Carol Dweck, "Goals: An Approach to Motivation and Achievement," *Journal of Personality and Social Psychology* 54 (1988): 5–12.

# Bibliography

Allen, D. W. "Hidden Stresses in Success." *Psychiatry* 42, no. 2 (May 1979): 171–176.

Barnett, Lynn A. "The Nature of Playfulness in Young Adults." *Personality and Individual Differences* 43, no. 4 (2007): 949–958.

Baumeister, Roy. *Meanings of Life*. New York: Guilford Press, 1991.

Beck, Robert, Thomas Cesario, A. Yousefi, and H. Enamoto. "Choral Singing, Performance Perception, and Immune System Changes in Salivary Immunoglobulin A and Cortisol." *Music Perception* 18, no. 1 (2000): 87–106.

Belluck, Pam. "Strangers May Cheer You Up." *New York Times*, December 4, 2008.

Berns, Gregory. *Satisfaction: The Science of Finding True Fulfillment*. New York: Henry Holt, 1997.

Burke, Ronald J. "Workaholism, Self-Esteem, and Motives for Money." *Psychological Reports* (April 2004): 457–463.

Carpenter, Gaylene. "A Longitudinal Examination of Wants-Out-of-Life among Mid-Life Adults: Implications for Event Managers." *Journal of Convention and Exhibition Management* 2 (2000): 45–57.

———. "Adult Perceptions of Leisure: Life Experiences and Life Structure." *Society and Leisure* 15, no. 2 (Fall 1992): 587–605.

Carruthers, Cynthia, and Colleen D. Hood. "Research Update: The Power of Positive Psychology: The Paradigm Shift from Problem-Solving to Optimism." *Parks and Recreation* (October 2005).

Chalip, Laurence, D. R. Thomas, and J. Voyle. *Sport, Recreation and Well-Being*. Palmerston North, New Zealand: Dunmore Press, 1992.

Chödrön, Pema. *The Places That Scare You*. Boston: Shambhala, 2002.

Coleman, Denis. "Leisure Based Social Support, Leisure Dispositions and Health." *Journal of Leisure Research*, 25 (1993).

———. *When Things Fall Apart*. Boston: Shambhala, 1997.

Coleman, Denis, and Seppo Iso-Ahola. "An Analysis of Stress-Buffering Effects of Leisure-Based Social Support and Leisure Dispositions." *Journal of Leisure Research* 25 (1993): 111–128.

Collins, Amy Love, Natalia Sarkisian, and Ellen Winner. "Flow and Happiness in Later Life: An Investigation into the Role of Daily and Weekly Flow Experiences." *Journal of Happiness Studies* 10, no. 6 (December 2008): 703–719.

Compton, David M., and Seppo Iso-Ahola, editors. *Leisure and Mental Health*. Park City, UT: Family Development Resources, 1994.

Conway, Patrick. "The Process of Perseverance." Center for the Study of Human Potential (1972).

Crocker, Jennifer. "Contingencies of Self-Worth: Implications for Self-Regulation and Psychological Vulnerability." *Self and Identity* (2002): 143–149.

———. "The Costs of Seeking Self-Esteem." *Journal of Social Issues* 58 (2002): 597–615.

Crocker, Jennifer, and R. K. Luhtanen. "Level of Self-Esteem and Contingencies of Self-Worth: Unique Effects on Academic, Social, and Financial Problems in College Freshmen." *Personality and Social Psychology Bulletin* 29 (2003): 701–712.

Csikszentmihalyi, Mihaly. *Finding Flow*. New York: Basic Books, 1997.

———. *Flow*. New York: Basic Books, 1990.

Csikszentmihalyi, Mihaly, and Isabella Selega Csikszentmihalyi. *Optimal Experience*. Cambridge: Cambridge University Press, 1988.

Davis, Martha, Elizabeth Robbins Eshelman, and Matthew McKay. *The Relaxation and Stress Handbook*. Oakland, CA: New Harbinger Publications, 2008.

Dattilo, John, Douglas Kleiber, and Richard Williams. "Self-Determination and Enjoyment Enhancement: A Psychologically Based Service Delivery Model for Therapeutic Recreation." *Therapeutic Recreation Journal* (1998).

Deci, Edward L. *Why We Do What We Do: Understanding Self-Motivation*. New York: Penguin Books, 1995.

Deci, Edward L., and Richard M. Ryan. "The What and Why of Goal Pursuits: Human Needs and the Self-Determination of Behavior." *Psychological Inquiry* 11, no. 4 (2000): 227–268.

Diener, Ed, Jeff Horwitz, and Robert A. Emmons. "Happiness of the Very Wealthy." *Social Indicators Research* 16, no. 3 (April 1985): 263–274.

DiLorenzo, T. M., D. M. Prue, and R. R. Scott. "A Conceptual Critique of Leisure Assessment and Therapy: An Added Dimension to Behavioral Medicine." *Clinical Psychology Review* 7, no. 6 (1987): 597–609.

Doidge, Norman. *The Brain That Changes Itself*. New York: Penguin Books, 2007.

Dweck, Carol, and Lisa Sorich. "Mastery-Oriented Thinking." In *Coping*. Edited by C. R. Snyder. New York: Oxford University Press, 1999.

Emmons, Robert, Ed Diener, and Randy Larsen. "Choice and Avoidance of Everyday Situations and Affect Congruence: Two Models of Reciprocal Interactionism." *Journal of Personality and Social Psychology* 51, no. 4 (1986): 815–826.

Ewart, Alan, and Steve Hollenhorst. "Testing the Adventure Model: Empirical Support for a Model of Risk Recreation Participation." *Journal of Leisure Research* 21, no. 2 (1989): 124–139.

Fisher, Marlo Jo. "Can Choirs Cure a Cold?" *Orange County Register*, March 31, 2001.

Frankish, James C., C. Dawne Milligan, and Colleen Reid. "A Review of Relationships between Active Living and Determinants of Health." *Social Science Medicine* 47, no. 3 (1998): 287–301.

Frederickson, Barbara. *Positivity*. New York: Crown, 2009.

———. "What Good Are Positive Emotions?" *Review of General Psychology* 2, no. 3 (September 1998): 300–319.

Freeman, Walter J. "Happiness Doesn't Come in Bottles." *Journal of Consciousness Studies* 4 (1996): 67–71.

———. "A Neurobiological Role of Music in Social Bonding." In *The Origins of Music*. Edited by N. Wallin, B. Merkur, and S. Brown. Cambridge, MA: MIT Press, 2000.

Frey, Bruno, and Felix Oberholzer-Gee. "The Cost of Price Incentives: An Empirical Analysis of Motivation Crowding-Out." *American Economic Review* (1997).

Gallagher, Winifred. *Rapt*. New York: Penguin Press, 2009.

Garfinkel, P. E., R. M. Bagby, D. R. Schuller, C. C. Williams, S. E. Dickens, and B. Dorian. "Predictors of Success and Satisfaction in the Practice of Psychiatry: A Preliminary Follow-Up Study." *Canadian Journal of Psychiatry* 46, no. 9 (2001): 835–840.

Gary, Kevin. "Leisure, Freedom, and Liberal Education." *Educational Theory* 56, no. 2 (2006): 121–136.

Goleman, Daniel. *Emotional Intelligence*. New York: Bantam Books, 2006.

———. *Social Intelligence*. New York: Bantam, 2006.

Gollwitzer, Peter. "Strong Effects of Simple Plans." *American Psychologist* 54, no. 7 (1999): 493–503.

Haworth, John T. *Work, Leisure and Well-Being*. London: Routledge, 1997.

Hills, Peter, and Michael Argyle. "Positive Moods Derived from Leisure and Their Relationship to Happiness and Personality." *Personality and Individual Differences* 25, no. 3 (September 1998): 523–535.

Howell, R. T., and G. Hill. "The Mediators of Experiential Purchases: Determining the Impact of Psychological Need Satisfaction." *Journal of Positive Psychology* 4, no. 6 (November 2009): 511–522.

Hyatt, Ralph. "The Art of Healthy Risk-Taking." *USA Today*, September 2001.

Iso-Ahola, Seppo. "Leisure Lifestyle and Health." *Leisure and Mental Health*. Park City, Utah: Family Development Resources, 1994.

———. "Leisure-Related Social Support and Self-Determination as Buffers of Stress Illness Relationship." *Journal of Leisure Research* 28 (1996).

Iso-Ahola, Seppo, and R. C. Mannell. "Social and Psychological Constraints on Leisure." In *Constraints on Leisure*. Edited by Michael Wade. Springfield, IL: C. C. Thomas, 1985.

Kalenscher, Tobias, and Cyriel M. A. Pennartz. "Is a Bird in the Hand Worth Two in the Future? The Neuroeconomics of Intertemporal Decision-Making." *Progressive Neurobiology* 84, no. 3 (2008): 284–315.

Kashdan, Todd B., and Frank D. Fincham. "Facilitating Curiosity: A Social and Self-Regulatory Perspective for Scientifically Based Interventions." In *Positive Psychology in Practice*. Edited by P. Alex Stanley and Stephen Joseph. New York: John Wiley & Sons, 2004.

Kashdan, Todd B., and Paul J. Silvia. "Curiosity and Interest: The Benefits of Thriving on Novelty and Challenge." In *The Oxford Handbook of Positive Psychology*. Edited by C. R. Snyder and Shane J. Lopez. Oxford: Oxford University Press, 2009.

Kasser, Tim. *The High Price of Materialism*. Cambridge, MA: MIT Press, 2002.

Kasser, Tim, M. Vansteenkiste, and J. R. Deckop. "The Ethical Problems of a Materialistic Value Orientation for Businesses (and Some Suggestions for Alternatives)." In *Human Resource Management Ethics*. Edited by J. Deckop. Greenwich, CT: Information Age Publishing, 2006.

Kasser, Tim, and Richard M. Ryan: "Further Examining the American Dream: Differential Correlates of Intrinsic and Extrinsic Goals." *Personality and Social Psychology Bulletin* 22, no. 3 (1996): 280–287.

Kasser, Tim, and Kennon M. Sheldon. "Time Affluence as a Path Towards Personal Happiness and Ethical Business Practice: Empirical Evidence from Four Studies." *Journal of Business Ethics* 94, supplement 2 (January 2008): 243–255.

Keeney, Bradford. *Everyday Soul*. New York: Riverhead Books, 1996.

———. *Shaking Medicine*. Rochester, VT: Destiny Books. 2007.

King, I. M. "Quality of Life and Goal Attainment." *Nursing Science Quarterly* 7, no. 1 (1994): 29–32.

Kyle, Gerard T., and Andrew Mowen. "An Examination of the Relationship between Leisure Constraints, Involvement, and Commitment." In *Proceedings of the 2003 Northeastern Recreation Research Symposium*. Edited by James Murdy, 2004.

Krebs, Ruth M., Bjorn H. Schott, Helmut Schutze, and Emrah Duzel. "The Novelty Exploration Bonus and Its Attentional Modulation." *Neuropsychologia* 47, no. 11 (September 2009): 2272–2281.

Krueger, Alan B., Daniel Kahneman, David Schkade, Norbert Schwarz, and Arthur Stone. "National Time Accounting: The Currency of Life." Working Papers, Princeton University (2008): 1–47.

Jackson, Maggie. *Distracted*. Amherst, MA: Prometheus Books, 2008.

Jones, Christopher D., Steven J. Hollenhorst, Frank Perna, and Steve Selin. "Validation of the Flow Theory in an On-Site Whitewater Kayaking Setting." *Journal of Leisure Research* (March 22, 2000).

Leary, Mark R., and June Price Tangney. *Handbook of Self and Identity*. New York: Guilford Press, 2003.

Levy, Joseph. *Play Behavior*. Malabar, FL: Krieger, 1983.

Limb, Charles, and Allen Braun. "Neural Substrates of Spontaneous Musical Performance: An fMRI Study of Jazz Improvisation." Published online, *PLoS One* 3, no. 2 (2008).

London, M., R. Crandall, and D. Fistgibbons. "The Psychological Structure of Leisure." *Journal of Leisure Research* 9, no. 4 (1977): 252–263.

Lykken, David. *Happiness: The Nature and Nurture of Joy and Contentment.* New York: St. Martin's Press, 2000.

Lyubomirsky, Sonja, Laura King, and Ed Diener. "The Benefits of Frequent Positive Affect: Does Happiness Lead to Success?" *Psychological Bulletin* 131, no. 6 (2005): 803–855.

Lyubomirsky, Sonja, and Lee Ross. "Hedonic Consequences of Social Comparison: A Contrast of Happy and Unhappy People." *Journal of Personality and Social Psychology* 73, no. 6 (December 1997): 1141–1157.

Lyubomirsky, Sonja, Kennon M. Sheldon, and David Schkade. "Pursuing Happiness: The Architecture of Sustainable Change." *Review of General Psychology* 9, no. 2 (2005): 111–131.

Mageau, G. A., Robert Vallerand, J. Charest, S.-J. Salvy, N. Lacaille, and T. Bouffard. "On the Development of Harmonious and Obsessive Passion: The Role of Autonomous Support, Activity Valuation, and Identity Processes." *Journal of Personality* 77, no. 3 (June 2007).

Manel, Baucells, and Cristina Rata. "A Survey of Factors Influencing Risk-Taking Behavior in Real-World Decisions under Uncertainty." *Decision Analysis* 3, no. 3 (September 2006): 163–176.

McAvoy, Leo H., E. Curtis Schatz, Mary E. Stutz, Stuart J. Schleien, and Greg Lais. "Integrated Wilderness Adventure: Effects on Personal and Lifestyle Traits of Persons with and without Disabilities." *Therapeutic Recreation Journal* (2001).

McCan, I. L., and D. Holmes. "Influence of Aerobic Exercise on Depression." *Journal of Personality and Social Psychology* 46, no. 5 (1984): 1142–1147.

Mills, Allan S., and Thomas S. Butler. "Flow Experiences among Appalachian Trail Thru-Hikers." In *Proceedings of the 2005 Northeastern Research Symposium.* Newtown Square, PA: U.S. Dept of Agriculture, Forest Service, Northeastern Research Station, 2005.

Mundy, Jean. *Leisure Education Theory and Practice.* Champaign, IL: Sagamore, 1998.

Nachmanovitch, Stephen. *Free Play: Improvisation in Life and Art.* New York: Tarcher Putnam, 1990.

Nadirova, Anna, and Edgar Jackson. "How Do People Negotiate Constraints to Their Leisure?" Abstracts of papers presented at the Ninth Canadian Congress on Leisure Research, 1999.

Neulinger, John. *The Psychology of Leisure.* Springfield, IL: Charles C. Thomas, 1981.

Nickerson, Carol, Norbert Schwarz, Edward Diener, and Daniel Kahneman. "Zeroing in on the Dark Side of the American Dream: A Closer Look at the Negative Consequences of the Goal for Financial Success." *Psychological Science* 14, no. 6 (2003): 531–536.

Nix, Glen A., Richard M. Ryan, John B. Manly, and Edward L. Deci. "Revitalization through Self-Regulation: The Effects of Autonomous and Controlled Motivation on Happiness and Vitality." *Journal of Experimental Social Psychology* 35, no. 3 (May 1999): 266–284.

Nyaupane, Gyan P., Duarte B. Morais, and Alan Graefe. "A Comparison of Leisure Constraints among Three Outdoor Recreation Activities: White-water Rafting, Canoeing and Overnight Horseback Riding." In *Proceedings of the 2002 Northeastern Recreation Research Symposium*. Edited by Rudy Schuster, 2002.

Parncutt, Richard, and Gary McPherson. *The Science and Psychology of Music Performance*. Oxford: Oxford University Press, 2002.

Perlow, Leslie. "Finding Time, Stopping the Frenzy." *Business Health* 16, no. 8 (1998): 31–35.

Pfaffenbach, Becky J., Harr C. Zinn, and Chad P. Dawson. "Exploring Satis-faction among Paddlers in Two Adirondack Canoeing Areas." Northeast Recreation Research Symposium, 2002.

Pieper, Josef. *Leisure, the Basis of Culture*. Indianapolis: Liberty Fund, 1998.

Podilchak, Walter. "Distinctions of Fun, Enjoyment and Leisure." *Leisure Studies* 10 (1991): 133–148.

Pritchard, Mark, Ian Patterson, and Gaylene Carpenter. "Serious Leisure and Self-Directed Learning." In *Leisure Challenges: Bringing People, Resources and Policy into Play*. Edited by Bryan J. A. Smale, 1990.

Propst, Dennis B., and Margot E. Kurtz. "Perceived Control/Reactance: A Framework for Understanding Leisure Behavior in Natural Settings." *Leisure Studies* 8, no. 3 (September 1989): 241–248.

Pyszczynski, Tom, Jeff Greenberg, and Jamie Goldenburg. "Freedom Versus Fear." In *The Handbook of Self and Identity*. Edited by Mark R. Leary and June Price Tangney. New York: Guilford, 2005.

Ratey, John J. *A User's Guide to the Brain*. New York: Vintage Books, 2002.

Reis, Harry T., Kennon M. Sheldon, Shelly L. Gable, Joseph Roscoe, and Richard M. Ryan. "Daily Well-Being: The Role of Autonomy, Competence, and Relat-edness." *Personality and Social Psychology Bulletin* 26, no. 4 (2000): 419–435.

Roberson, Donald N., and Vesna Babic. "Walking and Hiking as a Way of Life." Online submission to Educational Resources Information Center (ERIC. Ed.gov) (2008).

Rosenbloom, Stephanie. "But Are You Happy?" *New York Times*, August 7, 2010.

Ryan, Richard, and Edward Deci. "From Ego Depletion to Vitality: Theory and Findings Concerning the Facilitation of Energy Available to the Self." *Social and Personality Psychology Compass* 2, no. 2 (2008).

Ryan, Richard, Veronika Huta, and Edward L. Deci. "Living Well: A Self-Determination Perspective on Eudaimonia." *Journal of Happiness Studies* 9, no. 1 (January 2008): 139–170.

Rybczynski, Witold. *Waiting for the Weekend*. New York: Penguin Books, 1991.

Sarason, I. G., and S. Turk. "Coping Strategies and Group Interaction: Their Function in Improving Performance of Anxious Individuals." University of Washington, 1983.

Seligman, Martin. *Authentic Happiness*. New York: Free Press, 2002.

Sheldon, Kennon M. "The Self-Concordance Model of Healthy Goal Striving: When Personal Goals Correctly Represent the Person." In *Handbook of Self-Determination Research*. Edited by Edward L. Deci, and Richard M. Ryan. Rochester, NY: University of Rochester Press, 2002.

Sheldon, Kennon M., and B. Ann Bettencourt. "Psychological Need-Satisfaction and Subjective Well-Being within Social Groups." *Journal of Social Psychology* 41 (March 2002): 25–28.

Sheldon, Kennon M., and Tim Kasser. "Pursuing Personal Goals: Skills Enable Progress, but Not All Progress Is Beneficial." *Personality and Social Psychology Bulletin* 24, no. 12 (1998): 1319–1331.

Sheldon, Kennon M., Tim Kasser, Andrew J. Eliot, and Youngmee Kim. "What Is Satisfying about Satisfying Events? Testing 10 Candidate Psychological Needs." *Journal of Personality and Social Psychology* 80, no. 2 (2001): 25–28.

Sheldon, Kennon M., Tim Kasser, Kendra Smith, and Tamara Share. "Personal Goals and Psychological Growth: Testing an Intervention to Enhance Goal Attainment and Personality Integration." *Journal of Personality* 70, no. 1 (2002): 5–31.

Sheldon, Kennon M., and Sonja Lyubomirsky. "Is It Possible to Become Happier? (And If So, How?)." *Social and Personality Psychology Compass* 1 (2007): 1–17.

Sheldon, Kennon M., Richard M. Ryan, Edward L. Deci, and Tim Kasser. "The Independent Effects of Goal Contents and Motives on Well-Being: It's Both What You Pursue and Why You Pursue Them." *Personality and Social Psychology Bulletin* 30, no. 4 (2004).

Staempfli, Marianne B. "Adolescent Playfulness, Stress, Perception, Coping and Well-Being." *Journal of Leisure Research*, Third Quarter, 2007.

Tice, Dianne M., and Harry M. Wallace. "The Reflected Self: Creating Yourself as (You Think) Others See You." In *The Handbook of Self and Identity*. Edited by Mark R. Leary and June Price Tangney. New York: Guilford Press, 2005.

Tierney, John. "Ear Plugs to Lasers: The Science of Concentration." *New York Times*, May 4, 2009.

Yu, Ping, Jing-Jyi Wu, I-Heng Chen, Ying-Tzu Lin. "Is Playfulness a Benefit to Work? Empirical Evidence of Professionals in Taiwan." *International Journal of Technology Management* 39, no. 3/4 (2007): 412–429.

Vallerand, Robert J. "On the Psychology of Passion: In Search of What Makes People's Lives Most Worth Living." *Canadian Psychology* 49, no. 1 (2007): 1–13.

Vallerand, Robert J., Genevieve A. Mageau, Andrew J. Elliot, Alexandre Dumais, Marc-Andre Demers, and Francois Rousseau. "Passion and Performance

Attainment in Sport." *Psychology of Sport and Exercise* 9, no. 3 May (2008): 373–392.

Van Boven, Leaf. "Experientialism, Materialism, and the Pursuit of Happiness." *Review of General Psychology* 9, no. 2 (2005): 132–142.

Van Boven, Leaf, Margaret C. Campbell, and Thomas Gilkovich. "Stigmatizing Materialism: On Stereotypes and Impressions of Materialistic and Experiential Pursuits." *Personality and Social Psychology Bulletin* 36, no. 4 (2010): 551–563.

Van Boven, Leaf, and Thomas Gilkovich. "To Do or to Have? That Is the Question." *Journal of Personality and Social Psychology* 85, no. 6 (2003): 1193–1202.

Voelkl, Judith. "Go with the Flow: How to Help People Have Optimal Recreation Experiences." *Parks and Recreation* (August 2003).

Voelkl, Judith, and Gary Ellis. "Measuring Flow Experiences in Daily Life: An Investigation of the Items Used to Measure Challenge and Skill." *Journal of Leisure Research* 30 (1998).

Waterman, Alan S. "Two Conceptions of Happiness: Contrasts of Personal Expressiveness (Eudaimonia) and Hedonic Enjoyment." *Journal of Personality and Social Psychology* 64, no. 4 (1993).

Watts, Alan. *Become What You Are*. Boston: Shambhala, 2003.

———. *The Tao of Philosophy*. Boston: Tuttle Publishing, 1995.

———. *Tao, the Watercourse Way*. New York: Pantheon Books, 1975.

———. *The Wisdom of Insecurity*. New York: Vintage Books, 1951.

Wheeler, R. J., and M. A. Frank. "Identification of Stress Buffers." *Behavioral Medicine* 14, no. 2 (Summer 1988): 78–89.

Wittman, Bianca, Nathaniel Daw, Ben Seymour, and Raymond Dolan. "Striatal Activity Underlies Novelty-Based Choice in Humans." *Neuron* 58, no. 6 (2008): 967–973.

Yang, Haiou, Peter L. Schnall, Maritza Jauregui, Ta-Chen Su, and Dean Baker. "Work Hours and Self-Reported Hypertension among Working People in California." *Hypertension* 48, no. 4 (October 2006): 744–750.

Zeelenberg, Marcel, Eric van Dijk, Kees van den Bos, and Rik Pieters. "The Inaction Effect in the Psychology of Regret." *Journal of Personality and Social Psychology* 82, no. 3 (March 2002): 314–327.

# Index